CHRISTMAS
CAROLS
&
OTHER PLAYS

CHRISTMAS CAROLS & OTHER PLAYS

Jascha Kessler

CONTENTS

THE LAST TERRORIST

— farce in two acts

Perfect Days

Act I

PERSONS IN ACT I

THE WIFE
THE HUSBAND
HIS BROTHER

THE SCENE

The ultramodern kitchen. On the RIGHT, the breakfast nook; on the LEFT, the spotless stainless steel, chrome, and enameling. The ultimate-seeming appliances are operated, it would appear, from the small panel of controls on the wall at CENTER REAR. The whole place is large, comfortable, and humming with power. At the LEFT REAR, a door leads to another part of the house. Outside the large window of the breakfast nook nothing at all can be seen: the light is neutral; a pearly, misty light. A red, a green, and an amber light are flashing in a sequence of about three to five seconds' duration, followed by a thin, high bleep (at least five times repeated); but the control panel remains unanswered. The length of time becomes annoying.

Abruptly the backdoor (at RIGHT SIDE WALL) slides open: there is a great roaring from outside: it is the ceaseless din of traffic — trains, autos, trucks, helicopters, jets, and so on. THE WIFE slips through,, presses a button that closes the door, shutting off the noise and the lights on the panel. In the silence her breathing is hard. She leans back against the closed door in relief. Gradually her desperate expression calms; her face grows pensive, then quite blank. In one hand she carries a thick, folded newspaper. She is young, between 30 and 40. She wears an expensive silk kimono and heeled satin slippers; her hair is covered by a fine, gauzy silk scarf wrapped like a turban. But she is pale, her eyes ringed by shadows of hypertension; she slits them against the smoke of the cigarette she has drawn from a pack in her pocket and lit in the manner of the heavy smoker. From the control panel now another series of lights comes on: azure, rose, white; they are synchronized with tiny, pleasant chimes and buzzes. She hesitates, drawing deeply to steady herself, and regards the panel as if in momentary doubt as to the significance of their pattern. Her free hand feels along the wall and manipulates a pair of switches; over her shoulder, set in an oblique corner of the wall, a huge TV screen lights up and plays. She cocks her eye at it, half-annoyed But also half- reassured that the world continues; she smokes a while longer, staring at it. The smoke having cleared her mind, she crosses over to the complex of appliances and sets up a tray with a great number of items; then she carries it back to the glossy large table in the nook. She sits upright opposite the trays, draws herself a cup of coffee from the large urn standing on the table, and sipping,, the cigarette burning between her fingers, reads the newspaper at arm's length, reads all of it with terrific speed and utter lack of interest. When she is done, she puts it down, crumpled and misfolded, fills another cup of coffee, lights another cigarette, and slips into reverie as she gazes out the blank, sunny-shady window.

THE HUSBAND bounds into the kitchen and heads straight for the table. He is astoundingly rosy, brisk, strong, and spic and span in his tailored clothing. He has no ears. Sitting down at his place, he begins to dispatch the appetizing courses heaped on his tray. First he downs the juice; then systematically finishes one plate after another from the tray, accompanying his happy breakfasting with much clatter. He is hearty, jovial, just like the youthful executive Dads of the financial advertisements.

THE TIME

December 31st. Very early in the morning of yet another perfect day.

*   *   *

HUSBAND

Looks like another perfect day. Doesn't it.

WIFE

(In reverie, she responds without having heard him) Yes it does. Doesn't it.

HUSBAND

That makes the two hundred twenty-first perfect day. Doesn't it.

WIFE

Yes it does. Doesn't it.

HUSBAND

My, I'm hungry. Perfect days make me so hungry.

WIFE

Yes they do. Don't they.

HUSBAND

(Glancing at his watch.) Got off all right. Didn't they.

WIFE

Yes. Got off all right.

HUSBAND

Of course. Tell them I'd be back Sunday morning?

WIFE

That's when you're back?

HUSBAND

Of course. That's when I'm back. I don't have to tell you. Do I. That's when. Of course.

WIFE

I wasn't sure.

HUSBAND

As usual.

WIFE

I wasn't sure. What is it today?

HUSBAND

Monday. Of course. You know I leave on Mondays.

WIFE

Of course.

HUSBAND

To work.

WIFE

The work.

HUSBAND

My work.

WIFE

Your work.

HUSBAND:

Of course. To work. The work. My work. I'm so hungry on days like this! Perfect. The work. Perfect days. They'll be perfect — um — days like this — um — all week. Through part of next. As well. My, but I was hungry!

(He pours himself a great mug of coffee, adds much sugar. He reaches for the newspaper, turns it back to its original state by painstakingly refolding it: then he folds it and proceeds to read and drink busily. As he becomes immersed in reading, the Wife, lighting another cigarette from the butt of the old one, smokes steadily and speaks tenderly, meditatively, to the window)

WIFE

How surprised I was to notice, when I happened to look at the world this morning, that the sun moves. No matter what they say, it really moves. Up it came: up and up and up. Nothing could stop it. The black trees grew a silvery green. The misty gray air turned lavender. Slowly the glistening streets became visible, and the gardens glimmering wet, and the houses, and then even the shadowy snow-covered hills — as though it were all just being brought into existence out of the very emptiness. Suddenly a cool breeze passed, opening my eyes and turning the leaves. And then, as I watched, the red edge of the sun came up there, there at the end of the world. It grew and it grew until it was a round rosy platter, oh about the size of our fruit dish. And then it flattened, and it shrank, smaller, smaller, higher and hotter and whiter. Of course it moves. And changes. It is never the same.

HUSBAND

Now we're talking!

WIFE

And there was also the pale moon, stained as an old handkerchief, drifting off to the other side of the world, floating away down into the sea. The robins have returned. The sky was no longer a black and empty place, but blue, pale blue, blue as the veins in my wrist, and very high and very quiet. There will be roses to cut this week. How the dewdrops sparkled on the roses!

HUSBAND

We were coming to this. It was about time too. We've reached it, we've got it now. Admit it! That's what I say! Tell them!

WIFE

Kitty sat watching the robins: only the white tip of her black tail twitched hungrily, just so. It was all so still. And beautiful. And polite.

HUSBAND

Logical too. Of course.

WIFE

And pointless. I lit my first cigarette. Altogether pointless.

HUSBAND:

They don't guess the half of it!

WIFE

I had gone for the papers. There they were. Of course.
How do they come to be there, folded and wrapped? I
could assume they are — brought by — um — Mister
Daly, that man who came to the door when we moved
in, three or seven years ago, and asked if we wanted
news. Or was it Adly? Or was it Lady? Yes, I said, Mister — um — Daly, of course. Of course we need news.
He was glad. And polite. No he didn't smoke, thank
you. He only brought news. But now it could be someone else. Couldn't it. I could suppose that. Couldn't I.
Of course.

HUSBAND

Of course! If they knew even half of it! Hah! If they but
knew —

WIFE

Or somehow automatic. Many things are. Automatic.
The techniques. The boxes. Inside the boxes there are
motors and wires and gears. On the outside there are
buttons and switches and wheels. On, off. Up, down.
In, out. Simple. The boxes. Automatic. Either it's off or
it's on. Yet even when it's off, it's on. Which is strange
but true. Which means it's off only when it's OUT OF
ORDER. But that's hardly possible, they say. What
with the techniques. So you must never put your finger
in. Never. Never. And that — that is how the news
comes to be there every morning. I think.

HUSBAND

Obviously it has to be simplified. Otherwise it would
be incomprehensible. To them. Otherwise it would be

confusing. To them. Oversimplified. Is what it has to be. For them.

WIFE

But I'm not sure. I might be mistaken. As when I thought the sky was pale blue. It is not blue, they say. Or that the sun rose up and changed before my very eyes into a bright, white burning ball. It does not move, they say. It has all been simplified. It's bad to make the old mistakes, they say. But it is inevitable. I think. Or why do I make mistakes like that. *They* don't .

HUSBAND

And it's foolproof.

WIFE

They say that if they made mistakes everything would be turned off. Definitely OUT OF ORDER. Then what would we do? We would begin to die.

HUSBAND

It's settled for good. Now we know.

WIFE

If everything were definitely OUT OF ORDER. . . .

HUSBAND

(Excited enough to speak to her over his paper) Of course it's such old stuff now, But listen to the idea. *(Reads impersonally)* Instantaneous release of ten X ten solar units . . . vehicles utilize random path trajectories . . . invulnerable . . . delivery in three minutes . . . obliterates one million cubic megameters . . . forever. Once and for all. Forever and ever! And ever and ever. What do you think! Of that!

WIFE
Sounds somehow automatic.

HUSBAND
It is, it is! To prevent mistakes. They say.

WIFE
Oh. Of course. I see. *(Lighting another cigarette, she directs her attention now from the window to the TV screen. She presses her remote-control, makes the round of channels, and returns to the original. Gazing at it absorbed, she speaks, however, to him)* Well, what do you think?

HUSBAND
(He is reading again, and answers her queries from a distant part of his attention) What do I think?

WIFE
About last night.

HUSBAND
Oh. Yes. Of course.

WIFE
How did you like it?

HUSBAND
All right. Actually. Yes. Novel approach. Interesting development. Sort of a — um — reverse twist in there. It was all right. Almost ready to go. Good you thought of it like that. Yes. I was surprised. Really.

WIFE
What shall we call it?

HUSBAND

Call it? I Don'tknow. What shall we call it?

WIFE

What about — oh . . . "Operation" — um . . . — "Reverse Twist"?

HUSBAND

Reverse Twist is all right. I think.

WIFE

I wonder why it took so long to find it. Because when you have it, it seems obvious. Doesn't it. So unexpected, yet . . . so simple. So . . . natural, I think. How could we have overlooked it all this time? Where were we? What were we doing? Oh how stupid it makes me feel! But I am not stupid, am I?

HUSBAND

(Still reading and marking his paper industriously with his red pencil) Those things take time. Sometimes years. They say.

WIFE

Is that what they say?

HUSBAND

Um. Years. Sometimes.

WIFE

But it's *been* years. Don't forget that. Years!

HUSBAND

(Reading) I'llmake a note of it.

WIFE

Years. I was that sick of your old Double Jumper Routine. Only a routine, it seemed. Automatic.

HUSBAND

Um.

WIFE

Didn't it seem somehow automatic?

HUSBAND

Um.

WIFE

And what was it before that old Double Jumper Routine? I forget. What was that again? Remember? What it was? Now why should I forget. . . .

HUSBAND

(Reading) Boom Town? How could you forget Boom Town! Where would we be today without Boom Town?

WIFE

Boom Town? Boom Town? What was that? Boom Town?

HUSBAND

Yes. Boom Town. You always used to say, "There's just so much I can stand!"

WIFE

(Laughs abruptly, a gay barking laughter, her eyes glowing for a moment with the memory) Ah, oh! Boom Town! Oh. Oh. Oh. Yes, I'dforgotten Boom Town. (Quite expres-

sionless again, and still watching the TV screen) Now why
is that? Whatever happened with that?

HUSBAND

With that? We quit wildcatting. Renewed the land. Put
down roots. Built home. Settled in. Found commu-
nity. There were the children to consider. Older. Experienced. Attitudes change, they say. As you get older.
Experienced. Moreover, experienced.

WIFE

Oh. Attitudes.

HUSBAND

Yes. They change. Attitudes. That'swhy you forgot. Life
changes. Moreover. Changes. Life.

WIFE

Attitudes. I suppose they do. Life changes. How curious. I never noticed. First one thing. Then another.
That's why I forgot. Changes. You forget pleasure. You
forget pain. You forget everything. So that's why I forgot Boom Town. Forgot that I used to say, "There's just
so much I can stand!" It must have been long ago.
How strange. . . . *(Somber)* We haven't much time now.

HUSBAND

Yes. I'll make a note. Operation . . . Reverse . . . Twist.
Technique. Model. Patents? Research? So forth. And
— um — yes: Not . . . much . . . time.

WIFE

That way you'll remember. *(He reads his paper and doesn't
notice her taunt)*

HUSBAND

Um. That way I'll remember.

WIFE

That way you won't make a mistake.

HUSBAND

Um. That way you can't make mistakes, they say.

WIFE

That's why you've been successful.

HUSBAND

That's why I've been so successful.

WIFE

Um. *(She is gazing out the window, her voice neutral. He explains, looking over the top of his paper at the TV)*

HUSBAND

That's why I've been so successful. Yes. Because the techniques demand it. A record. Everything. That way you remember.

WIFE

Um.

HUSBAND

Yes. Because if you have no record you don't know what happened. If you don't know what happaned you can't hope to grasp what's happening. And if you can't understand what's happening you don't know how to prepare for what is going to happen. *(His tone is didactic: he has expounded these principles countless times, and patiently does so again)*

WIFE

(Startled, looking out the window, which is bright and blank) For what is going to happen?

HUSBAND

Um. As I've said, I think. Haven't I? Yes. Always said.

WIFE

(Neutral once more) Um.

HUSBAND

The future. We're going on. Into the future. Somehow. We should be prepared. It's simple. If you know what you're doing. Example: weren't we prepared when the waters were used? Suppose we hadn't been prepared! But we were. We were! All right?

WIFE

Um.

HUSBAND

If you can remember — can you remember? That was merely the first of our — um — difficulties. You've forgotten. Since then there have been so many — doesn't matter. Um. Anyway it's simple. If you know what you are doing.

WIFE

If. But what happened to your grandfather? He knew what he was doing. They say.

HUSBAND

Um.

WIFE

Didn't he. Well, did he?

HUSBAND

Um. He knew. Yes. But. It was just beginning then.
Actually. Primitive. No method. Crude techniques.
Unsystematic. He never knew what happened, they say.
That's what happened to my grandfather. I think.

WIFE

He wasn't unlucky?

HUSBAND

No. No no no. Unlucky! No such thing. How absurd
you are. How can there be any such thing? Unlucky!
Didn't he live a long time? Didn't he finally have his
son? My father. I wouldn't call that unlucky. Would
you?

WIFE

Um.

HUSBAND

And my father lived a long time too. And he knew what
had happened. Moreover, did he do well or didn't he
do well? And why did he do well? Technique! He knew
what was happening. He recorded. Clarified. Diversi-
fied. Consolidated. Would you call that unlucky?

WIFE

Well. . . .

HUSBAND

And then my father had his son. Me. Moreover, I've done — um — pretty well. Despite everything, I'm doing well. Even better.

WIFE

Well. . . .

HUSBAND

And despite everything I'm prepared for what is going to happen. In fact, in fact — I'm so well prepared that, that —

WIFE

Well. . . .

HUSBAND

(Looking at her for the first time. And she at him. They are expressionless) Well, what?

WIFE

I —

HUSBAND

Well, what? You know there isn't any time to lose. There's so much to do. We're on our way. Things are happening. Things will be happening. Inexorably. We're on the move. We must keep moving. On. Moving. Why just the techniques alone —

WIFE

Do you want to know?

HUSBAND

Um. Of course.

WIFE

Do you really want to know?

HUSBAND

Of course. I do. Um. You never know, I think.

WIFE

Do you?

HUSBAND

I should. I need to. Moreover everything may come to depend on it. Inevitably does, they say. Have I forgotten anything? Could I have forgotten anything?

WIFE

Your brother.

HUSBAND

(Somewhat puzzled, if not surprised) My brother? Why do you mention my brother?

WIFE

You never do.

HUSBAND

I never do? Why should I? It's been over twenty years. We drifted apart. I have no brother. He slipped into some other kind of orbit. No idea what's happened to my brother. Who knows where he is? Or what he's doing? He doesn't matter. He's out of it. My brother. Don't know why you should even mention him. My brother!?

WIFE

Why I should mention him. Just wondering. *(Her eyes drift back to the TV screen. She lights another cigarette, stifles a yawn. She is ready to let the subject drop. His eyes drift outside the window)* He came into my mind, I think. You would say it's about time. Wouldn't you say it's about time?

HUSBAND

What does that mean? Nothing at all, does it! No, I would not say it's about time. About time. Doesn't mean anything. At all. Can't . About time. *(He rises abruptly, brushes himself, rolls up his napkin, Puts away his marking pencil, folds the paper neatly and tosses it neatly into a basket. He goes round the table to her, and stands behind her chair, holding her head tenderly against him and looking absently out the window, through which is seen the luminous fog that has been there from the beginning)* Not at all. What were you thinking? About my brother. Thinking anything at all?

WIFE

(Watching the TV) I?

HUSBAND

(Squeezing her throat) You . . . were . . . thinking . . . ?

WIFE

I . . . don't. . . know . . . what. . . .

HUSBAND

(Throttling her) You were thinking: It's about time. *(Harder still)* What . . . is . . . about . . . time?

WIFE
(She has noticed nothing) I . . . Don't. . . know. Your brother?

HUSBAND
But why? *(Rapidly)* Why?

WIFE
I . . . don't. . . know. He just came . . . I think.

HUSBAND
(Murderously shaking her) When? Where?

WIFE
Into my mind. *(He relaxes his grip instantly, holds her head tenderly once more. She has noticed nothing at all)*

HUSBAND
Um.

WIFE
Tell me about him

HUSBAND
(Stroking her cheek absently. Now he watches the TV screen, and she is not listening to him at all) They say Mother favored him. He'd be the lucky one, they said. She thought luck was everything. Luck! Father believed in me. They say. Because I'd keep things moving. Develop things. Organize things. Right from the start there was that difference. But not enough was known. Picture not clear yet. I think it is now. Clear. Getting clearer. *(Longish silence as they stare into their respective focal points)* If it isn't really clear yet. . . . Mother was like you. She'd

get a notion. She would guess something. Not that she
knew. She'd come in upset one fine morning. No reason at all. She would say to Father, You see?! You see?!
*(The Wife starts, looks up at him, as he looks tenderly at
her)* There was nothing there. At all.

WIFE

There was nothing there. Although —

HUSBAND

Said she saw things happening. Which is impossible.

WIFE

Impossible. Impossible?

HUSBAND

Or at least unreliable. You think you see things happen. Merely *think* you do. At best, you're only remem-
bering them a little while afterwards. At best.

WIFE

(Trustfully) Like Operation Reverse Twist.

HUSBAND

(Taken quite off stride) Um. What?

WIFE

Like the Reverse Twist.

HUSBAND

Oh. Ah. Um. Yes. Which is why you *must* note things.
Records. History. Everything is in the past. In a sense.
Even discoveries have already happened. In a sense. All
we can do is make notes. That's the basis of the techniques. You see, don't you? You understand, don't you?

WIFE

Yes. Um. But —

HUSBAND

Take, for example, your Reverse Twist. Assume it was possible. Of course. Even assume it was probable. Of course. But now it has happened. Last night. Now it is today. So that, um, Operation Reverse Twist was already in the past. In a sense. You see? You *do* see?

WIFE

Yes. No. I'm not sure. *(After a silence, she cries out very loudly in orgasmic anguish — though not to him — and she is not in the least aware of her cry)* Darling! Oh darling!

HUSBAND

Anyway, my brother. Lacked my concentration. Like my grandfather, actually, in a way. As a boy he was wild. Wild as a boy. He'd always be a boy. Even if he is older than me. My brother.

WIFE

Older than you? I thought —

HUSBAND:

Well, we're really the same age. I think.

WIFE

Twins?

HUSBAND

Um. Actually. Yes. No. I'm not sure.

WIFE

I don't understand.

HUSBAND

Brothers. Twins. Same thing. Somehow got turned round, they said. He. I. Um. Us. Doesn't matter now, does it. Which was which. We're not at all alike, I think. You wouldn't know him.

WIFE:
(As though begging for reassurance) I wouldn't know him?

HUSBAND

Never.

WIFE

You would.

HUSBAND

Of course. I'd know him. Because. An old story. *(He is vague, rather distressed)* They say.

WIFE

I wonder if. . . .

HUSBAND

Don't. Doesn't matter. We're different. Always have been. And then . . . because . . . moreover . . . there are certain details. Details within details. Pointless. One of those things.

WIFE

One of which things?

HUSBAND

Natural. *(He is irritated)*

WIFE

Natural?

HUSBAND

Unimportant, I mean. A coincidence. Irregular. Pointless. Unfair.

WIFE

Oh.

HUSBAND

A mistake. Unfair. Incongruous. Odd. Unusual.

WIFE

Oh.

HUSBAND

Accidental. Abnormal. Erratic. Unfair.

WIFE

Oh.

HUSBAND

Unfair. Doesn't matter anyway.

WIFE

*(Her voice rising in a crescendo of sheer agony that he doesn't
notice in the least)* Are you sure? Are you convinced? Are
you perfectly certain? Are you? Are you?

HUSBAND

I hope you got me packed.

WIFE

(Her voice is quite ordinary) Yes, you're packed. Yes. Are you ready? *(She is up and leaving the kitchen)*

HUSBAND

(Looking at his watch, shaking his head in annoyance) I'm late. I shouldn't be late. It's risky.

WIFE

(Returning with two elegant, terribly heavy suitcases and an attaché case: they seem to weigh a hundred pounds each) Before you go —

HUSBAND

(To himself) If I skipped Honolulu, I could pick up some time.

WIFE

— I wanted to ask you. Would you call me? No. I know you're not allowed. But if I called, could I reach you? No. I'm not allowed. But — *(her eyes are drawn to the window)* — just in case?

HUSBAND

(Involved with his watch and calculations, he is matter-of-fact) Everything's taken care of. We're prepared for anything.

WIFE

As usual.

HUSBAND

Of course. For this week. And most of next week. I think.
Perfect days.

WIFE

But — just in case?

HUSBAND

Can't . Rules.

WIFE

(She sits on a suitcase) Just — in case?

HUSBAND

You *know* There's no such thing as "just in case." Not
allowed. The techniques.

WIFE

Um.

HUSBAND

*(Surprised by her doubt yet grasping its significance, he fi-
nally speaks directly to her — with growing exasperation)*
What *is* the matter with you? Why are you like this
today? You *know* it's not allowed. You know the situation is absolutely delicate. How can you be so irrespon-
sible?

WIFE

Um. *(To herself)* What a dummy!

HUSBAND

Sometimes I think you're not with me! Do you realize
what you're doing when you ask something like this?

No, you don't grasp it at all. Do you. Try to comprehend now: you are introducing a novel variable! At this moment. In history. Think of that. You want to do something like that at this enormous moment in history? Do you understand what a mistake a novel variable would be? *(He is even a little angry)* Under the circumstances? For all of us? A terrible mistake. Think of that. A terrible, terrible mistake. . . . What dummy?

WIFE
Who? Such a dummy, I said. Isn't it all so . . . it's just all so dummy.

HUSBAND
(Longish silence. Now he is petulant, even pleading) You know I would tell you. You should know this is part of something much bigger, and much more important than — I can't risk introducing a novel variable. Not now. No dummies. Everything's set up. Rules are. . . . Old mistakes. . . . They say that. . . . Or maybe . . . yes. A dummy might work. *(Glancing at his watch again, baffled, worried. Speaks to himself)* I'll have to skip Madrid. Can't be helped. What will they say in Nairobi? *(Turns on her in full rage)* You're my wife! Have you forgotten *that*, too? You can't do this to me. Not now. My wife?! Why if I'd known you would be the sort of woman to lose her nerve, I'd never have married — that sort of woman, I mean. Who'd want a dummy for a wife?

WIFE
(Responding suddenly with equal vehemence, pounding frail fists against his unfeeling chest) You're my husband! Don't forget that! I can't go on. As I have. What has happened to us? I have the right to know! What is happening to

us! Why, if I had known you would think only of the techniques, I would never have married —

HUSBAND

(Speaking sweetly to her, as though their voices had never been raised) You've never been like this, I think. What's the matter? You know nothing's happened to us. You know nothing's happening to us. You know nothing can happen to us. It's under control. We're not dummies, you know. Tell me.

WIFE

(She places her cheek tenderly against his breast. She keeps one eye on the TV however) It's nothing. Really. Just a little frightened. Haven't you ever been frightened?

HUSBAND

That's a mistake. It isn't something that — it can't be something that—

WIFE

Don't you know what it is to be frightened? I'm such a dummy.

HUSBAND

What?! You should have told me sooner. Why didn't you tell me? *(Over her shoulder, while patting her, he looks at his watch)* No, you're not. You're just my own . . . wife. And it's late. Now. I don't believe there will be time to—

WIFE

I did.

HUSBAND
(To himself) Have to cut out Saskatoon as well. Too bad. Risky. Tch. Risky. And Calgary? Tch.

WIFE
(In a low dreamy whisper: she is absorbed in the TV) I did. I did tell you. I did. I'm not such a dummy, you know.

HUSBAND
(To himself, thinking about his schedule) The past cannot be helped. What's happened has happened. Too bad. Gone. Can't be adjusted. We'll have to change the pattern for next week, is all. Which, of course, involves the week after. And so forth. For good. Um. Risky risky risky. Where's my margin? I've got to have some margin. But — no variables! *(He is both determined and panicky)*

WIFE
Last year, I think. I think I told you last year.

HUSBAND
(Rapidly, nervously, thinking out loud) Must alert the analytical boys. They'll team up with the factors to resynthesize the flow. That'smore staff. Overtime. Dammit. Office crowded now! Dammit. Yes. . . . But. . . . And. . . . Still, very risky.

WIFE
Or the year before. You made a note. You promised you'd remember. Now you've forgotten. Aha! You see! You see! Now who's the dummy?!

HUSBAND

(Coming back to her line of conversation without a break)
No. Not at all. How could I? *(Explains patiently)* Part of
the record. *You've* forgotten. Why we made this place.
You don't remember. You wanted something. I gave it
to you. Extended the complexes. Don't you remember?
We installed ourselves.

WIFE

(Sighing contentedly, whispering softly, eyes glued to the TV)
Yes. Yes. Yes. Yes, oh yes!

HUSBAND

(Hasn't heard her: enumerates all of its features with satis-
faction) Safe, now. Whole thing's automatic. Doors. Keys.
Perpetual lights. Permanent pressurizer. Stabilizer. Con-
ditioner. Electronic exterminator. Self-renewing garden.
Synchronized, miniaturized, and directed by self-en-
casing units: The Boxes. Automatic. Plugged in from A
to Z. Nothing can happen now. System engages itself.

WIFE

(Cries out in her dream of TV, as though in terror) Oh
darling! Oh darling!

HUSBAND

Except, of course, for an error. Marginal. But, we *have*
to have that margin. Oh yes. We'd be dummies if we
had no margin, wouldn't we!

WIFE

(Lamenting piteously, twisting his lapels in supplication)
Oh please! Please! Please, darling! Please, oh please!

HUSBAND

Just set the switch. It takes care of the rest. Nothing to surprise you.

WIFE

(In utter desperation) I'm frightened. Frightened, frightened! *(Last exclamation is moaned)*

HUSBAND

Don't worry. It's just like a dummy. It's automatic. You *do* understand?

WIFE

(Quietly watching TV again, as though She'd made no outburst) Yes. needn't worry. Of course.

HUSBAND

(Pats her head, lifts his suitcases as though they were empty) I'm off. I must go. Understand?

WIFE

(Looking coyly at him, she tries once more with a wee wheedling voice that knows it will get its way) But — just . . . in case?

HUSBAND

I think I'll be sorry for this. But, um, all right: "just . . . in case. . . . ."

(He consults his watch as he gives his itinerary. She has returned to the TV and doesn't listen. She lights a new cigarette, pours herself a cup of coffee, gets involved with whatever is showing or turns channels for amusement. As he matter-of-factly reviews his schedule, there may be a sequence of changes in lighting to correspond with the passing days. His

speech is not delivered monotonously But with variations and self-dra-
matization, to render it interesting. TV may weaken and fade in coun-
terpoint with lights)

Running behind badly . . . Um. ..I should be leaving
Buffalo at ten-thirty: only a brief reconstruction conference. Four to six-thirty, Buenos Aires: — they're having hydrostatic-ramp difficulties there, as well as local
recalcitrance — probably will require reportioning the
malleable districts. Hope they won't be stubborn. Odd
traditions surviving down there: they like friction for
its own sake! Then the native dinner at the Tenochtitlan
Hostal, where we'll cover social aspects of geobiological
refabrication, regarding particularly the introduction
of the prolific configurations. Leaving Mexico before
coffee — have to apologize for that, can't help it now
— and pick up four hours en route to Manila. Assign-
ment complete by midnight: merely recoding the hy-
pothetical transducers for omnivoltage capacity and
highload transference along the polar magnetic ducts.
Then Tokyo, for the nanoscalar air-bearings. Also take a
little looksee in at Kyoto: they seem to be concerned
about my schedule for those super-orbital disciplines.
Um. Maybe we could reactivate our planetary calen-
dars without using subtemporal circuits? Say, how about
that! Um. Hate to cut close corners like that: sets a bad
example. Well, we'll see. Melbourne by eight in the
morning. Packaging. Lunch. Wednesday: Munich. For
pneumatics, dynamics and stress-sensors. Best people
in the world there for that. Must come out of their
psychology, I think. Nothing that special involved, but
it's important to have it all molecularly identical, because unless it is . . . you can just imagine what. . . . oh
boy! Trust them in Munich for hydraulic barriers!
So . . . let's see, I was . . . Um. By three, Roma. Napoli

at four. Squeeze hard and get Palermo in by five. *(Muttering, vexed)* Can't understand what could be causing the hitch in that hyperplastic transshipment. They promised me that . . . they should know that. . . . They're still corrupt there, I imagine. Would they dare to skin us . . . ? Let 'em just try! Karachi for dinner; that would be eight-fifteen. I bet that committee will solve those synoptic variations in solar torques with that new tensor they've evolved. Personally, I don't care for their Oriental approach. Too spooky for me. But if it works, it will change even the most reliable basis for the techniques we have ever had. Won't they be thrown for a loop in Edinburgh! Heh heh! I told them to drop those Manchester-Cambridge empirics, I told them! Unreliable algorithms. If you ain't got algorithms, you ain't got nothin'. Well, Stockholm at midnight, for alloyed rotors. Which brings us, I think, to Thursday A.M.C. : Houston. Collocation of reports. Must watch out for them there: there are deals within deals. They say. Let 'em just try! Then on to Caracas: 4:40. Inspect hyper-hydraulic presses for proper phasing at macrovelocities. We'll get up into the mountains for some evening air. Say, weren't we scheduling them for a Totalization Festival that night? I think I could sit in on that. Can't harm. Might be interesting. To consider, I mean. Post-transference side of things. Ultimates and all. The Ultimates, the Ultimates. . . . I like Caracas. Change of pace. Why miss the chance? So then. It's now Friday noon: Singapore — check out designs and test rigs for reactor gear. New mockups. It will be a remarkable demonstration of advanced universal projection. Well ahead of schedule, too. Really fascinating the way time doesn't affect them. Chinese. Soooo Chinese. . . . Only *they* could think of it. Friday night is open. No. Ah, yes. The Bamboo Shrine Moon Motel in

Hong Kong. Dinner. Casual. Some people I must see, even if they're not ready to see me. *(Angry)* Some people never know what they want! What they *think* they want. As if we'd leave it to them to do the wanting! Or even the thinking. Dammit. Oh, I'll hear what they have to say for themselves. Show them we care. See them, talk to them. In person. Personal relations. Heh heh. *(Dark now: small, hot spot on the top of his head, as he speaks to himself sinisterly)* They'll know . . . what . . . to think . . . then. Um. Saturday morning bright and early, very busy: Vladivostok. Then St. Petersburg at 2:30. Stuff of theirs is still formative. But promising. Very. If it can stand adaptation. The cycle there, as I see it . . . *(Greenish-tinted light perhaps)* . . . seems to be not only polyphasic and hypermutational but also regenerative. They've come up with rather unusual self-deducing control servos. Nifty. Have to give them credit for their initiative. I always had a soft spot for the right thing in control servos . . . Built-in, too. . . . At five o'clock the top directorate of Aesop meets: Paris. Formality. I'll insist on it, though. Formal dinner in Monte Carlo. A bore. I'll insist on it, though. And then . . . *(Lavenderish light)* . . . for a nightcap. Tangiers. And recapitulation of our finality sequences. The Ultimates again. Have to look at the results. Every week. I don't really like contemplating those damned results. Need a drink for that. Techniques demand it, though. Ultimates and all. You know what I mean. Then, Sunday morning — and I'm back again! If something tricky doesn't happen. Somehow. Expect me. Have I forgotten. . . forgotten anything? No. How could I? After all. Well, then. All right? All right!

(He does not wait for her response, which is not forthcoming in any event, but brushes his lips over the top of her head, mechanically, and

slips out the door, which has opened at his approach, and which re-
mains open on the void. The din of traffic enters like a Niagara as the
door slides open; but it is as nothing compared to the incredible decibels
of an extraordinarily-powerful motor that starts up and moves away,
rapidly shaking the very house with its power. The door slips to. There is
the silence, the machine silence, of the kitchen again. The WIFE, look-
ing at the TV, assents somnambulistically)

WIFE

All right? All right. Dummy! *(She stretches, yawns luxu-*
riously as though waking for the first time today)
All . . . right. . . . *(She emits a burst of laughter)* Dummies! *(She smiles at the TV, not really seeing it anymore)* all
right! *(She switches it off)* Dummies. *(She is answering*
an unheard voice) All right. *(She looks about the room*
contemptuously, as though she is a complete stranger in it)
Half-dead. *(She goes to the window, hisses at it)* all right.
(She turns around, lights a cigarette, seems to be making up
her mind about something) Half-alive! *(She goes out the*
other door with brisk steps, returns with a large make-up
box, seats herself — half-turned away from audience —
and, by the garish light emitted from the box, makes up her
face, muttering to herself in mounting anger) All
right . . . dummies . . . all right . . . dummies . . . all
right all of us alright . . . what dummies we are!

(She stops in mid-phrase as she becomes conscious of a faint, sensuous
drumming heartbeat that is neither in the house nor outside — it may
be done by electronic pulsation. It will steadily grow louder. At a paral-
lel rate the light diminishes. As though hypnotized, she rises, closing the
box — her makeup completed — glides languorously backward to
FRONT CENTER, her hips moving inside her kimono in the sugges-
tion of the dance that would accompany the drumming beat. Then she
glides, still dancing from the waist down, backward to STAGE RIGHT,
where she comes to rest with her back against the door, as the drumming

is loudest. By now it is dark: the drumming abruptly stops with the appearance of a man's figure in the door at STAGE LEFT. He is tall, well-dressed: indeed he wears the same clothing as her husband had worn, although it is crumpled and used hard. In fact, were it not that he has ears, he might seem to be her husband himself. He wears dark glasses. He carries luggage identical to her husband's, although it is quite worn and seems to be too heavy for him He sets it down and steps forward into the kitchen a pace, which now is lit only by the luminous control knobs at rear, and perhaps by the grayish light of the TV screen. The walls can have receded at this point. His face is calm, in repose. When she speaks, her voice is passionate, yet poised and luxurious: a much richer voice than she had used heretofore. Perhaps a spot grows on her slowly from overhead)

WIFE

Is it you? At last?

BROTHER

(Nearly inaudible) Um.

WIFE

I've waited for you. So long. I've waited for you so very long.

BROTHER

(Nearly inaudible) Um.

WIFE

Now you're here. *(Takes off her kerchief. Her hair is set perfectly for evening. There is actually a diamond pin spar-kling in it. She whispers)* Well?

BROTHER

(Quiet, noncommittal) all right.

WIFE

(She drops her kimono. She wears a long luxurious night-gown or is it a peignoir?) Well?

BROTHER

All right.

WIFE

(Feverishly) Wait. Wait. *(Unhooking her nightgown, she lets it fall to the floor, revealing a glamorous, backless, and low-cut evening gown. Spotlight may sparkle on her. There is enough light from a spot on his head now to reveal a trace of a smile on his impassive face)* Now. Well?

BROTHER

(Softly) Yes. All right.

WIFE

(Holding out her arms) At last. At last. At last. It must be you! At last. *(Crooned)*

BROTHER

(Reassuringly) All right. Yes.

WIFE

But you do want me? You will take me? At last?

BROTHER

If there is time. *(He steps forward a pace. His hands seem to open a little toward her. The spot on his head grows and fades almost imperceptibly: this "pulsing" is not strong enough to be disturbing but merely happens, slowly and rhythmically. His head is bowed and contemplative)*

WIFE

Free me? Save me?

BROTHER

If there is time.

WIFE

I have been alone. Too long. Always. Now you've come.

BROTHER

Um.

WIFE

Oh you don't have to answer. You don't have to promise. Wait. If there is time.

BROTHER

If there is time.

WIFE

(She moves towards him almost imperceptibly. He waits, unaware of her approach. Finally, she will be in his arms . . . at the point noted below) Last night, somewhere between sleeping and waking, you came. I don't sleep much. I seem to have lost the habit. Though it is not really necessary, they say. Sleep. Because it is a delusion. A disappointment. Sleep. Moreover it is dangerous, they say. They say that sleep is very dangerous. Because that is the way we are approached, that is the only way now that we can be approached, they say, and reached, they say, by . . . by. . . .

BROTHER

A novel variable?

WIFE

Yes. That. Last night — if it was last night — I can't remember — in the dark of that room, in the silence, in the utter isolation of that room, we were lying on our bed, alone, together . . . yet I thought of you.

BROTHER

And you were thirsty.

WIFE

Very thirsty. How long had it been? I was parched. How long since I had been touched, since I had been opened, since I had been filled? I was in darkness, in the silence. Was that my breathing I heard? I was not sure. It was cold. I was naked. I was sinking into the cold. My ears ached. My head ached. I was growing heavy.

BROTHER

Heavy. Heavy.

WIFE

Heavy. So heavy. I was a piece of scrap. Broken metal. Sinking through the coldness of the stone of the earth. And as I sank, slowly, into the deeper cold, I could feel my knees, my belly, my breasts. *(She does so with her jeweled hands)* And they were no longer a part of me. They belonged to a cold body, someone else's cold body. The hands that touched them were another's hands. Sinking. Where was I? How long had I been falling? After the third day. . . .

BROTHER

You were no longer thirsty. After the fifth day. . . .

WIFE

I wanted to die. To kill myself. Die. Yet I'd grown used to this darkness. Time. There was no such thing as time.

BROTHER

You were hungry.

WIFE

I wanted to pick the cherries. There were cherry trees nearby, all around me. I could smell the ripe cherries. An orchard. I was in an orchard. And then I thought of you. At that moment.

BROTHER

You were lonely.

WIFE

So lonely. All those years, how long had it been? Following him, from one life to another. And I had never thought of you. Though you were there all the time, I had never thought of you. Don't you find that strange?

BROTHER

Is it strange?

WIFE

Very strange. Nothing else I have thought of is so strange as that. I was on the bottom. I had sunk down and down — through the transparent darkness, the cold darkness that pressed upon me, heavier and heavier, until now I was on the bottom, under the stone. Nothing but the burning cold and the thick silence of a hundred hundred miles of frozen stone. I was on the bottom, among a few scattered, broken shells and stars. I was not afraid any more. I was on the bottom. And then I thought of you. For the first time. *(She laughs a short, gay laugh)* And I worried about you. Someone I had never known or even heard of! Worried! Don't you find that very strange? *(She has reached him. She looks up into his impassive face)*

BROTHER

Is it?

WIFE

Anything might have happened to you! Our world has changed over and over again. Yet we have gone on. Until now, when it seemed . . .

BROTHER

That you thought of me.

WIFE

(She caresses his face, his head, shoulders, arms, while speaking) How I, how I have *needed* you. How I have needed *you*! You must have starved. While he lunched. Alone and aching and cold while he rested. You might even have died, while he was contracting the future. Anything was possible!

BROTHER

Anything.

WIFE

(Embracing him hungrily. He is impassive) How did I know it was you? I can't remember my childhood. My girlhood. My men. My marriages, even all my children. Yet — when you came into my mind I recognized you!

BROTHER

That is very strange.

WIFE

(She kisses him passionately about the face, speaking all the while) And then, I wondered — how would I ever find you? Could I live until I found you? Would I be able to speak to you? Would you hear me? And if I cried out to you in that emptiness, "Come! Come to me!" would you come? But now I have found you. Where have you been?

BROTHER

(Stage has grown fairly light by now. It grows slowly, steadily, inexorably brighter- — until the light is unbearable) Here.

WIFE

Here?

BROTHER

Here. Somewhere near. Always. *(He seems to be searching vaguely from behind his dark glasses. Silence: he is baffled by what he fails to recognize)* . . . He went away. One night. A long time ago. Alone. Empty-handed. Never returned. Never will return. I stayed. Here. It was my home. Hard to remember, But somewhere here. . . .

WIFE

He went away?

BROTHER

Ran. Away. If he hadn't run away. . . .

WIFE

He ran away?

BROTHER

Disappeared. Vanished. Up the creek. Into the hills.
Gone. Had to. I would have —

WIFE

(Clutches him) Killed him?

BROTHER

Killed him! If he'd stayed here. If he'd had the courage.
If he weren't such a thief, such a swindler, such a coward. I'd have —

WIFE

(Incredulous) Killed him? Oh, darling!

BROTHER

Got away by luck. Sheer luck. He always had it. Luck.
And he *needed* it! Luck!

WIFE

Killed him? *(She laughs)*

BROTHER

(Angry) Killed him! Yes! Cut him down, and chopped
him up, and thrown away the pieces! *(Calmly)* Family
matter. *(Distant, ruminative)* You never heard about it?
He has a way of talking. Oh, there is nothing he wouldn't
say, wouldn't do. . . . And you were never told?

WIFE

No. Yes. I'm not sure. *(Faintly, far-off there is a sonic boom)* I was just wondering. . . .

BROTHER

Don't . Doesn't matter. Anyhow. It's over. Done with. Forgotten. But if he came back . . . here. . . .

WIFE

(She whispers loudly at his ear) He will. He always does.

BROTHER

If he ever tried. . . .

WIFE

He will. On Sunday morning. Our anniversary. Sunday. Or some day.

BROTHER

Although it happened so long ago. . . . It really doesn't matter —

WIFE

(Another sonic boom, somewhat stronger) That's his. He's passing.

BROTHER

It's been so long since. . . . No one remembers. Anymore. World changes. People change. No one cares. I don't either. . . .

WIFE

(She has released him. She begins to drift away, backward, almost imperceptibly. By the end of the action, she will be

once more pressed back against the door at right — if walls have gone, she is pressed against the invisible barrier that limits room) We have so little time now. This is *our* moment. Our *enormous* moment.

BROTHER

(Quietly, to himself) Though I've thought about it so long, it doesn't matter, in the end. What matters is now. I'm ready. Finally. To begin. Never mind what happened. It's gone. We're moving ahead now, to the future.

WIFE:

(She is exuberant: she begins in full joyous voice — yet her enthusiasm diminishes as his voice grows stentorian) So much to discover! Our selves! *(Another sonic boom, stronger)* That's his! *(To herself with relief)* He's passed. *(Aloud)* We still have our lives. And so little time. We must begin. But where?

BROTHER

(Starting low and rather indecisively, but gathering momentum and power and exaltation, gradually, until the very end) Because, now that I'm here. . . . Where I've always been. . . . In a sense. . . . We are going to start. Again. From here. Where I have always been. Here, somewhere.

WIFE

Yes! That is what I meant. That is what I have always wished, always. Do you see my toes, my tender little toes?

BROTHER

Never mind what is happening. I am going to do it my own way! All right.

WIFE

Yes. That is what I mean. Do you see my feet, my pretty feet, with their fine ankles?

BROTHER

Never mind what they say is going to happen.

WIFE

And my round calves? So cool to the touch. . . .

BROTHER

Never mind them, the others who have failed in their miserable blind purposes and ways. Never mind the rules, the clubs, the societies, the companies and committees, the judges, the juries, the banks, soldiers and sailors and syndicates of space, the politicians of the world and their police, the philosophers, psychologists and professors and priests and prophets and poets and panderers and prostitutes and people of the professions in general, the people, the people and people and people. . . . It is my way that matters now. My way only. From here.

WIFE

Yes. That is what it will mean. And my legs, my long, strong legs . . . ?

BROTHER

From the ground up. And up. To choose a site, if such there be, that has truly natural advantages —

WIFE

— My knees that are so smooth and round. . . .

BROTHER

— Something solid amidst the ancient swamps and sands and marshes where I've always struggled, where I have been lost again and again, yet going on step by step, hand over hand, a place exposed to the skies, yet sheltered from the changing winds of the inevitable and prolonged bitter seasons, a site dry and warm yet abundantly watered, where the roads shall meet —

WIFE

— And these firm and straight thighs that are like polished marble: my so full and lovely legs?

BROTHER

— Meet, meet! Yet will not cross or tangle, where there is light and quiet and safety . . . *(Sonic boom, louder yet)* . . . and the air is free and fresh, the food tasty and tender and newly grown in neat gardens visited by bees and watched over by song birds, where we shall walk and ride and swim and run, dance and sit in places conveniently planned and commodiously arranged, where the materials are cheap and lightweight and strong and adaptable, easy to use and keep clean, where there are centers for shopping and temples for prayer and meditation, for exercise and games, information and entertainment, for working and playing —

WIFE

— And here is my deep belly: complete and round and yielding. It is a secret fountain, and it is framed by my wild and slender sides. And here, here are my breasts: like soft birds. Do you see my body, my desirable body?

BROTHER

— for eating and meeting, for judging and speaking, and squares for hospitals and schools and cemeteries, prisons and libraries and factories and theaters and offices and prisons and parades and parks and gardens and prisons and —

WIFE

Or my shoulders of old ivory, my arms like alabaster vines, warm and strong and light as feathers on your heart, and my neck like a milky column of —

BROTHER

— And all of it full of my invented healthy families, spreading over the great green and tree-lined boulevards, spotlessly broad, branching across the lands, across the world, bridging the seas, diving below the seas, above the valleys and over the earth and beyond, beyond, growing beyond, spreading — *(Another sonic boom, louder yet and closer. Fills the stage)*

WIFE

— And, and my head — do you see my head? Like a blossom, a flower of the morning, and my lips soft and covered with honey, my eyes like coral grottoes through which the deep-sea waves drift with changing lights, my hair like a delicate and living thing? Do you see? For you. All. For you. Now. But now. While there is time. (She sways in supplication) Do you see? My body, my beautiful body? *(Stage is very bright now)*

BROTHER

— Spreading and growing, everywhere the same, everywhere equal, everywhere together, the many as one, now and forever, united, like, like, like —

WIFE

— My simple, my spontaneous, my musical, and utterly original body My beautiful, human body? *(Very loud sonic boom indeed)*

BROTHER

— And yes, it is one, like one vast radiant incorporation . . . *(His tone is exalted, thrilling)* . . . a scintillating body, a city golden, ruby and emerald, an organism, jeweled and sparkling and glowing with the brightness of many suns, and governed by one and only one law, governed, I say —

WIFE

(Whispering piteously, desperately, for the last time) It is all I have. It is all there is for me to give. It is all there ever was for you. . . . For you. . . . For me. . . . My life. . . .

BROTHER

(Triumphantly) — Governed, I say, with the same indivisible justice and meaning and mercy for all, from here, from now on, for ever . . . and forever, and ever and ever and everand foreverand everand everand everandever foreverandeverandeverandeverand — *(With a flourish, he removes his dark glasses as he ecstatically pronounces his last andevers: he has no eyes!)*

(Blinding flash. A sonic boom rocks the theater!)

Silence. Darkness.

*   *   *

The Dummy

Act II

Persons in Act II

ALFRED O'MEAGER: "The Watch King," whose time is up.

MADELEINE O'TOOLE: wife of DANIEL O'MEAGER, and mistress of ALFRED O'MEAGER: an alcoholic, and a clairvoyant.

DOCTOR KILDARE: A medico.

ABRAHAM O'TOOLE: President of the World, an administrator.

PATRICK ISAAC O'TOOLE: General Of The World, no better than he should be, but no worse, either.

DANIEL O'MEAGER: Director Of World Publicity, a demagogue, who loves not wisely, though too well.

The Scene

A sort of hospital room in a high place, its furnishings simple and elegant. Beside the large window that is the Left Wall there is a chaise longue facing the enormous TV-Screen in the wall at Left Rear; placed conveniently near the chaise is a small portable bar; at Center Front is a low settee that will hold three persons quite comfortably. On the Center Rear Wall is a great clock with several kinds of hands moving at various speeds: it is too complex for Us to read — perhaps it keeps the times of the solar system as well as of the globe. Below the clock, the bed in which ALFRED O'MEAGER lies in coma, kept alive by the wires in his scalp, chest, groin. These "nerves" and "vessels" come from shiny chromium valves in the wall beneath the clock and from the little, elaborate chromium machine standing beside the bed on his left. This machine is silent as it pumps and registers. On the patient's right a low bed table with a lamp, some medicines, hypos, trays of the usual paraphernalia.

MADELEINE O'TOOLE O'MEAGER lies on the chaise, rather reclines in languid ease, her face half-turned from Us; she fills a martini glass from the chilled decanter on the bar. She is dressed in a sequined, hobbling cocktail skirt that reveals only her shoes, a transparen't blouse reveals a great, pendant ruby between her breasts; her auburn, ankle-length hair is thick as a horse's tail. On the Right Rear Wall is the door to the corridor. Outside the great window and over the towers of the vast city, it is afternoon.

DOCTOR KILDARE is examining the lengthy taped ribbon that has been printed off by the machine at O'MEAGER'S side; he marks certain interesting passages. (This tape is produced at a slow steady rate through the entire action; it curls down on the floor, but no one pays it any attention, even if they have to step through it.) Meanwhile, the TV shows a newsfilm: fighting, rockets, places, or seems to be broadcasting it, from the lights and sounds we hear.

DOCTOR KILDARE adjusts some of the tubes and wires and changes some dial settings on the machine; he may attach others that he reels out of the wall, and he may seem to be reaches checking the planetary clock. MADELEINE O'TOOLE's arm languidly to press a button on the bar top: though the channel of the TV is switched, the same sort of images appear: deafening battles in rain, beneath the sea, charts, maps, tactical arrows, radar, etc., and another voice drones in another exotic language. DOCTOR KILDARE examines the patient's body behind the lifted sheet; he rearranges the large un-conscious head's position on the pillows, and examines the closed eyes: it is a handsome, leonine head, quite gray. MADELEINE O'TOOLE tries another channel with the same results; the next language is also exotic, incomprehensible, and painfully sad with the weight of battle and defeat. Is there no sign of consciousness in the patient?

DOCTOR KILDARE shrugs in his elderly, experienced manner, watches the TV a bit, watches MADELEINE O'TOOLE fill another glass. The door has opened quietly to admit the PRESIDENT OF THE WORLD (formally dressed, morning coat, boutonniere), and the GENERAL OF THE WORLD (a muscular Air Force type, bemedalled, showing signs of tension, yet tailored to perfection too), Both are O'TOOLES, father and son. The PRESIDENT regards the DOCTOR closely, but the GENERAL's eyes are drawn to the TV-screen, which he watches emotionlessly, except that he begins to nibble at a fingernail. MADELEINE O'TOOLE pays no attention to them, and they give none to her after their first glance. When the screaming of the mortar shells becomes deafening, and the flashing lights of their explosion becomes intense enough to trouble the audience, the GENERAL walks casually over to the remote control next to MADELEINE and switches it off, after which he goes to the patient, and, alongside his father, bends over him silently, hands clasped behind his back. For a long, interminable minute they quietly contemplate O'MEAGER. When MADELEINE speaks, her voice is

hollow, abstract, commanding — never drunken. Yet no one answers her, or even seems to have heard her.

THE TIME

It is late in the evening of December 31st.

* * *

MADELEINE

He is not asleep. He is not awake. How is he? *(Silence)*

PRESIDENT

I don't understand. *(Not spoken to her)*

MADELEINE

He is not alive. He is not dead. Where is he? *(Silence)*

GENERAL

I don't understand. *(Not spoken to her)*

MADELEINE

(Chuckling to herself) There are some things we can't understand yet. Ah. Excuse me. That phrase is out of fashion. *(Pours another drink)*

PRESIDENT

Doctor?

GENERAL

Doctor!

DOCTOR

Frankly. . . .

PRESIDENT

Yes?

GENERAL

(Urgent, a little threatening) Frankly . . . ?

DOCTOR

(Unruffled, undaunted by their sense of their own authority) Frankly — I'm puzzled.

GENERAL

(Annoyed) Puzzled? You? For god's sake! *(Indicating the complex of paraphernalia)* Then what's all this?

DOCTOR

(Vaguely, somewhat surprised, flustered) Oh this . . . It's . . . I thought you knew . . . Surely . . . it was your request . . . ? I mean, I was advised that . . . Well I understood that you . . . But I would never have given him the extreme. . . . That is. . . .

PRESIDENT

Never mind.

DOCTOR

This treatment is the ultimate —

GENERAL

(Hand involuntarily over his eyes, nauseated, mutters) I don't want to know.

PRESIDENT

Never mind.

MADELEINE

He doesn't want to know.

DOCTOR

(To Madeleine) He doesn't want to know?

MADELEINE

He doesn't want to know. "General of the World," he calls himself! First in death, last in life!. Bravest of the brave! And he doesn't want to know! Cheers! That's what I say.

PRESIDENT

Perhaps it's better not to avoid the issue. Now. Tell him, Doctor.

DOCTOR

Well it's no secret. Really. People have merely forgotten it. This thing's been out of use since — oh, I forget when. The . . . er, law, however, clearly states that the apparatus must be available and ready. At all times. In case. In case. . . . Though this is the first case in all *my* practice.

GENERAL

What is it?

DOCTOR

This technique's out of your line, General . Some witty interne once dubbed it THE DUMMY. The name stuck. THE DUMMY. I've even forgotten its medical terminology. Anyway it's unimportant . As I said, it's just not called for . . . these days.

GENERAL
Never mind what it isn't. What *is* it?

DOCTOR
A life surrogate. That's all it is. Really. Nothing much.
Not to you, I suppose. A substitute existence. A kind of
replacement. For the time being. For the time being
only, you understand. A continuation. For the time
being. . . .

GENERAL
(Deeply shocked) I would hardly call this a life. Or even
a . . . substitute. I don't understand. You're joking. It's
one of your grisly damned medical jokes. A joke, isn't
it!

MADELEINE
He doesn't understand. How could he? No, it's no joke.

DOCTOR
You don't understand, GENERAL. As I've said, it is
old-fashioned. Science once hoped — once upon a time
science hoped.

PRESIDENT
(Nostalgic) That was before your time, GENERAL. Just
before your time.

GENERAL
What Don'tI understand? *(This is an order to explain)*

PRESIDENT
Tell him

DOCTOR

As I recall, the group that developed this technique —
under my direction, as a matter of fact — I had a theory
about — well, it's unimportant now. . . . My group
had been working for years on a method for extending
the usefulness of the organism. A lot of effort was ex-
pended on this problem. And money. You can't even
imagine how much. *(Laughs)* Public money. Military
money. Private money. Even *(Addressing Madeleine)*
Church money, oddly enough. It was thought, or so it
seemed then, that more time was needed. For everything. For everyone. There was not enough, you see.

MADELEINE

Time. More and more. The last resource.

DOCTOR

Time, yes. If only, you see, there were more time for
each life, so much could be learned, so much could be
done to avoid the misery and frustration caused by the
lack of time. And by the time that we found out how
we could — well, things had changed. I don't remember how exactly. Haven't you been struck by the way
everything has seemed to turn into its opposite lately?
It's a phenomenon that ought to be studied. I mean . . .
(Eager) . . . if the philosophy of the hour says we must
try to —

GENERAL

(Peremptory) Go on.

DOCTOR

(Brought back) Oh yes. THE DUMMY was the answer.
At first. But it was mishandled. I'm ashamed of the

medical profession, whenever I think about it. Someone has a lot to answer for. Partly it's my own fault, I
think. Because if I had known then what I know now
—

PRESIDENT

Never mind, Doctor Kildare. Never mind.

DOCTOR

It was turned into nothing more than a clinical trick for
rejuvenating expensive people. It was sold. Can you
imagine that? They *sold* it! "The fast . . . the modern,
way . . . to take a good . . . rest. . . . î And sold to certain groups, General. *Certain* groups, mind you. Now,
I admit, the temptation was —

PRESIDENT

Never mind. Go on. *(Peremptory)*

DOCTOR

Then there was a technical breakthrough. It was simplified. The government took charge. It was something
for everyone. That seemed very important. They said
everyone had the right to be given — I mean, everyone
was equal, of course, so that —

GENERAL

Oh, politics, you mean. Go on.

DOCTOR

But only for a short while. A very short while indeed.
Novelty of the thing. The novelty passed. Very soon.

MADELEINE

I wonder why.

PRESIDENT
(Nostalgic) That was before your time, GENERAL. Tch.

DOCTOR
Yet it seems Just the other year. But. . . . After all. . . .
Why *force* people? If they don't want . . . to go on. . . .
If they can't be made to see that . . . After all, though,
why force them?

MADELEINE
Can you blame them?

DOCTOR
Still, it was a pity. I for one never got to — I mean, to
us it remained potentially useful. I mean, it *could* have
been useful. We hoped . . . There were possibilities for
the future . . . alternatives . . . horizons. . . . We were
still free to . . . *(He's dreaming again)*. . . . I mean . . .
That is . . . *(He's at a loss to put it tactfully, yet accurately)*
Well, at the very least, it seemed a way to handle people
who'd just Couldn't anymore. I mean people who'd had
an overdose of . . . well, things. If treatment were be-
gun early enough, then, you understand —

MADELEINE
I don't think the General understands yet.

GENERAL
I think I do. Go on.

DOCTOR
(Encouraged, he grows scientifically excited) When I think
of the fascinating lines of research THE DUMMY might

have made available to us: There was so much to be done! So much. . . .

GENERAL
(Suddenly quite stern, as he sees where this is leading) You're wrong. Absolutely. Mere fantasy!

DOCTOR
But no, General! THE DUMMY could have given us time. More time. I used to think that might even have been its great gift to us. For instance, listen, imagine taking a man who had run right through his resources, and putting him into, er, suspension. Like this. *(Indicating O'Meager)* In order to —

GENERAL
(Grimly challenging him) Go on. Go on.

DOCTOR
(Scared) It doesn't matter. Our work was cut off. Abandoned. Forgotten. Pity. Such potentiality. There were no more funds. All of a sudden. The money just dried up. Overnight. As if they had decided. . . . Yet after all, why force people? Why force them? When there was time, I mean . . . once upon a time. . . .

PRESIDENT
(To himself, really) That was the least of it.

GENERAL
What?!

DOCTOR
Nothing. Really. Nothing much.

GENERAL

What do you mean?

DOCTOR

(Bursts out in brave indignation) Well, of course there were abuses! Is that my fault? There are always abuses. What can you expect? People have a way of perverting anything. That's the trouble. That's history.

MADELEINE

Perversion. Self-abuse.

DOCTOR

And of course THE DUMMY was so easily perverted. all licenses for General distribution were suddenly revoked. Pity.

MADELEINE

I wonder why.

GENERAL

(Exasperated) Get to the point!

DOCTOR

But seriously, it was nothing. Really. Nothing much. Like drug addiction, it became, you see, a sort of, er, medium.

GENERAL

(Alert as a wolf) A medium? Medium for what?

DOCTOR

We — I mean we doctors — were never clear about the *what* of it. Or the *how*. These things are subjective. Like pain. But the *why* is simple. Like any other addiction, it seemed to satisfy a craving. A deep craving.

MADELEINE
A profound and universal craving.

DOCTOR
Just for a while, though. Instead of giving the illusion of real time, it used time up. It literally devoured it, like an uncontrollable fire. Faster than fire. The victim was aged by it phenomenally: he lived a virtual lifetime in a week. Just the reverse of its original purpose, you see. That didn't do at all. No good. Waste of time. Waste of people. That was wrong.

MADELEINE
How things have changed.

GENERAL
(Interested) How did they work it?

DOCTOR
Now that was a well-kept secret. But there must have been an irregular system for resetting the thing *(Indicates the machine)* all wrong. Basically it's a very unstable mechanism. I never did understand why anyone would want to fool around with a medium. *(Laughs, embarrassed)* Anyway, not one like this!

MADELEINE
Oh, you don't understand, do you?

DOCTOR
Yet, after all, here we are. *(Shrugs at O'Meager)*

PRESIDENT

Yes, here we are.

DOCTOR

But Mr O'Meager isn't Just people, is he? So when he was finally found, I mean when we had tracked him down at last, it was decided that, despite everything, THE DUMMY was to be used. Er —

PRESIDENT

— for its original purpose.

DOCTOR

(Relieved) Precisely.

GENERAL

(Enraged) It was *decided*? To Use THE DUMMY?! Now wait a minute there, Doctor, just you wait a minute!

DOCTOR

I was merely following the procedure required. Clearly, the law prescribes that —

GENERAL

Law? I don't give a damn about law. There is no time for law now, Doctor. For god's sake, look at him! Law? What I'm asking you is, who gave that order?

DOCTOR

Yes, well, yes. I see.

GENERAL

Doctor!

DOCTOR

You can't expect *me* to say: I'm his doctor. Frankly, I'm not free to answer you.

GENERAL

You're not free, eh? Doctor, you do know who I am? *(Tugging at his revolver holster's flap)* You do understand that I can put you right the final last hell out of your scruples here and now. I'll give you just three seconds to —

PRESIDENT

(Holding up a restraining hand) He's right. We have very little right left. If we can't respect a doctor's oath of secrecy, we'll have lost that, too. Along with everything else.

MADELEINE

Along with everything else.

GENERAL

Now, Dad, Just can that moralistic crap — Mr. President, I mean. I think I understand your concern for principle. But can we be realistic, at least now? How much time do you think there is, a week? Forty-eight hours? *(He glances at the great clock)* A day? Can I guarantee you even a day?

MADELEINE

You can guarantee nothing

PRESIDENT

I don't understand you.

GENERAL

(Glances out the window. Is it a shade darker outside?) The fact is, I can guarantee nothing, not really. As of last week. *(Takes a deep breath, and whispers)* As of Sunday.

MADELEINE

You guarantee nothing. *You* never could guarantee anything. *You!?*

GENERAL

So let's think. Let us think. If I didn't give the order to continue him, I mean, O'Meager . . . and you didn't . . . .

PRESIDENT

No. How could I, you fool!

GENERAL

Precisely. Then who did? And you, Doctor — you wouldn't make such a decision all by yourself . . . ?

DOCTOR

(Scandalized) General O'Toole! That would be against my, er —

GENERAL

Against your hypocritical oath. Precisely. Medical ethics! Thank you for that. And she didn't . Or couldn't. Or would she? To feed her insatiable lust for — *(Glancing at O'Meager)*

MADELEINE

(Coldly scornful, addressing them for the first time) You forget yourself, General. I *am* your sister.

GENERAL
We're beyond that sort of thing. What I demand to know is —

PRESIDENT
Remember what she is. Keep your head screwed on, General . Tight!

MADELEINE
Yes, remember what she is. She does. Tight does it. Tight!

GENERAL
(Baffled) What? Remember what *she* is?

PRESIDENT
In any case, it's nonsense about his medical oath. We are beyond that sort of thing. He's only pretending. Aren't you, Doctor? Pretending? *(Longish silence)* At this moment, what is the significance of an antique formula pronounced fifty years ago at graduation by a young doctor in a moment of profound inattention? Nothing, really. *(Longish pause)* And remember, you can't force people any more. *(Pause)* But, he would tell us if he knew. Am I right? *(Pause)* Consequently, I don't believe he knows himself. Do you, Doctor?

DOCTOR
(Ashamed, looks at his trembling hands) Frankly, General—

GENERAL
(Impatient) Well?

DOCTOR

. . . I don't . It just seems to have — happened. Some-how.

PRESIDENT

Precisely. It's like everything else that has been happen-ing ever since we — *(gestures at O'Meager)* — oh, I for-get when. Despite everything we have done. Despite everything. Decisions are made. Orders are given. Events follow. But it is not known how. Believe it or not, we are spectators.

GENERAL

I don't accept that view of things. I refuse to. Why, if I believed that —

MADELEINE

I believe it.

DOCTOR

Frankly, I don't understand why we cannot do some-thing about this, this awful —

PRESIDENT

We . . . are . . . spectators. You, General of the World, I, President of the World. Merely spectators. Consider this: with all the power of our offices, with all the ma-chinery of social manipulation in our hands, at the very summit of our civil evolution, we find ourselves here, baffled and utterly helpless before this — this uncon-scious man. If he *is* unconscious. If he *is* a man. THE DUMMY! Look at him: Alfred O'Meager. The Watch King! Mr. Time Himself! THE DUMMY! *(Laughs a short bitter laugh)* We are spectators, like it or not. *(Long-*

ish pause as they stare at the figure in the bed. Madeleine pays no attention to them, merely refilling her glass) . . . It is like a dream. A dream I have had many times before.

GENERAL

Mr. President, now is no time for your dreams. There is no time now. Please. No dreams.

PRESIDENT

Why not? *(He gazes out the window, which has grown several shades darker. The sky may even show momentary blazes in the distance, like heat lightning)* I dream that I am in my office. The screen is flashing: Attention! Attention, please! Attention!

GENERAL

You have no screen in your office.

PRESIDENT

Alarm bells are ringing! Emergency! Emergency, please! Emergency!

GENERAL

There are no bells in your office.

PRESIDENT

Nevertheless, that is the way it is.

MADELEINE

That is the way it is.

PRESIDENT

I press the keys. I press the secret keys, the keys in the top right-hand drawer of my desk. Key One. Key Two. Key Three: Nothing happens. I am confused. I think, perhaps I have mistaken the sequence? Perhaps! I press them again in reverse order. And nothing happens. Nothing!

MADELEINE
Nothing.

PRESIDENT
Nothing at all. Do you comprehend this? Do you? It is a terrible dream. I wake up and touch the switch and my room lights up, as usual. Precisely as usual. I am all right. It is very quiet. Very, very quiet. The horror; The horror has not come. I am dreaming. Only dreaming.

GENERAL
Please, Mr. President.

PRESIDENT
How often it comes to me, that dream. Crystal clear, like a vision: the screen, the bells, the secret keys in the drawer of my desk. Like an ancient premonition. What does it mean? As if, once upon a time, there was a way for me to lead us, a way for us all to go. . . .

GENERAL
(Sternly) Mr. President!

PRESIDENT
Now I understand.

MADELEINE
You do not understand. How could you?

PRESIDENT

Now I understand. This! *(Points at THE DUMMY)* This is infinitely more terrible. What shall I press now? I have no buttons to press! *(Short laugh)* Absurd. Of course.

GENERAL

Absurd. We have not got to that hour yet. I'm disappointed in you. If I had ever thought you would crack—

PRESIDENT

Or perhaps I am really dreaming now. It wouldn't surprise me. Look at him: Alfred O'Meager! THE DUMMY? Do *you* believe it?

MADELEINE

No. You are not dreaming. *(Silence)* Neither are you awake.

GENERAL

Hush, you!

MADELEINE

Fool!

GENERAL

Bitch!

MADELEINE

Killer!

GENERAL

(Makes a gesture at her, his hands are a strangler's clenching hands) You rotten, boozy, whoring psychic! If I'd

ever thought you could really see what you say you do
see —

DOCTOR

(Imperturbably resuming his medical manner) Frankly,
General, I'm also puzzled — aside from this peculiar
matter of the decision to keep Mr. O'Meager on with
us . . . for the time being, of course, merely for the time
being — I am puzzled as to the reason why?

PRESIDENT

Precisely.

GENERAL

I don't understand.

PRESIDENT

Perhaps it suits someone'
s purpose.

DOCTOR

Yes. If you consider, for example, what it would mean
to . . . that is, the, er . . .

PRESIDENT

. . . Or perhaps it's really as absurd, as meaningless as
it seems to us? If we had something to go on, some clue
to THE DUMMY..

DOCTOR

Precisely. Because, the truth, after all, is that we abandoned this technique for a fundamental reason.

PRESIDENT

(Surprised) Oh?

DOCTOR

Yes, I mean, aside from the new laws passed against the unnecessary preservation of life, there was the subjective matter of pain.

PRESIDENT

Pain?

DOCTOR

I suppose it is hard to imagine what real, true pain is like. Sheer pain. Almost impossible, I suppose.

GENERAL

(Scandalized) Doctor! You? If you of all people can't imagine it —

DOCTOR

(Patronizing the General's youth and ignorance, he lectures sinisterly) General, you don't understand. There is pain . . . and there is pain. There is suffering. And there is suffering. You are thinking of ordinary pain.

GENERAL

Ordinary?

DOCTOR

Ordinary pain. Frankly, yes.

GENERAL

What do *you* call ordinary, Doctor Kildare?

DOCTOR

Oh, ordinary, ordinary. . . . Try to imagine this, General. Ordinary is as though I were to burn you slowly, burn you ever so slowly, through your skin, through your flesh, your bones and blood, through your nerves into your very cells, slowly, slowly burning you everywhere hotter, until you were filled throughout your body with slow scorching fire, until there was no room for your own self in your own body *(General has been shuddering involuntarily as though feeling this "ordinary pain")* until at last I was squeezing you entirely into the uttermost corner of yourself, and then until you had been squeezed out of yourself into nothing, into nowhere — and I could do that you know, I could do that to you — that would be ordinary pain. You can imagine that, can't you?

PRESIDENT & GENERAL
Ordinary?

DOCTOR
Frankly, yes. It is merely relative. Like life.

GENERAL
Oh, well. . . . *That.* . . . *(Relieved)*

DOCTOR
Yes. *That.* Yet even that kind of pain comes to an end: it ends precisely where you end. But — when we discovered there was another sort of pain —

GENERAL
(In great anxiety) Please, Doctor, don't .

DOCTOR
(Relentless) — a sheer pain, an excruciation. . . . A pain that is, I am afraid, clinically indescribable — precisely because it is subjective pain, the pain of Being, per-

haps. I don't put it well. When we began to appreciate
that aspect of things, well, then, frankly. . . .

PRESIDENT

We are beyond that now. It hardly matters. Let us look
at the situation as it is.

GENERAL

(Much relieved) Thank you. We must think now. It's
time.

PRESIDENT

*(Gestures at the whole world: there are more noticeable
flashings in the distance)* Granted, we now find ourselves
in this situation —

GENERAL

(Impatient) Go on.

PRESIDENT

Granted this present situation, the only realistic hy-
pothesis is that he was on to something. *(Pointing at
O'Meager)* Something big. If we had a clue, if we might
begin to imagine what —

GENERAL

You're still dreaming. What! Him? Alfred O'Meager?

PRESIDENT

Yes.

GENERAL

Please, Mr. President. *(Barks contemptuously)* This is no
time for a joke.

DOCTOR

I don't understand.

PRESIDENT

Something big. Call it what you want. World Welfare.
Something important. After all, it is about time.

GENERAL

Optimist!

DOCTOR

Science fiction. Speculation.

MADELEINE

Wishful. Go on.

GENERAL

Go on! World Welfare? Now you sound like Daniel.

PRESIDENT

Why not? What's wrong with that? When Daniel
O'Meager speaks —

MADELEINE

— the world listens.

PRESIDENT

Precisely.

GENERAL

If I'd had any idea you'd been listening to that demagogue —

PRESIDENT

Who can avoid hearing him? Sometime or other. Who can avoid it? After all, he *is* our Director of World Publicity!

GENERAL

I thought you had more sense than that. At least. This is becoming a farce. *(Looks out the window)* Tch. A farce!

PRESIDENT

(Looking from him to Madeleine to the doctor) I beg your —

GENERAL

God damn it!

PRESIDENT

(All dignity) I beg your —

GENERAL

I beg yours, too, goddammit! Daniel O'Meager is a fraud.

DOCTOR

Frankly, I've sometimes wondered about him. Maybe, I mean, if there were a tain't of truth in what he declares, it would make all the difference between, well, this present situation of ours and, er, the future of, er, well, the world . . . ?

GENERAL

A bitter and defeated fraud. Believe me.

PRESIDENT

I don't understand.

DOCTOR
I don't understand.

MADELEINE
Go on. Brother! Go on. You surprise even me . . . a little.

PRESIDENT
(Curious) What do you know about this, Madeleine?

MADELEINE
I? I? Nothing. Nothing, really!

GENERAL
Don't believe her.

MADELEINE
Really, nothing at all. Am I my husband's secret-keeper? Whatever Daniel O'Meager preaches officially to the world he preaches in his sleep. I can assure you of that. Demagogue he may be, but he's a simple one. He believes what he says. That is the worst kind.

PRESIDENT
Of course.

GENERAL
Nonsense: You're lying. You cunning woman. You soft-bellied whore, you. You filthy, mangy witch. You cold, cruel, calculating —

MADELEINE
Names, mere names.

PRESIDENT

General! If there is something we should know, then now is the time —

GENERAL

I could murder you, you evil, mocking, poisonous —

MADELEINE

You won't.

GENERAL

(Surprised, exasperated) I won't? I won't?

MADELEINE

Come closer, General. Look at me. Closer, O'Toole. So, so. . . . Closer. Look into my eyes. *(He is bending fondly over her, quite entranced)* Look, Patrick. Deep. Deeper, dear. Look. So. So, So. . . . What . . . do you . . . see?

GENERAL:

(Dulled mystification) I don't understand.

MADELEINE

You see everything as it is. Will you murder me, now?

GENERAL

I don't understand —

MADELEINE

Will you, my dearest General?

GENERAL

(Succeeds in pulling himself away, awed) No. Not yet.

PRESIDENT

Is this the time for yet another riddle?

MADELEINE

And why not, Mr. President?

PRESIDENT

(Ignoring her) Patrick, I asked you a question. I want the answer.

GENERAL

Sir!

PRESIDENT

Daniel O'Meager has been speaking to the world for ten years. He has spoken and there have been these ten years of uninterrupted peace. I give him the credit. We were desperate: he has calmed, he has convinced, he has converted a lost world. He has given us an obedient and orderly population. For once there has been justice and plenty. Enough for everyone. As he himself says, **ENOUGH FOR EVERYONE!** I don't know how he has done it, but done it he has. I give him the credit. It has been like a miracle. His miracle. I give him the credit. He has the gift, all right, the gift! He has the gift of tongues. I, even I, acknowledge that. And I assure you I am not the only one. The whole government in fact believes that without his public voice, and his voice alone, we could have, well, we would have —

MADELEINE

— come to this before now. *(It is fairly dark outside the window towards which she gestures idly. The sky is lit by silent lurid flashes coming closer)*

PRESIDENT

Precisely. For that at least we must be grateful

MADELEINE

Fool. Oh, you fool, fool, fool!

DOCTOR

I don't understand.

GENERAL

(Casually as though he is revealing information of the slightest importance merely) She's right. You don't have to pin another medal on him, or hand him another honorary degree.

PRESIDENT

I don't understand.

GENERAL

(Again casual as he turns to consider the comatose Alred O'Meager) Daniel O'Meager, Director of World Publicity, has been working for me.

DOCTOR

For you?

GENERAL

Oh, he's honest. Says only what he believes. **ENOUGH FOR EVERYONE!** I think he even believes what he says, if he believes anything. Nonetheless, he is a fraud.

PRESIDENT

(Stunned) For you? Working for *you*? *Our* Daniel?

GENERAL

For you. For us. For me — what difference does it make now? What difference did it ever make, really?

MADELEINE

(Laughs) None at all!

GENERAL

Are you laughing at me? You devil!

PRESIDENT

But I don't understand. How could you? Your office is quite separate — I mean, it's legally separated from any possible tampering with —

GENERAL

I'm sorry, Dad. I am, truly. You must realize it was the only way. There was nothing else. Everything else had been lost. I had to have more time. Somehow. Some way.

PRESIDENT

So that you — you dared?! Everything lost? Everything?

MADELEINE

Almost.

GENERAL

Everything.

MADELEINE

Oh.

GENERAL
Everything known, that is.

MADELEINE
Ah. But what you don't know, General. . . ?

GENERAL
And so Daniel came along then with his dogmas and
doctrines and his golden tongue.

PRESIDENT
What have you been up to? Patrick, what have you been
doing?

GENERAL
What in the damned hell do you imagine we have been
doing? The only thing possible, given our circumstances.
Conquering. Conquering and controlling. The only
thing left us: power. Over. Through. Under. Behind. In
everything. Everywhere.

MADELEINE
Almost.

GENERAL
Everything. Everywhere, I say! Everything known. . . .

MADELEINE
Ah.

PRESIDENT
But really, I don't understand, son. The world has been
at peace. Comparatively. We have grown rich, tranquil.
Even almost happy. During these last ten years we have

been approaching a time of universal clarity and com-
prehension. We have been nearing, if I might suppose
it, the fulfillment and, why not, why not dare to guess
it — the realization of our most ancient human hopes,
and our most daring of prophecies. So what is there left
to conquer, or to control?

GENERAL
(Bitterly) Everything.

MADELEINE
Almost.

GENERAL
Everything, I say! Everything known. *(To the President,
with condescension, but in tones of generous pity too)* You
have been listening to Daniel too long. I'm ashamed for
you. I am sorry. Believe me I am.

PRESIDENT
Answer me.

GENERAL
What was left for us to conquer? What in the world was
left? We had everything else in our hands.

PRESIDENT
I don't understand you.

GENERAL
I'll tell you. Ourselves, Mr. President. Ourselves. That
was all we had left to aim at.

PRESIDENT

You are mad! Patrick! You *are* mad, aren't you? You dared to think — *(drops to the settee, fatigued, joined by Doctor Kildare, who suddenly seems tired and very old)*

GENERAL

Not mad. Not at all. Think about it. We ourselves are all we had left. Yes, I dared. But it is too late now, I am afraid. Ask her. I have no more information.

MADELEINE

Life is a fool's paradise.

PRESIDENT

Darling, how can you? Life is, life is, life is. . . .

MADELEINE

. . . Mostly our waste of time.

GENERAL

I'm afraid we've lost the last battle. For ten long years, oh, how I have fought to avoid this! But I'm afraid I've lost.

MADELEINE

And you're afraid. You should be.

GENERAL

Who isn't?

MADELEINE

I'm not.

GENERAL
(*Dismissively, with a gesture suggesting her unimportance*)
Oh, you. . . .

MADELEINE
And *he* isn't . (*Indicates THE DUMMY by pointing at it
with her chin*)

GENERAL
I don't—

PRESIDENT
One thing at a time, for pity's sake. What were you up
to? What have you been doing, Patrick!

MADELEINE
Maybe it would be best not to speak of it. Wait for your
demagogue. He's coming.

PRESIDENT
I can't wait.

MADELEINE
He's coming, I tell you. (*President gestures impatiently*)

GENERAL
(*Sighs and commences his explanation, as to innocent and
ignorant children*) Cultivation. Concentration. (*He is met
by blank, incredulous stares*) I haven't Daniel O'Meager's
golden tongue, so I'll put it in my own way, you understand —

(*Daniel O'Meager enters. He is a smooth, even plumpish, healthy man,
exuding natural warmth, assurance, conviction and well-being. Is he*

*simple, or an arch-hypocrite, or a consummate conspirator? It is anyone's
guess. He breaks before he can reveal whatever truth he knows. He
crosses the room and stands looking down at his father, halfway between the bed and Madeleine's chaise)*

PRESIDENT:

(Distracted) Oh yes, come in, Daniel. It's all right. Yes,
that is your father there. Or was. Or will be. I'm not
sure. He's under treatment. The Doctor says it is all in
order, I think. I mean, I think he believes so.

DANIEL

(His voice is quiet and formidable) I don't understand.

MADELEINE

It doesn't matter.

GENERAL

(Continuing as though Daniel had never entered) . . . So
that you might say we've, well, we've been, well, weeding. Selectively, of course, but nevertheless, weeding.
The Doctor is beginning to grasp my meaning, I hope?

DOCTOR

*(Shows signs of distress, fear, guilt. He gets up, goes to the
window, the bed, Madeleine, the machine, paces near the
door: his hands wring each other. He reseats himself on the
settee, puts his head in his hands, and groans)* Oh. Oh.
Oh.

PRESIDENT

But I —

GENERAL

(Continuing as though he had not been interrupted) About ten years ago. When I was appointed. You have all forgotten — oh, how short our memories are! — you spoke of peace and happiness on earth. Yet this was coming all along. While you slept. You have forgotten, haven't you, how much trouble was brewing everywhere in the world. Daniel O'Meager hadn't taken up preaching yet. He was still singing, or pretending to sing. What actually was he doing? Ask him. What was it you did? *(Daniel doesn't respond, only looks down abashed)* He is ashamed of his past.

PRESIDENT

(Making excuses) It was a time of transition. Things had not yet stabilized. The world was confused. We were still groping for our present accommodation —

GENERAL

(Applauds) Spoken like the veteran politician! Transition! Confusion! Disorder! What do you take me for, Abraham O'Toole? It was a time of anarchy! The world was slipping into madness: collective and individual. The earth was shaking itself to pieces, like a ship in a typhoon. And there was no captain, no crew, no rules — and no one with the presence of mind or the force of will to take the wheel. Anarchy, did I say? No — revolution! Everywhere. A thousand revolutions. And not merely a tribe, a state, or even a continent in disorder, but — everyone, everywhere! Merely to be born at that time was to have been born mad. Yet in ten years you've all forgotten what those times were like. The disease of life was raging through the earth on a scale so incredibly vast that —

DOCTOR

(Groaning) Yes. Yes.

MADELEINE

(Acidly) The cost of living was too high.

PRESIDENT

Aren't you exaggerating? Patrick, you slept safely in your own bed every night, didn't you?

GENERAL

(Unimpeded, snorts) Huh! Ten years ago revolutions were flaring out like boils. The signs were that clear — if you were not blind and complacent and impotent. The esoteric gangs were forming. Mobs and riots, sabotages of laboratories, breaks in communication, failures of energy, exploding ships, falling airplanes; mutinies; the police conniving with bandits and working for the syndicates; strikes and shutdowns; looting, rape, murder. Waves of suicides. Cities on fire. Governors marching by night against the central authority. And in the central command? Resignations, coups d'états, mock trials and firing squads! Orders and counter-orders and civil war among the ministries. Chaos from top to bottom and inside out. . . .

PRESIDENT

Yet you slept safely in your bed —

GENERAL

Am I exaggerating? Am I? Is my memory playing tricks on me? Can you really have forgotten all that? And that was merely the symptom before the terrible final outbreak. And it would have come to much worse, too, and much sooner, gentlemen. It would have become the final human disorder. And it would have been inevitable, irreversible, and immutable.

PRESIDENT
Yet you slept safely —

GENERAL
Mr. President. Mr. Master Politician: when your wife, my own mother, was discovered to be the arch-plotter of that sophisticated group of cannibalistic assassins —

PRESIDENT
Patrick, please. I don't like to recall —

MADELEINE
— the dramatic circumstances. It was nothing unusual, not really. What is terror, after all?

PRESIDENT
It was a time of —

GENERAL
— transition. Yes. But — transition to what ? I ask you!

DANIEL
These disturbances are periodic in nature. We have it seen them before. We were, however, at the threshold of the new, the greater —

GENERAL
— world society. Yes, yes.

DANIEL

And humanity was struggling towards maturity out of a long and troubled adolescence. THE GREATER WORLD SOCIETY! When our dreams and hopes —

GENERAL

Can that crap, Daniel. Fabricate your memoirs some other time.

MADELEINE

(Laughs) Some other time:

GENERAL

There was only one alternative, if we were to survive.

MADELEINE

And you, of course, were the only one with the guts to seize that alternative. Go on, General. Tell them.

GENERAL

There was nothing else to be done with men but to . . . weed them out. Perhaps it was too late. Even then.

MADELEINE

It has always been too late.

GENERAL

I took the challenge — *and* the risk. I dared. I alone. Give me credit. And so . . . I established . . . the Nuclear Factor Operation.

PRESIDENT

You? *(Looking at him with fear)* You? the NFO?!

GENERAL

Oh, please, Mr. President. We are not on stage now. Don't act for us.

PRESIDENT

But I do not understand.

GENERAL

Well, I guess it wouldn't have done as public information, would it? My demagogue, Daniel, took care of the public information. Daniel spoke of the New Freedoms Organization, the Neefoe. People would have been too terrified, if they had guessed what the NFO stood for. We couldn't have had that, could we? They would have lain awake nights wondering, Am I next? Tonight? Tomorrow night? The night after? When? How could we have restored our precious peace and prosperity?

MADELEINE

Peace. Prosperity.

GENERAL

The Doctor knows about it. He could tell you. Doctor? *(They all look at him for explanation. The Doctor glances round at them, and buries his face in his palms again, groaning)*

DOCTOR

Oh! Oh! Oh!

GENERAL

We had to work fast. Under pressures. A Master Plan was devised and set in motion long ago. So secretly that none of you knew much of it. Even to you, the NFO was no more than a rumor, eh, witch? *(Smiles maliciously at Madeleine)*

PRESIDENT

Patrick, how could you?

MADELEINE

(Mockingly) How could you, Patrick!

GENERAL

Oh, it has been hard enough to carry on all these years. A world of secrecy. A world of information withheld from everyone. A world of stupid lies everyone publicly swallowed, thanks to Daniel O'Meager.

DANIEL

(Muttering bitterly) A world of spies and counterspies digging beneath all the houses and through the walls, worming their way into everyone's life. Lies and spies and more lies.

GENERAL

At first it seemed impossible. Too much to be done, and so little time. Almost impossible. In fact, the one thing that has kept me from giving up like the rest of you, was the goal we were working for.

PRESIDENT

That you, oh my son, my son, my very own son, that you, General Patrick Isaac O'Toole, should justify the means of NFO by its end!

GENERAL

We are beyond means. Beyond ends. No, let me express the simple truth: the NUCLEAR FACTOR OP-

ERATION is automatic: it calculates by itself for itself. It is an impartial judge. *(Offhandedly)* One of Alfred O'Meager's clocks, as a matter of fact.

DANIEL

My father? You used one of *his* clocks?!

GENERAL

Why not?

DANIEL

I don't understand. How could you? He never would have allowed —

GENERAL

Why not?

DANIEL

My father is neutral. His time is the same for everyone. Our family has always been neutral. That is our tradition. It is even our motto. Neutrality! It is what I have always believed. We have never, never meddled with the world.

GENERAL

Precisely! Who else could judge impartially!

DANIEL

I don't understand you. You mean to tell me —

GENERAL

— Even "judge" is the wrong word. There is no judgment. The NFO is a life-selector, pure and simple. It does not judge, not in your sense of the word. It is neutral, yes.

MADELEINE
Annihilator!

GENERAL
Crazy slut!

MADELEINE
Exterminator!

PRESIDENT
And I swore at my last inauguration to ferret out the
leaders of the NFO! To bring them to international
human justice. To stamp out every single agent and cell
and procurer. To save humanity once and for all from
the most insidious, cruel, and evil criminal conspiracy
in all memory!

GENERAL
Daniel, he has been spending too much time listening
to you spout. You ought to sue the President for plagia-
rism.

DANIEL
I am, at least, a prophet with honor in his own house.

MADELEINE
(*Laughs deeply. By now the room is dimming, lit only by
the dummy, and a few small indirect lamps*) Oh, god! Am
I the only one who knows?

GENERAL
(*Ignoring her*) Now come, let us reason together. Try to
rid yourselves of your old prejudices. For a moment.
Just try.

PRESIDENT & DANIEL

Prejudices!

GENERAL

Prejudices. Yes! Because — nothing and no one is sacred. in the last analysis, nothing and no one is immune or safe from judgment. No, let's call it evaluation: evaluation by the central clock of the NFO. And mind you, no one knows where that clock is or how to reach it. It is safe from tampering. It cannot be perverted. It was set in motion once and for all.

PRESIDENT

Who did it? You?

GENERAL

I, we, who knows? What does it matter now? Like history, it cannot be set back. Like time itself. Neither you, nor I — nor even I — can change it or stop it. That was the way it was set up. We are powerless. The key was, er, broken . . . or hidden . . . or . . . um . . . lost.

DANIEL

But, General—

GENERAL

And human life, the life of each single one of all the billions of us, wherever we may be, is available to it for evaluation. And of course selection. The selection must be made. There is no alternative: it must! And it is made on the best principles we have . . . under the circumstances. . . .

DANIEL

Circumstances?

GENERAL

So that, we, it, *It*, I say, has been . . . weeding men out.

PRESIDENT

Patrick!

DANIEL

General!

GENERAL

— Yes, weeding men out. But weeding them fairly —
in terms of . . . survival.

DANIEL

Survival? Mere survival? Is that all — ?!

GENERAL

Wait: Daniel, you mustn't let sentiment speak. Not here.
Not now. . . . The optimum survival of essential men.
In order to leave only the essential mankind. There is
no longer room for anyone else. Perhaps there never has
been. We have weeded only in proportion to population. Naturally.

MADELEINE

Beginning with 5 million — per month.

GENERAL

(Coyly) Something like that, yes.

PRESIDENT

I am shocked! I cannot speak. I cannot think.

DANIEL

(*In pain and fear*) And how many of us have disappeared since you started the NFO? Tell me that?

GENERAL

Who's counting? Does it matter?

DOCTOR

(*Groaning still*) Oh, oh, oh.

GENERAL

(*With genuine humility, even compassion*) Mr. President. Father! Abraham! Try to see this thing rationally. At least now. You are thinking in terms of ten years ago — That's the past, why, That's ancient history!

PRESIDENT

Our lives come from the past.

GENERAL

But the past is dead. It died long ago.

MADELEINE

I pity you, Patrick. If you only knew what you have done.

GENERAL

(*Pays her no attention*) We of the NFO have been working for the future. We've sought Increased Power, for Increased Action. Increased Action, for Increased Being. And that is the goal, that has always been the goal of human life. Isn't that true, Daniel? If I could ask everyone in the world right now what he wants, if I could shout, if they could hear me, they would answer: Increased Being! Isn't that true?

DANIEL

I suppose so, yes. Of course. That's what I hoped. Of course. **INCREASED BEING! HUMANITY! FOR EVERYONE!**

DOCTOR

(Murmuring to himself) Increased being? But that would be so painful, so much more terrible than simply dying. Dying simply. Can you force people to accept more pain, more and more pain? Can you?

GENERAL

Defeatist! Aren't we still alive? Here! Alive! Now!

DANIEL

I suppose so, yes. That's what I hoped for.

GENERAL

But ten years ago everything was about to be lost, and lost forever.

MADELEINE

Almost everything.

GENERAL

We were falling, falling, falling. . . . From anarchy to chaos, from chaos towards extinction. all of us. Together. We felt it coming, and we were afraid. Extinction. Absolute extinction. It had to be stopped before the end, before we lost everything.

MADELEINE

Almost everything.

DANIEL

They were frightened and guilty. They lusted only to kill and to destroy — the others. The others. Always the others.

GENERAL

Now, thanks to the NeeFoe, we are all one together. Only the inessential among us were selected from humanity. And sent out.

PRESIDENT

How do you mean — we are all one?

DANIEL

Inessential? Sent out?

GENERAL

How sheltered your lives have been. How idealistic you are! The NFO is not a political movement. It has no leader. NeeFoe is impartial. It selects from everyone, from ourselves. Mankind to it is merely — mankind. There is nothing else. We are all one, together.

DANIEL

But what right had you — ?

GENERAL

Daniel, my dear demagogue, no matter what you may say, there is *not* enough for everyone. There is no room in the future for *everyone*. You will say —

DOCTOR

It is not ethical!

PRESIDENT

It is not just!

DANIEL

It is not fair!

GENERAL

Precisely. But — it is necessary! We are our own crop.
We sow ourselves. We must weed ourselves. Necessary.
Only way. Perhaps it's unpleasant to hear it?

DANIEL

But — General!

GENERAL

I'm sorry. You must accept it. I did. I do. There was no
other way.

ALL *(Except Madeleine)*
(After a pause) I understand.

MADELEINE

But, General —

GENERAL

(Satisfied he has convinced them, he speaks quietly, exhausted)
Yes, Madeleine?

MADELEINE

— You have failed.

GENERAL
(Very quietly) Not yet. We are still fighting.

MADELEINE
And you have lost.

GENERAL
Not yet.

PRESIDENT
Then why are we here? What are we doing waiting here
with Alfred O'Meager?

MADELEINE
Perhaps you were right. *(Slyly)* Perhaps he *was* on to
something.

GENERAL
What do you know about it, you sullen, open-legged
cunt, you?!

PRESIDENT
She is my daughter, Patrick. Enough of that from you.
(Is he showing concealed authority?)

DANIEL
She is my wife, General. *(Also threatening?)*

GENERAL
(Defiant?) And my sister!

MADELEINE
We are beyond all that. Now.

DANIEL

What do you mean?

GENERAL

Maybe you should ask THE DUMMY, Mr. Director
of World Demagoguery? *(Scornful)* See if it answers!

DANIEL

I don't understand.

PRESIDENT

Never mind. Never mind. The wind is coming. Never
mind. *(The sky is very brightly lit up by a slow flare. Silence. It is beautiful light. The room is quiet. We hear the
fain'test ticking and whirring and pulsing from the machine. They seem to be contemplating the patient)*

DANIEL

(Ruminatively) My father — ? Was he — ?

MADELEINE

Daniel, what do you think you would do if you knew
you had only twenty minutes to live?

DANIEL

(With desire and tenderness) I think — I think . . . I would
make love to you, Madeleine. Madeleine, would you
let me? Make love? To you?

MADELEINE

You know twenty minutes aren't enough. For love.
Daniel. Daniel, be serious for once.

DANIEL

(Sadly, defeated again) I am. I was. I'm sorry. It isn't enough? I thought it was. Enough for everyone. Madeleine. Enough for everyone else. Why do you ask me now, Madeleine? Now, when Father is . . . my father is. . . . You. . . .

MADELEINE

(Filling her glass again) Because . . . perhaps that is all there is left. Twenty minutes

DANIEL

Now you be serious, Madeleine. This is no time for one of your moods. You're bored, That's all. Infinitely. Your mind is upset, isn't it, when you are bored? Life seems futile then, and you are not responsible, are you? How I love you like this! If I could — *(his hands go out to her as if to wish to embrace her very tightly)*

MADELEINE

Do I look strange to you? Do I sound moody? No, Daniel. No, it isn't that. *(She glances up at the clock. Daniel's eyes follow hers)*

DANIEL

What do you see?

MADELEINE

Suppose twenty minutes is all you have. Tell me one of your stories, Daniel, one of your dear, bedtime stories.

DANIEL

Now is not the time to —

MADELEINE

Imagine it: every night for ten years you have told me a bedtime story to help me go to sleep. And all the stories were different. You always had enough stories, and every story was different. Even if it was the same one every night. Tell me that one. I want to hear that one.

DANIEL

I forget.

MADELEINE

Twenty, nineteen, eighteeen minutes. What do you think now, Daniel? I want to hear what you think. Speak. Something. Anything. Now that I have put you under sentence of death, what can you announce?

DANIEL

What are you saying? I don't understand.

MADELEINE

Have you a theory? Have you more of the same soft sweet reassuring words? Oh, how sinister a preacher you were, dear! Can you tell me the story of your life once more? How you were born (like everyone else). How you grew up (like everyone else). How you left home (like everyone else). Of your suffering, your struggles among the wicked and the wretched and the ruined of the world. And how at last you won fame and fortune singing, at first for mere pennies, and then later, when notoriety was yours, for platinum contracts. And then how when you lost your voice you began to talk, talk, talk, talking all day every day to the whole world, and how your voice was everyone's voice. That was the story I liked best. Oh, I never believed it, Daniel — it was too true, too typically you. Too-too true. Your voice was everyone's. The story of the demagogue. Wonderful! *(He laughs delightedly like a child)* Is there anything else, anything more? No? Oh, Daniel, Daniel, where now are your words, where now your faith? Can you find it in fifteen minutes? Is there enough now even for you? Enough for anyone? Speak, Daniel!

DANIEL

Madeleine... I... You... My fahter and you — ?

MADELEINE

Enough of what, Daniel? May you be goddamned! Enough what?

DANIEL

Enough, enough! What difference does it make? Life, I suppose. Enough life. Is what, I suppose. I mean. . . .

MADELEINE

(Laughs cuttingly) We are beyond that now.

DANIEL

I don't understand.

MADELEINE

Didn't you hear the General? There is not enough life. There never has been enough of that. It takes too long to live. Much, much too long. Who can reach it? It is too far away.

DANIEL

You don't understand, Madeleine. That is not what he meant. Oh, you weird, perverse, thrilling cursed creature! If I could, just now — I don't care who's watching!

(He has clutched his genitals feverishly, and now begins to unlatch his belt) That is not what he meant. You know he was only talking about natural resources: all those billions of inessential mouths to feed. Billions of inessential bags of guts crawling over the surface of the globe like the spineless slugs they are.

MADELEINE
(Watching him closely, she has teased him by suggestively stroking her pubis and moving her thighs languidly) Daniel, Daniel, Daniel! Hear me: my brother is a professional killer. Nothing more. He is merely the instrument of the angel of death. It is his nature. He was made that way. Look at him. He knows nothing else but death. Who else could have planned and carried out the execution of more than three billion people in less than ten years? Silently. Secretly. He was chosen for that, whether he liked it or not, whether he wanted it or not. At first he even suffered. Didn't you, Patrick? *(The General smiles at her agreeably)*

DANIEL
You don't understand. Oh, you don't ! *(He is staring at her lubricious hand)* You know only your own — I mean, he has been conserving our lives. Life itself is his to care for. Without him we would have been . . . well, we all would have —

MADELEINE
— come to this before now. No, Daniel, you are wrong. As usual. *(Abruptly she stops teasing him, and becomes strict, queenlike)* Wrong, wrong, wrong! Ask him!

DANIEL
General? What is she saying?

GENERAL

And how I have suffered! Every unnecessary human life I was forced to send out was like the stab of a long, red-hot needle into my heart. And I was forced to! Ah! Forced. No one in the world can be forced anymore . . . yet the General of the World was. Forced! For the sake of the living. Eh, Doctor?

DOCTOR

Yes. It has cost him everything.

MADELEINE

Almost.

DOCTOR

Well, yes, almost everything. You don't understand. Frankly, I don't see how he has kept his mind. under the circumstances.

PRESIDENT

Don't exaggerate. You felt nothing. How could you? It was merely your duty, Patrick. Am I right?

MADELEINE

Or, if you did, it was like a vague cry of desolation from the back of your mind somewhere.

PRESIDENT

The cry of those extinguished billions became like one, fain't, fading cry. . . .

GENERAL

How well you put it. Father! I'm glad you understand.

DANIEL

And I, too! I believed what I believed. Because I am made that way. Is there anything wrong with hope? I hope for myself, and I hope for all the others. There is enough hope for everyone, at least? Madeleine?

MADELEINE

(Cuttingly) No excuses, Daniel. Twelve minutes. Perhaps eleven. Think faster.

GENERAL

Ah, leave him alone, you sultry, adulterous witch: You'll twist him into a tangle. Leave him alone. He knows nothing.

DANIEL

(From one to the other, desperately) Madeleine. . . ? My father . . . ?

MADELEINE

Think better, Daniel. Think harder. You may even make it in time. Your father . . . ?

DANIEL

(Anguished) I . . . ! I . . . ! I . . . !

PRESIDENT

(Takes Daniel gently by the arm and leads him back to settee) Don't push him. You will kill the poor man, Madeleine. Must you? *(An edge to his voice)* Must you?

MADELEINE

(With weary bitterness) Does it matter? We are beyond that now. It doesn't matter any more . . . He's as good as dead.

PRESIDENT
How can you! He is your HUSBAND.

MADELEINE
I can. And I must. He ruined my life. What there was
of it. Life. If not for — *(Looks longingly at O'Meager)* —
for him, I'd have given in long ago. It's your fault, too.
You got me into this, this — horror! *(She is suddenly a
soft, weeping woman)*

PRESIDENT
I'm sorry, my dear. It had to be done. Like being born.
It hurts. Then you forget. That was merely the beginning. And now — unless I am greatly mistaken, you
are on the point of betraying us all! *(He is suddenly firm
and commanding)*

MADELEINE
It doesn't matter any more, Father. *(She avoids his eyes,
and looks down into her glass)* Doesn't matter.

PRESIDENT
*(Lifts her chin looks into her eyes searchingly, then slaps her
face)* No, you don't! You had a job to do, Madeleine. I
think you have performed admirably. I'm proud of you.
Or, I was proud — until today. Until now. Something
tells me things are not turning out right. If this mission
fails — if you go wrong now, daughter, you will have a
lot to answer for. I warn you. There is no more time.
(Silence. Her eyes are defiant. He slaps her on the backswing)
Do you understand?

GENERAL

(Laughing with boyish delight) This is more like it! I thought we were just about wound up. Finished. Dad, you surprise me! Oh, this is more like the real thing. Was getting a little thick and slow in here. I like a good twist to the mystery. Let's play it out to the end. I want to see how it comes out. Where. Why. When . . . ? *(During this speech, he has energetically risen, gone to the window and slid it open. Outside it is quite dark. There are sporadic tearing explosions in the remote distance, audible now. Nothing to disturb the voices on the stage yet)* I'm ready. I'm listening. What have you two been up to? Devils!

PRESIDENT

(Contemptuously) I haven't left *everything* to you, General.

MADELEINE

Almost.

PRESIDENT

Not everything, though. Still, you've been useful, Patrick. No one else but you could have done this, er
—

GENERAL

(Reporting) Nearly eight out of ten, Mr. President!

PRESIDENT

Yes, yes, yes. I give you the credit. I have to give you the credit. But now — the key is missing. . . .

GENERAL

I never had it.

PRESIDENT

Of course you never had it, fool! It would have been too
great a temptation for the like of you, or anyone, for
that matter. Nevertheless, there is a key. Or there *was* a
key. . . . If it could be found now . . . Perhaps. . . .

GENERAL

Do you think — ?

PRESIDENT

O'Meager knows. Knew. all along. He's hidden it.

MADELEINE

It doesn't matter any more.

PRESIDENT

Oh yes, it does, Madeleine. It matters very much indeed. If we knew, even now, if we knew, we might understand how —

MADELEINE

(Mournfully, sadly, hauntingly) And I say it doesn't matter. We are beyond that now. Don't insist, Father. Don't.

GENERAL

(Catching the President's drift at last) I *knew* she should
have been watched more carefully! She's betrayed us all!
I see it! I'll murder the damned — *(rising again with his
strangler's reflex)*

PRESIDENT

If it is not in one of his clocks. . . . Or if it is not a clock within a clock. . . . Or if it is not a pattern of clocks, a web, or maze, or code of clocks. . . . Or if it is not a clock at all. . . . Clockery! What is Alfred O'Meager without a clock? It must be time! Time! The key must be hidden in time. . . . Somewhere. Somehow. Think, gentlemen, for the love of god! Think! *(There is a very faint wood-block ticking, syncopated in a complex, jazzy rhythm, modulated in volume, too, throughout the auditorium or theater: it can be heard, but not clearly, and it disappears and reappears irregularly in various places)*

GENERAL

Or a control. A control of controls. The ultimate control! But how, but how, but how?

MADELEINE

(Laughs)

PRESIDENT

Why are you laughing?

MADELEINE

Even Daniel, poor deluded Daniel, the dupe, the duper, the demagogue of demagogues, Director of Dreams and Doctrines, Dogmas and Desires, our Prophet of Peace and Plenty — even Daniel knows better than that! Don't you, Daniel? *(Daniel has sunk to his knees beside her, and she is stroking his head, which lies in her lap)*

DANIEL

(Resigned) I do. I always did. Despite everything.

MADELEINE

(Laughing) Almost!

DANIEL

(Quietly protests) Everything! Everything known!

MADELEINE

Poor thing. He has faith. Ignorance and faith. Nothing else can be done for you, Daniel. You are like everyone else, after all. Hope may help you, though. Hope may help. Hope, Daniel! *(The President and General are sitting facing each other, straddling the settee, scribbling notes and equations, handing each other the tear sheets from their pads. They are in deep concentration. The Doctor peeps over the General's shoulder)* . . . Five minutes, Daniel. Perhaps less. Can't you hear? Can't you tell? *(Muffled distant explosions punctuate the rhythmical jazzy ticking)* What do you say, Daniel? Have you anything to say to us?

Daniel

(Sepulchrally, impassively regarding audience) How many despairing men have wished for the words they needed for their last testimony! Their defense. Their defiance! And I, and I, and I. . . .

MADELEINE

Hush, my poor, dear demagogue. You have nothing to say. You don't understand. Give them a chance to find O'Meager. Hush, hush! *(The ticking is louder. Now they all seem to hear it. The President looks up with sudden insight and eagerness)*

PRESIDENT

Doctor, I've got to speak to O'Meager. I've got to know!

DOCTOR

I — I don't know what you're talking about. I can't touch him! You can't force me! I don't know what will happen if he's. . . . *(They are shoving him at the dummy)*

GENERAL

Who does this old fart think he is! Move, medico! *(Thrusts him away from the bedside in impatience)* Another coward! Another traitor! *(Begins to yank dripping tubes out of O'Meager)* This will settle our problem once and for all!

PRESIDENT

Patrick!

GENERAL

What difference does it make now?

MADELEINE

Oh, my god, General. What do you think you're doing?

GENERAL

If he has a minute more to live, That's too much! We're through taking orders from Alfred O'Meager! He can't force us any more! Let's see him as he really is! Let's hear him!

PRESIDENT

You imbecile! You insane boy scout! You, General the World? You don't even suspect what you may have done!

O'Meager's our arch-enemy! He's behind these insur-
rections! These confusions! Who do you think is the
mastermind of our human defeat? If we live through
the next hour, if we can push them back, we may still
manage to —

MADELEINE
You won't. You can't . You don't understand. We are
beyond all that now. War and victory, love and hate,
life and death. You still don't see it? *(Their voices are
now amplified by concealed microphones and reproduced
in tense, hysteric hoarse whispers from every point in the
theater. It is now a shadow play: the stage has grown darker
as the power fails in the hospital; in the distant skies there
are blinding, lurid, brief flashes of colors that are gorgeously
reflected on the walls of the hospital room. They will move
in the transfigured patterns of light. When O'Meager speaks,
his eyes open and stare unmoving straight up)*

PRESIDENT
What? What have we done? We're innocent!

DANIEL
We have done what we could! What will happen to us?

GENERAL
Where is it?! Where is it?!

DOCTOR
What's happening to us? Where is it?

MADELEINE
What do you want?

PRESIDENT

The key! The key!

MADELEINE

Still harping on that key? What key?

PRESIDENT

Madeleine, I beg you! Show us. You're the only one who can see.

MADELEINE

It is not up to me, anymore. Not up to me. It never was. Don't ask me what I see. Don't ask me what I know. It is of no use to you. It never was. Poor things. Poor, blind things:.

PRESIDENT

Whom then? Whom shall we ask? O'Meager? But he's not here any more. Or if he is . . . ?

MADELEINE

He is. Here. He is. He hears you. Ask. *He* is the key.

GENERAL

Who, O'Meager?! Madeleine, for the last time, I warn you —

MADELEINE

And you, oh, my brother! *You* have just turned the key! The door is opening. You stand here, waiting, watching. As the door swings wide, you will look out into another world, another time. You will walk towards it soon, and you will see nothing beyond that door, you will hear nothing beyond that door. It will be dark, and it will be silent. It will be — nothingness. But you will go into it. Whether you wish to or not. And when you have stepped through that door —

DOCTOR
(His eyes popping) Oh. Oh! It is not true. (Groans)

GENERAL
I don't understand. I don'tbelieve you. You really are a crazy clairvoyant cunt!

MADELEINE
Wait. Watch.

PRESIDENT
Oh, my god: He's here! He is here!

(O'Meager's large, white eyes have opened. His voice will be relentless, soft, low, powerful: an old man, an old, old man who need not insist in order to be heard: it is a voice that plunges all into frozen suspension)

O'MEAGER
Yes. Of course. I am here.

DOCTOR
O'Meager, are you all right? We did the best we could.

O'MEAGER
Of course, Doctor. You've done exactly right. What I wished. You could not have done better.

GENERAL
And now we have you, O'Meager! And I brought you out of it! I brought you back!

O'MEAGER

Yes, General. Of course. You've done exactly right. What
I wished. You could not have done better.

PRESIDENT

O'Meager!

O'MEAGER

Yes, Abraham. Of course. You've done exactly right.
What I wished. You could not have done better.

PRESIDENT

Listen to me, O'Meager! As President of the World, as
your old friend, as a man —

MADELEINE

— As a blind soul. Deaf! Dumb! Blind!

O'MEAGER

Hush, Madeleine. Yes, Abraham?

PRESIDENT

We need you:

O'MEAGER

You need me? Am I your father?

DANIEL

You are mine.

O'MEAGER

We are beyond that now.

MADELEINE

You loved me.

O'MEAGER

We are beyond that now.

MADELEINE

Yes, I know. We have always been.

PRESIDENT

But we need you, O'Meager!

O'MEAGER

Am I your god?

PRESIDENT

We can't live without you. Your clocks are like the beating of our hearts. Live without them? Without you. . . .

O'MEAGER

Yes?

PRESIDENT

Chaos! Right now, it seems as if the world is coming to an end!

O'MEAGER

An end. Yes. An end. In any case. . . .

PRESIDENT

Are we beyond that, too?

O'MEAGER

In any case. . . .

GENERAL
(Soft, desperate, impatient) Answer us!

O'MEAGER
In any case . . . in any case . . . in any case . . .

PRESIDENT
Do something, Doctor. He's going under. He's going
out.

DOCTOR
*(Quickly snatching a hypodermic syringe from the table and
injecting him as the light goes weird)* This damned
DUMMY! You never know what it's going to do. Can't
predict . . . *(Fiddles under the sheet)* This goddamned
DUMMY . . . ! *(Exasperated)* Well, it's very old, of
course, and frankly —

O'MEAGER
In any case . . . what can I do for you? Nothing, nothing at all. . . .

MADELEINE
Almost nothing.

O'MEAGER
You have wasted the world. Polluted and wasted the
world. The waters — wasted and gone. The earth —
wasted and bare. The air — dirtied and fouled. The
hills and the valleys polluted, filled with oils and grits
and muck — black, stagnant, fecal muck. Even the spaces
between the worlds: full of poisoned, floating junk. All,
all has been wasted. Muck. All you have. Muck. Even

life, life itself — wasted, poisoned. Muck. Filth and muck!

PRESIDENT, DOCTOR, GENERAL

We have tried.

DANIEL

We've tried.

DOCTOR

We have tried.

O'MEAGER

Muck! Muck! Muck! Muck!

ALL

Yes, but —

O'MEAGER

Only fire remains to you. It is burning now. It will burn your muck to nothingness. Can you see it? Can you? No, you are blind. You come to me now, crying, like children. What do you want from me?

PRESIDENT

Do something. Before it's too late.

O'MEAGER

It is. Too late. It is. Too late. Muck. Muck. Muck. Muck! Too late!

MADELEINE

(A tender whisper) Almost?

PRESIDENT
What do you mean, MADELEINE?

MADELEINE
There is a way.

PRESIDENT
Tell us! Quick!

MADELEINE
Out! The way is — out!

PRESIDENT

O'Meager, is she right?

O'MEAGER
Yes. Of course.

ALL
What? How? Where?

O'MEAGER
But not for you. Perhaps . . . not . . . For you . . . Perhaps . . . In any case . . . For you, perhaps not. . . .

President & GENERAL
Doctor, do something!

DOCTOR
(Diddling beneath the sheet) I'm trying! I'm trying!

DANIEL

Madeleine, darling Madeleine! For god's sake, will you do something? I appeal to you!

MADELEINE
(Dashes glass down) all right, Daniel. I will! *(She goes toward the bed steadily, her hands strangely held before her, somnambulist, priestess)*

PRESIDENT
Madeleine, what are you doing?!

DOCTOR
(Frozen, hands under sheet) Don't touch him!

MADELEINE:
(Disregarding them, she picks up O'Meager's head tenderly, and puts it to her breast as though it were a babe at suck) Time, gentlemen! Time! Twenty minutes! That is all there was for you. You have no time left. No time at all.

ALL
Madeleine!

MADELEINE
(Turning to face them, regal, the head in her arms) But — I give you, out of my kindness, and out of his generosity, greetings — Alfred O'Meager's greetings!

O'MEAGER'S HEAD
Yes, of course, Madeleine. You've done exactly right. What I wished. You could not have done better.

MADELEINE

I give you these seconds, these uncountable seconds, these moments in the nothingness which shall be your eternity, for you, for us all, forever. Find yourselves — here, now, before it comes! For it *is* coming. Coming. The time was set — and the time is up. It is the end. If you have wings, fly away, fly far away. Now, now, now — !

O'MEAGER'S HEAD

Now. . . . In any case . . . now. . . . Exactly what. . . . What I wanted. . . . Of course. . . . In any case. . . . Now! Now . . . !
(It has grown utterly dark, except for the luminous head of O'Meager.)

A blast of light blinds the theater.

*   *   *

CRANE, CRANE, MONTROSE & CRANE

— farce in one act

for Fred Nicholas

Persons

JEREMY CRANE: An aging businessman in his late 50's who is struggling with things.

AARON CRANE: His brother, a man in his early 50's who has renounced things.

BONNIE MONTROSE: Jeremy's executive secretary, about 30. Her métier: managing most things.

The Place, The Time

Jeremy Crane's office, high above the city. Late afternoon. Midwinter.

The Scene, The Action

This executive office is well-equipped, perhaps a small computer running and rapping at intervals, handled by Miss Montrose with the self-absorbed, complex and confusing routines of the computer-operator. She can run other machines as well, calculators and typewriter, and so forth. Jeremy Crane's desk is clean, except for the intercom to Miss Montrose, which intercom system is live for the house. There is a comfortable armchair or settee for the visitor, and a chaise longue, or coffee table large enough to serve as a chaise, with a sort of platform, or headrest, at one end.

Jeremy Crane is conservatively dressed; Aaron Crane may wear more relaxed clothing; Miss Montrose is quietly attractive in her taste. Jeremy may be prepared with a box of unsharpened pencils, which he will work at unconsciously much of the time. Aaron will have time to light and enjoy some good puffs on a fine panatela, while he plays with black-lensed, designer sunglasses.

Before the curtain rises, if there is one, we hear a steady beat of office sound: computer printout, typing, calculator, scored for the beat of a fast clock. Aaron is disclosed "reading" *Fortune*. He has been waiting for Jeremy to speak. Jeremy, slouched in his executive recliner-swiveller, is watching Aaron intently. They are brothers: they understand each other very well indeed. The pace of their speech follows from their deep knowledge of each other and of things. Jeremy's mouth is lit by malicious smirks as he watches Aaron's disguised preoccupation with Miss Montrose, despite his pretense of indifference to her attractions. She may, in passing with an armload of folders, computer printout, film cannisters, and papers, and in the course of arranging her desk and Jeremy Crane's, drop something near aaron. She will crouch efficiently to retrieve it, but she does not acknowledge his surveillance of her. It is a pantomime of animal sensuality played with restrained ruthlessness. She will at last settle at her desk, becoming instantly remote and silent in her work and her absolutely impersonal control of the executive scene.

MORAL

Boost a booster. Knock a Knocker. Fuck a sucker.

                           *   *   *

                         JEREMY
Montrose .

                         AARON
Montrose?

                         JEREMY
Montrose. You like her.

                         AARON
Pretty thing.

                         JEREMY

Bonnie Montrose. You like her.

                         AARON
Pretty thing.

                         JEREMY
Damned clever cunt. Montrose. You'd be surprised.

                         AARON

Bonnie Montrose. I'dbe surprised.

JEREMY

She'll do anything. You'd be surprised. Real estate.
Import-export. Legal work. Research and development.
Mixed portfolios. Including insurance. Export-import.
Screws my competition to hell. History. Psychology.
Every trick in the bag. Mythology. My Bonnie.

AARON

History. Psychology. What more do you need. Mythology.

JEREMY

Input-output. She'll do anything. You'd be surprised.
She produces. Take time, real time. Who understands
it. Bonnie knows it, like the palm of your hand. Real
time. Output-input. Markets it too.

AARON

You make it sound. Montrose. An interesting proposition to look at. But I wonder. Jeremy, wouldn't it be
better not to —

JEREMY

I always played it rough.

AARON

And I'm a quitter.

JEREMY

Did I say it.

AARON

I'm a quitter.

JEREMY

I didn't say it.

AARON

Not worth it. Poor Noah. Phoo! Not worth. Not. O, one dark, cold day they'll come in and find you. Just like Noah! Remember Noah, next floor somewhere. Wasn't it? Phoo! And what will Queenie say then. What will poor Queenie do then!

JEREMY

She'll buy a new coat to keep herself warm. Or find a new house in the spring.

AARON

Poor thing!

JEREMY

Too bad. Too bad.

AARON

Jeremy, think of it. Try to imagine it. Have pity. You should. Don't you have pity? What will Queenie do then.

JEREMY

Queenie. She'll shop. What does Queenie do now! What did she ever do? Shop: box of candy, basket of fruit. Then a new cologne. And a new suit. Shoes and the rest of it. What will Queenie do?!

AARON
Bu it's hard on them. Still. Women. Have pity. Some
pity.

JEREMY
Hard on them! Too bad.(Laughing) What's hard on
them. *(Senile)* Nothing's hard then. So what! I'm mort-
gaged. I'm collateral. I'm funds and annuities. Hard on
them? There'll be a vault for me, and the safety box for
Queenie. It's all in trust. Poor Queenie.

AARON

Jeremy, I'm talking to you, you know. Listen.

JEREMY
In fact. Hard on them? Hard on us too. Harder. In fact.
Hardest on us. *(Silence)* Come back in with me. I need
you. Be my friend. *(Young again)* Now. Listen. *(Silence)*
Aaron. I'm talking to you. In fact.

AARON

Jeremy — now what have you been up to? JEREMY!

JEREMY
I like it rough.

AARON
You'll be sorry. What have you been up to.

JEREMY
The rougher the better.

AARON

You'll be sorry. One late afternoon they come in here. They find you in that chair. Remember Noah, next floor somewhere? With your pants down around your frozen white ankles. Is it worth it.

JEREMY

There's a first time for everyone. I don't care. Listen. There's nothing new about it. We've been through it. It's the same old thing, isn't it. May not seem that way, but — but it is. You know. Say, listen. I'm fed up any-way. Why shouldn't I be. Who cares. It's rough. Listen, fella. I know. Rough! Rough! You know.

AARON

Is it worth it. Is it? They buzzed his buzzer. Noah. Knocked his door. Noah. Not a sound, not a whisper. They opened, they went in. Noah. He was staring at his lap. His hands were broken open. In the ashtray on his desk, a cigarette burning, its tip stained red. Who was that chippie? Noah! Who was she? Who knows her.

JEREMY

Who doesn't . A chippie, a chippie. Some Vassar girl. Cunt with a habit. Fifty bucks a trick. Worked this building. Everybody knows her.

AARON

Noah. Cherry-colored lipstick on him. Who was there. No one. No one was there. Phoo! And he was definitely dead.

JEREMY

Noah. Slob. Phoo! They were hard on him. They were
never good for him. Things. Noah. Too bad. Slob!

AARON

(Outraged, pacing) Natural-born sonofabitch like you.
Don't touch me! *(Jeremy is not even within reaching distance of him)* Don't try it! Fucking bastard. You!

JEREMY

But have a listen will you. I can't make it without you,
Aaron. Aa Aaron?

AARON

(Senile, mocking) Aaron, I can't make it without you,
Aaaaron.

JEREMY

I can't , Aaron, I can't .

AARON

Aaron, I can't Aaron. And why not. Why.

JEREMY

What do you mean, Why not. Ca-can't you see. Do-
Don't you hear. *(Abject, self-pitying)*

AARON

I'm not looking. I don't listen.

JEREMY

Help. Advice. Someone I can trust.

AARON

Oh no you don't . Not this time.

JEREMY

It's what I need. A brother. I need. At least. Like you.

AARON

Move along there. Next, please. Say, keep it moving
down there. Next. all right, please. What's yours? Form
a straight line. No exceptions. Next?

*(Miss Montrose whirls round, scooping up a file of papers, bringing
them to Jeremy to sign, scornfully indicating the line on each sheet,
which Jeremy signs automatically, unaware of her. She is watching Aaron
coolly)*

BONNIE

We'll take this, and that, and this. Drop them, cancel
this . . . and that . . . and this. . . . It'll work. It'll work
out. For the time being.

(She is watching Aaron with contempt during his self-congratulation)

AARON

(Young again, demonstrating his fitness) I'm retired, you
know. Quit when the quitting was good. Two lungs,
two kidneys. Stomach hard as a board. Hit me, hit me.
(Strikes himself with her hand) You see? Hard! Hard hard
hard.

BONNIE

Anything else?

JEREMY

Always comes down to this. Well not always. Aaron,
you I need. Listen . . . they're out there. They're waiting for me to make a move. You Don't know what it's
like these days. I can't even lift my head. One slip, one
goddam slip and . . . we're through. Put yourself in my
place, Aaron. Try to imagine it. Pity, try. Have a little
pity.

AARON

Heart, lotsa heart! Sinuses clear as bells. 20/20 eyes.
Plus or minus. I hear you, plus-or-minus one decibel.
Mouthful of teeth. Plus or minus. Bowels. I'm intact.

BONNIE

I don't believe it.

AARON

Intact!

JEREMY

And I'm not.

AARON

Did I say it.

JEREMY

I'm not.

AARON

I didn't say it.

JEREMY

This time it won't be easy. They're watching. One slip . . . and we're nothing. Less than nothing. Say, you can't even imagine it. No more probations. How do you like that! No more hearings. What it takes to live like this . . . ! Think of it. Imagine. And have pity! Right, Bonnie?

BONNIE

Yes, Mr. Crane. Of course.

AARON

Intact! Two legs, two arms, a bladder. What more do I want. I eat, I sleep. The world is all there. What more do I need!?

JEREMY

A man needs. Don't ask. A man needs something. *(Pause)* Something more *(Pause)* You know? *(Pause)* Right, Bonnie?

BONNIE

Of course, Mr. Crane. Yes.

AARON

What more do you want, the whole world? Who do you think you are. What kind of crazy idea. Something more.

JEREMY

I don't know. Something. Right, Bonnie? *(But Bonnie doesn't hear. She has returned to her station, and is keyboarding away at the computer)*

(Silence)

AARON

So you called me. Me of all people! Me!

JEREMY

Ca-can't handle it alone. This time it won't be easy. Not easy. Not alone.

AARON

There are banks. Go to the banks.

JEREMY

The banks. It's not so simple. Who needs banks. There isn't a bank that would. Besides, the way they treat you — it's sickening. Things have reached a point, I tell you, things have reached such a po-point . . . I don't need banks.

AARON

(To Bonnie) So, you called me?

BONNIE

(Without addressing him) Yes, of course. Mr. Crane. A loan. It is not easy.

JEREMY

Never saw anything like it. Stainless steel, That's what we're up against! They're waiting like walls. You don't know. Just waiting for me.

AARON

Why call me — you misery, you crud.

JEREMY

Go away. Who called you! Get out.

AARON

So I came. I'm here. What is it, you cramp, you crumbling turd.

JEREMY

Remember, I'm here too. Been here all this time. So here I am, minding my business — I can't get out, anyway — how could I get out, I ask you, how? — and, bing-bang, snip-snap, tick-tock . . . we've had it. That's the way it is. You're sitting at the red light, everything quiet, everything in order, ten o'clock by the music on the radio on a sweet Sunday morning and — whoom! Out of nowhere it comes. Crash! Smash! Sons of goddam bitches. The verdict is — they lost control. It's just manslaughter. Just! No, you can't imagine what it's like here now. Nothing satisfies them anymore. You don't remember how it happens, do you.

AARON

I settled my accounts.

JEREMY

(Twenty years younger) Where's your bottom line, hah? You forget patents? You forget discounts? The hot cash boys? You don't remember things, do you. I got a process here. Little guy in some lab, see? Worth millions easy.

AARON

Sure.

JEREMY

Hundred million.

AARON

Long shot.

JEREMY

Yeah yeah. What do you say, say a billion. Say two. Gross national, multi-national. Communications. Grab you?

AARON

Sure sure. I like them odds.

JEREMY

Easy. Easy. Little guy in a lab. I fund him. Deductible. Anyway, last week, listen, last week I was in Reno, you know —

AARON:

(Startled) Where's Queenie?

JEREMY

What about Queenie?

AARON

Reno!

JEREMY

Reno, I said. You don't know what things are like. Listen, I was in Reno last week —

AARON

What were you doing in Reno?

JEREMY

Went to meet The Put. You know what The Put wanted for another fifty? Oh he's into me all right, into me, but good. . . . You know what The Put grabbed me for?

AARON

I said, What were you doing in Reno.

JEREMY

Hold onto your balls. Listen: thirty percent: off the top: one month to repay. Think I took it? I took it. Signed and sealed. Fifty million. Cash. Ink still wet on the bills. Ten, fifty, a hundred million? Don't mean a thing to The Put. . . . Nowadays . . . Aah, what do you know. You don't know. Inventory is total. Saturation campaigns. Attack them, drown them, lose them in the dust. Nail down the take. No matter what. And moreover the staff has to be handled . . . oh so delicately. You just don't know. What do you know. We get it all in C-notes. Hundred mail sacks full. Whole plane load. Means nothing to The Put. Nowadays. You talk cash? Percentages? Inside and outside? Nothing to him.

AARON

So you went to Reno.

JEREMY

Sure I went to Reno. Why not. Example: I tell you what it is. Nowadays. There's a human relations outfit in this town, and it's one helluva big operation. And for a New Year's present, they send round the highest-priced girls on the list. Do the job right in your office. You don't know! Right in your office. Right, Bonnie?

And who do you suppose gets the top billings? Of course. Top ratings? Of course. That's what it is. Nowadays. So who called you.

JEREMY

AARON

Broke off everything to get here. And I got here.

JEREMY

What for.

AARON

You shit.

JEREMY

Listen, Don't bother me.

AARON

All right. Now I came, though, now that I'm here, it's been a long time, so now . . . what about Queenie. How's Queenie. I'd like to, uh —

JEREMY

Fuck off now, brother. I'm busy. Right, Bonnie?

BONNIE

Yes, Mr Crane. Of course. *(Miss Montrose is typing and working super-efficiently)*

AARON

Oh. Well.
(Silence)

JEREMY

I know I shouldn't ask. But there's no one else, actually. No one. Is there, Bonnie.

AARON

I think you should pray.

JEREMY

After all these years!

AARON

Praying is good for you. You'd be surprised. Better pray.

JEREMY

I'd be surprised.

AARON

You'd be . . . better. Better off. Pray.

JEREMY

Surprised. . . . I was thinking. You know, Aaron, I was just thinking about things. . . .

AARON

Or ask your son. Where is George, anyway. Must be forty, forty-five by now. He's your son, isn't he. You should be a grandfather by now, and look at you! What do you know. You make me sick.

JEREMY

George is a student.

AARON

When I was his age.

JEREMY

What does he know. He's an idealist. Theoretically.

AARON

When I was his age.

JEREMY

It s all been worked out for him. That's the way things
are done now. There are methods. There seem to be.
He says there are methods. Nowadays. So why bring
him into it.

AARON

Well it's just too bad then.

JEREMY

George. I send him his allowance. He marches. They're
marching again. These days they're always marching.
One thing or the other. They rally. They block the streets.
Male and female and whatnots. Every type and then
some. They shout, they sing. They fill the streets with
their bodies. They want the right to life. They like animals. They like trees. They want to breathe. all right.
Well, I had morals too. They want protection. Do they
vote? They don't vote. They chant. Money. They want
money. Everybody owes them. Money. Love. It's blood
money. It's blood. They throw firebombs. They hold
hands in the desert. They preach. They cash my checks.
They are on camera! Rights, my rights, your rights,
everybody's rights. Out there. In the bedroom They
practice on their body. Dress it. Undress it. Feed it.
Build it. Buff it up. Everything is the body. Make it
pure. Yet how bad are things? Nowadays, how bad.
Things could be worse. But do they listen? They got
headphones. They are deaf. Their brains don't grow up
somehow. Well, all right. I don't know. Honestly, Aaron,
is it morals or what. What is it.

(Aaron leaps into action with handheld microphone.
Music fills house with his voice over the guitar tape of
"Annihilator Soul," Punk-metal, deadpan, with incred-
ible energy, and without reference to anyone in office
either by gesture or direction. His singing ends as suddenly
as it began, shattering Jeremy's meditation, which resumes
again, quite unbroken)

All the time you see us, we'll be on our way, tata!
Taking what is mine, cuz now I'll have my day, tata-ta!
Dom-in-a-tor So-o-ul, he take what's in his way!
Ta! Move in on them!
All the time you see us, ta! we'll be on our way! tata!-ta
Passive ways to pull you down, tear them up and smash
them in, tata!
We'll have our day, tata-ta tata-ta!
Dom-in-a-tor So-o-ul!

JEREMY

Punk, you. You punk. Merely.

AARON

You know right is right, and wrong is wrong,
We'll sing all night, come hear our song!
You know you may shoot, and you may kill,
But we'll stomp and shout till we get our will!
For you's the old and we's the young!
And we's the bold, we's the strong
And we's the many, and you's the few!
So victory's ours, despite your powers . . .
Do what you may do
Do what you may do
Do what you may do
Do what you may do

We'll step right over, we'll step right in
So come on over! We're gonna win! win! win . . . !
Do what you may do
Do what you may do
Do what you may do, do, do. . . .
Yah . . . ! Yah . . . ! Yah . . . !

JEREMY

Let me poll you, Aaron. Can the son help the father. I ask you. Even if I beg. When I was his age! I don't know. George is maybe forty-five. Don't I send the punk his lousy allowance. But now, you —

AARON

I'm retired.

JEREMY

Don't congratulate yourself yet. *(Shouting)* You think you're so smart?!

AARON

Try something. Come on, slob, just try. Slob.

(They both leap suddenly agile into karate posture. Jeremy responds to Aaron's feint with passes; Aaron blocks and attacks. Formal karate grunting, passes and blocks: loud middle-aged karate noises and breathings. Evenly matched, they come to that recognition and bow deeply to each other)

AARON

You see? Impeccable. I'm in training.

JEREMY

(Older again) I can flush you down the tube. Any time I like. Right, Bonnie?

AARON

(Older again) Hmn. Hah. Hmn.

JEREMY

(Raging, senile) Down the goddam tube. You don't think I can, but I can. *(Coughing, strangled)* Go-go-goddammit.

AARON

(Compassionate) Here, drink some water. Let's sit down a bit, shall we. Right, Bonnie? *(Accomplices, they help to carry Jeremy to his executive chair, comforting him)*

JEREMY

(Bleary, senile, suspicious) What do you think, I'm zorko? I know what you think. But I'm not going to zork. I won't. Oh no. Zorko, he thinks! Leave me alone. In fact. Who needs you. He thinks I'm zorking. Wants to wipe my ass for me, yet. Who needs you. *(Talks to intercom)* Bonnie, bring me the file on Aaron Crane, will you, like a good girl?

BONNIE

(Breaking off her concentration on Aaron) Yes, Mr. Crane. Of course.

JEREMY

(Humming happily and senile to himself) We'll show him. The tube, the tube, we'll flush him down the

goddamned tube, the boob! we'll flush, we'll flush, and
we'll flush him down, down, down . . .

*(Aaron nonchalantly lights himself a fresh panatela, as though nothing
of what follows remotely concerns him. Bonnie brings out a voluminous
file, stations herself beside Jeremy's desk. She is impassive, except perhaps
for the professional flicker of amusement or interest as Jeremy holds up
photographic documents for her inspection, flashing them at Aaron,
who does not look at them, but at her instead. Jeremy gloats and chuck-
les to himself like a panderer, a demon of vicarious lechery, chuckling
with scorn and ribald triumph. It is possible to use this bit in the form
of a sales demonstration: i.e., screened hardcore porno slides)*

JEREMY

Ah hah, brother of mine! Scandal. Scandal and corruption. Corruption and degradation and lechery. Oh ho!
Do you see? Lechery and decadence and rebellion. Right,
Bonnie? Look at that: my my my! Perversion. Subver-
sion, reversion and conversion. Hee hee. You see? Shock-
ing. And funny too. Right, Bonnie? Humiliation. Di-
version. Inversion, proversion and deversion and
postversion. Tsk tsk tsk . . . And fore-version! And
preversion and unversion, and, and, dear dear dear. . . .
Disgusting! Despicable! Where! When! How! To whom
and with whom and how many times! What types! What
techniques! Oh, what you haven't been up to, and down
to! Up and down, and down and up! And so the world
goes round. Tsk tsk tsk. . . .

AARON

I deny everything, of course .

JEREMY

(Calm, self-satisfied) Nobody knows what you've been
doing with your life. But we know. Right, Bonnie? He

denies everything, of course. But don't we know, Bonnie
dear?

AARON:

Impossible.

JEREMY

You're my brother. It's our business to know.

AARON

You wouldn't dare.

JEREMY

Try and stop me.

AARON

How much.

JEREMY

Nothing doing. It's not for sale. Is it, Bonnie. But — if
they happened to get curious about you. . . . *(Cackling)*

AARON

You can't prove a thing. I was never there, Jeremy. Never.
You can't pin it on me. *(Shouting)* I'll sue you, Jeremy.
Tell him, Bonnie! I'll shave every hair off your ass —

BONNIE

Then you wouldn't have a case, Mr. Crane. Who could
help you then? Isn't it better to have a case.

JEREMY

A case? With my experience at manufacturing? My kno-
whow in merchandising? I can prove what I like. Lis-

ten, my boy, you're tagged and ticketed. Nobody's innocent, so who'll believe you. Besides, I hold all the invoices.

AARON
(Reasonably, as to a madman) Jeremy, now look here, Jeremy —

JEREMY
(Shouting) Don't you "Now look here, Jeremy" me! I've had enough from you! I'm fed up to here with you! I'm on your case!

AARON
(Addressing himself to Bonnie, who remains impassive) Filth, you know. You know, lies?

JEREMY
(Smugly) Your case is an open book to me. All accounts are in. Cross-filed and double-checked. Now for that old bottom line. Oh brother! Right, Bonnie?

BONNIE
(Bonnie listens to them both tactfully, objectively) People prefer something solid, you know. I know I do.

AARON
Fabrications. Forgeries. Freaks. Sales promotion!

JEREMY
It adds up. The machine says it all adds up. Yours!

AARON
(To Bonnie) You do see what it is? You know what's wrong? It's blackmail. Extortion. He's a tax maniac.

JEREMY

I can run you through the machine backwards and forwards.

AARON

Creeping bureaucrat! Propagandist! Torturer! Bonnie, you do see how it is?

BONNIE

It would be better if you could show me. Perhaps I haven't seen it all. Your case.

JEREMY

Through the goddamned machine. Forwards and backwards. And what do you think he'll look like then, eh, Bonnie? A fine, a lovely printout, eh, Bonnie? We will supercompute his ass off!

AARON

(Anguished) Terrorist! That you could do this to me, your own brother!

JEREMY

Like the poet says, I would stop at nothing.

AARON

Your very own brother?!

JEREMY

Who else?! We'll fax you to hell and back!

AARON

Can he do that, Bonnie?

JEREMY
(Triumphant laughter) Tell him, Bonnie. Go on. Go on.

BONNIE
Yes. And no. It's too bad. Yes and. No. It's hard. Isn't
it. No one likes a soft case. *(Silence)*

*(Miss Montrose leaves her workstation and enters a space of her own.
The brothers Crane have disappeared into a silent confrontation of one
another)*

Mr. Crane. And Mr. Crane. Two men. And I am only a
woman. I've asked myself what is to be done for you.
That is, what I could do, if there is anything I can do
that you couldn't do for yourselves. Everything you do
here, in the way of business — and it's all business,
isn't it — I can do as well as you. Better. In fact. Because I learned it all from you. Things. It is all yours,
this world, and it's all for you. And now we're in it
together, aren't we. So we ought to stick together, I think.
We ought to pull together. Isn't that right. What could
we do without each other. Not much. Very little. Nothing at all. In fact. And yet.
And yet, why ask me? What do you want from me. Do
you know? I'm nothing. Just your girl. Miss Montrose.
Bonnie Montrose. Better than most. But all you know
is my name. That's all. You have nothing else. My voice?
My face? Perhaps my hands? Don't deny it. And you
want me to say yes. And That's all you want, isn't it. I
have so much more, but that's all you want. You want
me to say yes. How can I? How can I offer to say yes to
you both. It's illogical. Or say No, not to both of you.
That's not logical either. Two men. And I'm only a
woman. But — if you knew what you wanted. . . .

(Silence)

AARON
(Fraternally) Something's wrong. Jeremy. Jeremy, what's wrong?

JEREMY
Listen, Aaron. I don't. . . know . . . what they're thinking. Out there. I'm afraid of them. I don't know what they want. They are leveraging me up and down till I don't know where I am. It's no buy-out. You think it's a buy-out, but it's no buy-out. I got one tough case here.

AARON
Inexcusable. How long's this been going on.

JEREMY
Who knows. Forever. Does it matter now.

AARON
You can tell me. Who else, after all. Come on. Jeremy.

JEREMY
You're the only one I can ta-ta-talk to. Listen. Aaron.

AARON
(Soothing) Listen. I've come. Finally. Put your mind at rest. Can you do that.

JEREMY
There's so much to tell you. Things. Where do I begin. History. It's been so long. Anyway. Listen now. You

know, they're afraid of me. Out there. They don't know . . . what I'm thinking.

AARON

I'm here now. I'm with you. Now.

JEREMY

And you'll come in with me. Now, yes? You'll take my case? Yes?

AARON

If that's what you really want.

JEREMY

You'd better. I'm telling you. You'd better.

AARON

So I'm in. I'm in. If that's what you want. Count me in. I don't like it, but I'm in. You can depend on me. One thing I hope — I hope it's not . . . CONSOLIDATION INCORPORATED!?

JEREMY

Why'd you think of that.

AARON

Or INCORPORATION CONSOLIDATED!? Because if it is. . . .

JEREMY

No. No, no, noooooo! Nothing like that. Are you slipping? What makes you think of that. Oh brother, you must be slipping.

AARON

Because that's when I quit, you know. When the quitting was good. That table. Those twelve men. That morning. forty lawyers waiting outside. I'm telling you. Because, if that's what it's about. . . . No thanks. It's been good to know you. That's all, brother. I wash my hands here and now.

JEREMY

Christ, no. Nothing like that. Right, Bonnie?

BONNIE

It was a bad quarter. Rotten season. The world was in deficit. All budgets out of control. A hole in the sky. Eruptions. Meltdown possible. Such seasons are periodic in nature, though no one comprehends the rhythm, much less the fundamental cycles involved. Comets, maybe. Anyway, it was bearish. Men were filled with doubts. That they had faith, oh yes, that they believed things could turn up again, is true, too true. But — confidence was lacking. You must have confidence. My private analysis of the situation is that men didn't understand because they didn't see things straight, you know. Or couldn't after all. If men can't, they can't, you know. But in a way it all made sense — to me.

JEREMY

Of course. *(To Aaron, gleefully)* You see what I mean? Oh, Bonnie, oh! Oh, what a girl!

AARON

(Caught up in his own memories) Bankers and lawyers. Chairmen. Vice Presidents. CEO's. Managers and assistant managers. Stocks, bonds, pension funds. Short

notes, mutuals, holders of holders of holdings. Around
that table, from sunrise on, fighting over piles of —
you just can't imagine. They were smashing in the ceil-
ings, the thing was going under, what a beating they
were taking! Top men, respected figures, conmen bas-
tards, gilt-edged advisers! Securities were pyramiding,
securities were collapsing: combines of churches and
companies and colleges, collapsing! Foundations squab-
bling over the pieces of collateral, over those piles of —

JEREMY
(Holding up a censoring index finger) It's done every day,
you know.

AARON
— piles of . . . paper! Fighting all morning around that
table. Well, it seems that some guy bought in secretly.
With ten million. Dentist. Now where does a dentist
get hold of ten millions. . . . Jesus!

JEREMY
Orthodontist.

AARON
I mean, what the hell! A dentist.

JEREMY
Anyhow, he pledged a lot more than he actually had.
We all do it. We do it every day. It's natural. Right,
Bonnie? I pledge yours? You pledge mine?

BONNIE
Very natural. Anticipation. It keeps things going. If
things are going to go at all.

AARON

A dentist! All afternoon round that table. I know. I suffered. I was there. I saw men wrecked in the prime of life: the best men in my generation. Ruined. *(He acts out his description)* Urping, burping, hacking away. Slurping down syrups, gobbling up tons of Tums, and sucking lozenges, and puffing on adrenalin. They were squirming and burbling. They were farting and gasping. They were yawning and they were groaning and choking. There was no air left to breathe.

JEREMY

They were in conference.

AARON

Some conference! All morning, all afternoon round that table. . . . Gimmee three! I'll take one! You can't do that! Oh no? Boost the shares. Buy them out. Cut them off. Ante up. Shake them down. Fifty cents on the dollar. Ten cents on the dollar. A penny! Zero on the dollar! Drop those pricks in the bucket. Squeeze their dummies. Kill that report. Shut those shysters up. Where's the fixer! Put the fix in. Produce the proofs. Stick it up your own damn country. And as for proxies — Jesus! Those proxies!

JEREMY

Rough, rough. You go public, you got to expect the proxies. Leverage your ass to the moon.

AARON

All day long round that table. He won't sign? Bring in ten more. Send it overseas! Where's that judge? Call in Morgan & Morgan. Who? Bought who out? In? Up? I

want his father. No good, he's finished. Get me the son!
Who? Ask the Governor. No good. Call the General.
Write the President. Cut that crap. No, kill that story.
Stuff her. Bring him round. Kick them out. And then,
the proxies — oh god, oh god!

BONNIE

I remember that affair. It was a classic case. You have to
study cases, you know. Cases are all we have. I have
studied it, and it seems to me that the situation was
unnecessary. It would not have deteriorated so badly
had it not been for —

AARON

You don't know! That is one case you can't imagine.
That's when I saw my first one. Oh my god! The shock.
Dead on that table. Cut to pieces. He was carried out.
You don't know, if you haven't seen it for yourself. You
can't imagine, if you haven't seen one yourself.

BONNIE

And yet it happens every day. It's life, you know. It is
natural.

AARON

Did that slow them down, do you think? Did that stop
them? No. Oh no! Chairmen and directors all inter-
locked and losing their VIP pants scrambling for the
phones. Hundreds of millions running wild, the thing's
out of control, and Canada and Mexico too, all tangled
into the deals. . . . Oh god. Oh god.

JEREMY

Typical, typical.

AARON

I don't exaggerate. You couldn't fix it. It can't be fixed. So what do you want. So I got out. I had enough. Sold my shares right there. Everything I had, I gave up. Willingly. They said to me, You crazy? You stupid? It's going up, they said. It's going to go up again. up and up and up! But enough's enough. I got rid of the thing. Phoo! Too much trouble. They wanted their names on their doors. Sit behind a door, worrying? A door with my own name on it waiting. Waiting for what. For whom. Worrying. Phoo! Not me. I retired. So what do you want now, Jeremy. Jeremy?

JEREMY

(Dreaming, fondly, cajoling) Remember our first one, our very first? Listen. Remember? AMERICAN LIMITED?

AARON

(Happily, joining him in laughter) AMERICAN LIMITED . . . ! Thrill of a lifetime. Sure, never nothing like the first deal. Now she was something; she was a baby! From cave to chateau. When I think of it. Corn to caviar. I have to laugh. Quite a deal. A real deal. Cotton to chincilla. When I think of it. Pork to platinum! Cider to champagne!

JEREMY

Ashes to airplanes. And dust to dynamos . . . ! Yeah. Had my name written all over it. Yeah. CRANE —

AARON

— & CRANE.

JEREMY

And it went on up.

AARON

And up.

JEREMY

And up! all the way! Does it matter now. Nobody remembers anyway. An old story. One for the books.
Though it was really something while it lasted. I forget
the half of it. After all. It wasn't so much.

AARON

(Reverting to his story) So they laughed at me. Their name
was on the door. Sure. But, when it came tumbling
down later, a year and a day, and they came tumbling
after — who did they call? They called me. Yeah. How
did I know! they said. Oh, listen, I said. Don't call me,
I said. But who could put it together again, they said,
who but me? I said, Oh yeah? With all my resources,
and all my smart men, I wouldn't, I couldn't put it
together again. . . .

JEREMY

Aaron. . . .

AARON

Say, listen, Jeremy. If it's s what I think it is, the answer
is no.

JEREMY

Aaron . . .

AARON

Absolutely no. A thousand times no. *(In operatic recitative)* Non-non, non-non, non-non!

JEREMY

Aaron. . . . Aaron. . . .

AARON

You're in shock.

JEREMY

Oh.

AARON

You're exhausted. Used up, you know?

JEREMY

Yes. Yes. What are we going to do.

AARON

You'll make it. I'm retired, you know.

JEREMY

But you promised!

AARON

Of course. What is the matter with you.

JEREMY

Why should I trust you. The things you've done. You'r
not to be trusted. You're capable of anything. After the

things I've seen!

AARON
Well, yes. And now I'm going to the museum. If you need me, just call.

JEREMY
Hey there!

AARON
Just call. You'll make it.

JEREMY
Hey! Treat me like this! Why come here and treat me like this.

AARON
For the walk. Nice afternoon. Still nice. *(Putting on his sunglasses)*

JEREMY
What"s doing at the museum.

AARON
Retrospective exhibit. Marvelous things. Some old. Some new. All retrospective by now though. Things. There used to be such things!

JEREMY
Like what things

AARON
Oh, things. Of, um, sorts. Objects. Subjects. Arranged things. For, um, contemplation. You coming? Come.

JEREMY

M-m-me? Out? There?

AARON

Well, yes. In fact.

JEREMY

Come back. Sit down. You're not going anywhere. *(Takes up a sawed-off shotgun from behind his desk)* I said, Co-co-come back! *(A blast in the air)*

AARON

(Casually returning, removing sunglasses) Remember how much I used to like peanut butter sandwiches? With ham slices. Black bread. Had to have them for lunch, every day, individually wrapped. Also raw carrots, celery, salt, cheese. And a brownie. Apple. Two paper napkins. Now it doesn't . . . seem that . . . important. Lunch. You reach a point. . . . Sooner or later you reach a point. . . .

JEREMY

No. Of course I'm not angry. Who's angry. *(But he holds the weapon trained on Aaron)* Lots on my mind, is all. Lots happening. You understand. Seems to be happening. Leave it at that. Let's.

AARON

Or perhaps there will even be a breakthrough. I'd like that. I, uh, I'm waiting for that. It depends. Some time or other. Perhaps a breakthrough is coming. But I wouldn't count on it.

JEREMY

Don't be foolish. If it's not one thing, it's another, as the poet says. Still, why not? A breakthrough. . . .

AARON

That's what I mean. You know, sooner or later you reach a point in life. . . .

JEREMY

No! There's a limit, and that's all! I ca-ca-can't explain it now. I didn't call you back for that. There must be a limit. There always has been a limit. . . .

AARON

And yet there is none, you know. Though you go on. There never has been. No limit, none at all. On and on and on and. . . . But if it's coming, if there's a real breakthrough coming. . . .

JEREMY

What I mean. That's the point!

AARON

Exactly. Suppose there is. Well, anyway, I'm retired.

JEREMY

I never expected you would help. Did I.

AARON

I'm only your brother, after all. So bag it. Mark it. Call it a day. (Silence)

(Jeremy replaces gun behind desk and swings into action, as briskly as though starting his working day. Miss Montrose has set the pace and *beat by reactivating her machines at full level)*

JEREMY

No, I don't like it. Ipso facto. Yes, ipso facto. Say — but you remember AMERICAN LIMITED. Now, that was interesting to begin with. If we arranged to . . . *(Buzzer of his intercom sounds)* Just a sec. Hold on, Aaron, will you. Yes? *(Gabble of voices on his intercom)* Listen, Aaron, what I wanted to talk about: you remember INCOR-PORATED AMERICAN? Supposing we floated her again, eh? Sure There's a long way to go; but now's the time. Before we're out of it. What do you think, hey? *(Buzzer of intercom)* Just a sec. Hold on, Aaron, will you. Yes? *(Gabble of voices)* You know me, baby, I wouldn't sell you short, would I. (He is speaking both to intercom and to Aaron, winking) Trust me. Tell you what: you keep a kicker, Aaron baby, eh? Always keep a kicker anyway, don't you, Aaron baby. . . .

(Aaron has not bought any of this. He speaks into Jeremy's intercom now, which is live in the house).

AARON

You *are* a prick. *(He has switched off the intercom and turns to Bonnie)* When my wife died, you know, it was a surprise to me. Who'd have thought of that! I felt I was finished. One hell of a surprise. She died. And I felt I was finished. *(To Jeremy)* You don't remember what I was like. You don't care. How could you. You don't know. You don't imagine.

JEREMY

I'm a busy man, you know. *(Jeremy flicks on his intercom and addresses it, live in the house)*

AARON

(Meditative) If not for your Queenie, I could never have made it. *(To Bonnie)* Queenie's the wife. Queenie's a woman. Queenie's not like the others.

JEREMY

(To intercom) Once you've got the women going for you, think of the possibilities. . . .

AARON

She's some woman. Queenie took care of me. She bathed me. She fed me two soups a day, one thin, one thick. She changed my clothes for me. Washed me. Gave me her breast. You don't remember how I was. Awful. Queenie understood though. Queenie helped me. Tucked me in. After the funeral, Queenie even . . .

JEREMY

(To intercom) Like the poet says, Too bad! But you got to fight it. Fight it! You got to!

AARON

Queenie was good to me. She nursed me back. Showed me things. You don't know, you can't imagine. *(Talks to him via Bonnie's intercom, live in the house)* Jeremy — I love that woman. Queenie.

JEREMY

(To intercom) Yeah. Yeah. So?

AARON

So now I suppose I got to show you my gratitude. *(Also to intercom)*

JEREMY

(To intercom) Of course! You owe it to me! Come on, Aaron! I forgive you. Why shouldn't I forgive you. Listen, I have no ti-ti-time left now anymore. I can't discuss it. Believe me, that's the way it is. Why discuss such a matter. Sure, it matters. But there are more important things too, aren't there. More important things.

AARON

Well, it's not for sale. Some things are not for sale. *(To intercom)*

JEREMY

What do you mean! What things! Things are always for sale. *(To intercom)*

AARON

Life. Death. *(To intercom)*

JEREMY

(To intercom) Not today. Not yet. Tomorrow? All right, tomorrow. Maybe yes, Maybe not. It depends. Not for sale just now. Listen, who knows? These things don't matter anyway. *(Has turned to put that to Aaron)*

AARON

I thought I'd just remind you. Because. *(His hand seeks out Bonnie behind him, and happens to light on her breast; she holds him)* Because women get involved in these things. Somehow.

JEREMY

(Turning back to his intercom, satisfied) Of course. I've thought about it. There are problems. Naturally. Com-

plicated. But, consider it from where I sit. I can't think of everything. Can I think of everything. I can't . I can't.

AARON

Who can.

JEREMY

Who wants to.

AARON

(Has released her and is involved near Jeremy) But — you have to.

JEREMY

That's why I asked you. Why I need you. You can. And you're ready. . . . Ready?

AARON

Who is.

JEREMY

Ready or not, get set, and . . . here we go! *(Buzzes his intercom)* Miss Montrose? *(No response; she is making up)* My new secretary. Want you to meet her. She's made all the difference in things. I want you to meet her, Aaron. You remember AMERICAN CONSOLI-DATED? Of course. *(Buzzes)* Miss Montrose!

BONNIE

Yes, Mr. Crane. I'm ready.

JEREMY

I want you, Miss Montrose. In here. Please. And, oh, yes, dear Miss Montrose —

BONNIE

Yes, dear.

JEREMY

Miss Montrose, the plans, too.

BONNIE

What, Mr. Crane? What did you want?

(Bonnie and Aaron are facing each other along Jeremy's desk, studying one another intensely)

JEREMY

The plans. I said, The pl-pl-plans. The new things. Uh, I . . . ne-ne-need you. . . . Uh, Miss, uh. . . .

AARON

Montrose. Bonnie Montrose. *(Miss Montrose responds to his naming of her and goes. Aaron takes his time and then goes the whole way)* Jeremy. Let me ask you a question.

JEREMY

Shoot! Go on. Go on, shoot!

AARON

Have you thought of . . . dying. *(Miss Montrose has returned and stands behind them at attention, two long tubes of blueprints under her arms)*

JEREMY

No. Uh. No. Should I. Think of it. Dying. Should I, uh, die.

AARON

I didn't say it.

JEREMY

I should. Shouldn't I.

AARON

Did I say it.

JEREMY

Think of it. Dying. I should.

AARON

After all, it's s your only defense. Your only real defense. In fact.

JEREMY

Think. I don't. . . want . . . to . . . th-th-think. . . .

AARON

Everyone says that. Don't you believe it, Jeremy. It's
not true. You must think. You must.

JEREMY

No. Listen. To live. Think of living instead. There are
still some things, I think. I, uh, I want to think about
it. Some more. Please.

AARON

That's your trouble. It's not true at all. There's no time
to think.

*(The stage is dimmer. Jeremy is aware of Miss Montrose behind them.
After he has introduced them, she places the plans in his grasp and he*

settles back, fading out slowly in his executive chair, content, his eyes disappearing gradually. Gradually, Miss Montrose will assume control and command of the action, leading subtly and inevitably to an over-whelming conclusion)

JEREMY

Miss Montrose. Mr. Crane. My brother.

AARON

Montrose?

JEREMY

Montrose. Bonnie Montrose.

AARON

Pretty thing.

JEREMY

You like her.

AARON

Pretty thing.

JEREMY

One damn clever cunt. She'll do anything. You'd be surprised.

AARON

I'd be surprised. Interesting proposition. Though . . . I wonder.

BONNIE

I beg your pardon. The plans. You wanted something. The plans are not all ready. Not at all. All the plans are not ready. At all. Mr. Crane, you planned, didn't you, you planned, Mr. Crane —

JEREMY

Aaron, you know. You know Aaron?

BONNIE

Aaron, yes. Of course. Your brother. You were saying, Mr. Crane. . . .

AARON

Discussing things. Just things in general. Subjects. Objects. I've been out of things, Bonnie. Retired. I now have time for some things. Other things. My brother Jeremy here believes, on the other hand, that things have changed. I don't know. I'm not sure. There may be an explanation, you know.

BONNIE

Yes I'm sure there is. And alternatives. *(A lobby sort of Muzak may be faintly introduced here)* There are ways, Mr. Crane. And there are means. Always. No matter what. But — not many, you see. Not too many today. Fewer, that is. Fewer every day. Here and now, however, here and now, for instance, we are trying to imagine, trying to think . . . to begin with. Despite alterations in things. Trying to know. We should try, Mr. Crane. We should. Try, shouldn't we. Try. Mr. Crane, try!

AARON

It's hard. Well, it's always hard. Isn't it. I mean it's hard to begin with. To imagine. But there it is.

BONNIE

It should be. Hard. Oh, yes there is work to be done.
Lots of work. But I don't mind. Really. It's all in the
job. It depends what, though, doesn't it. It all depends,
Mr. Crane.

*(The action until the end is a love-dance, which may employ the entire
office for its performance. Their hands will preoccupy themselves with
the technicalities of mutual preparation for love, clothing, et cetera, as
they move and speak with gravity and rarefied humor)*

AARON

Does it ever end. Does it ever. Can we finish ever finish
it. Can we.

BONNIE

It never seems to end. It is not simple. Mr. Crane. It is
not easy.

AARON

And there's so much to be done. Even now. Right now.
Isn't there.

BONNIE

Always. And he's so tired. He finds it hard to keep up
with things. To keep it up and going. And I have so
much. And I have so much. I have to do so much for
him. It isn't simple. Not, it isn't easy. I try, though, I
do try. I do everything I possibly can to keep things up.

AARON

I know. You are very good. I understand you are really
very good. Very. I hear.

BONNIE

Do you. Do you. Perhaps. Perhaps not.

(They may have reached the chaise by now, or a couch. She may have covered Jeremy with Aaron's jacket. The action will require choreographing)

BONNIE

It's all a risk. Carefully calculated; yet still a risk. You know. And the odds are large, the odds are long. Mr. Crane was willing to try though, to take it on, the risk. I was new to it all, of course. Although I've been around myself. I've had some background. And I've had some training. The case itself is not new to me. In fact. You understand. It's an old, familiar sort of case, it seems. Sometimes it seems as though we're born for it. In fact. And then, you pick up the rest as you go along. Things. In life. You understand.

AARON

I think I understand. Of course. You are concerned for him. Very. You'll help. Yes. all you can. In fact.

BONNIE

It's my job. That's why I'm here. *(Smiling)* Of course. I am. Your brother. After all.

AARON

My brother. Of course.

BONNIE

And so things went along, you know. Of course. After the first little surprises, things do go along. all right. You learn where the problems are. You begin to find little solutions for them. Tricks. You know. You size up situations as they come along, you learn to see it coming after a while, you learn to feel it coming, and to feel a little clearer about it, a little clearer all the time, little by little. Until you know where you are, you think you do. And you think you know what's happening, you think you do. And what you think you're doing. And the things you're doing begin to form a pattern. Even a habit. And so you do them. And then, when you think you've got it down to the point, when you've reached that point — ah, things are not that simple. You couldn't know. You didn't imagine. Things are not that simple. Are they. Are they.

AARON

Did I say it.

BONNIE

They should be, though!

AARON

I didn't say it.

BONNIE

Well, shouldn't they?

AARON

Did I say it.

BONNIE

No, they are never simple. It never is. But then, you reach a point. In life. Whoever you are, sooner or later you reach a point. Don't you.

AARON

You do. Yes. Sooner or later. You must.

BONNIE

And one thing is after all pretty much like another then, isn't it. Well, not always.

AARON

And you think there are some things still. . . . You imagine there may be some things still. . . .

BONNIE

That seem to be so important! That you depend on, as much as you depend on life! And you know they may not be there at all! And yet —

AARON

(Finally kneeling to enter her) And yet? And . . . yet . . . ? And. . . .

BONNIE

Yet — it is! You know it! You know it is! It is! It is! It is!

(As Miss Montrose clasps him, the lights have gone, and the sounds of the office have risen steadily in the house. The last two speeches are to be interwoven rhythmically as ejaculations of passion, physical and intellectual)

*   *   *

CRANE, CRANE, MONTROSE AND CRANE was first produced at THE AMERICAN PLACE THEATER in New York City. It was directed by Rick Edelstein. The cast was:

Jeremy Crane: Louis Zorich
Aaron Crane: Michael Tolan
Bonnie Montrose: Margaret De Priest

CHRISTMAS CAROLS

a play in two acts

ELEANOR STEINER: née CASEY, sculptor, from Chicago, presently separated and suing for divorce, about 40.

HENRY FRANKLIN: Dolores' lawyer, about 55.

VICTOR JOHNSON: doorman, handyman, Black, 45.

SAMUEL ADAMS: Deputy D.A., Black, about 40.

SOLOMON JUDAH: Hannah's dead husband, Black, 45.

LIZ FRANKLIN: Henry" wife, perished on the ANDREA DORIA, at 35.

GEORGE SIMONSON: Herbert's younger brother, nuclear physicist, died some three years ago, at 45.

JACK GARNET: Dolores' husband, lawyer, dead a year, at 49.

DAVID GLASGOW: Victoria's fourth husband, recently dead in San Quentin, 40.

BOBBY STEINER: Eleanor's child, very ill, asleep, nearly 4 (non-acting).

The Place and the Time

Dolores Garnet's apartment overlooking Central Park, high up at Nine Ninety-Nine Fifth Avenue. A vast, elegant penthouse, all living room during this play, comfortably, tastefully furnished with a mixture of quality things, books, pain'tings and sculpture from the Modernist Period up only until the 1940's. At least three sitting areas can be used, But the central one should have for Dolores a comfortable sofa facing the audience, which she occupies regally; whether she sits or occasionally moves from it, she dominates the room. At opening a tremendous Christmas tree has just been secured by Mr. Johnson and Hannah Judah; atop a ladder and having just cut away about three feet of tree that crowded the ceiling, he will tie a very large silver-and-gilt Baroque wooden carving of the Archangel Michael to the truncated crown, from whence it looks down upon the action. The process of decorating the tree will continue through most of Act I. They are in no hurry, and neither is the company. They are sheltering here from the great storm; they drinking casually, comfortably, as they wait for dinner. Christmas Eve has been slouching towards them through a dim afternoon that presaged the onset of the blizzard that roars in through Act I, increasing its force as the annual ritual drama of the season devolves towards midnight, squandering the common hope raised by perennial rumors concerning the Prince of Peace.

Dolores Garnet wears a peignoir-cum-hostess gown affair, versatile and very expensive. She never troubles to close it modestly, since she is not at all self-conscious; rather, as she is so volatile, her filmy wrapper often comes undone. One of her characteristic attitudes is to settle in a corner of the sofa, legs tucked under, a pack of cigarettes constantly in one hand, which she also uses to clutch her gown to her now and then; in her other hand there is always her silver lighter and a cigarette burning, although she may not drag at it often. Appearance to the contrary, she is not in deshabille, but wears a diamond necklace, an elegant tiara, and a diamond bracelet; she also wears stockings and elegant slippers. It is just that she seems constantly to be coming undone. Her hair is elaborately coiffed, and she wears a long fall with curls; it is long hair, too long for a woman her age, and it tends to stray later on, even wildly. Heavy makeup, perhaps peach to march her gown; nevertheless, dark shadows under her eyes denote the insomniac.

Victoria Glasgow is a tall woman given to striding about as though she had come in boots and jodhpurs straight from The Hunt. She may still wear her blue-black hair swept up from her forehead in the severe exclusive girls' college manner; her face is powdered dead white, her eyes are broodingly dark, with dark shadows and heavy lashes; she may wear a basic-black crepe tea-dance dress; it looks as terrifically expensive as it is, and is set off by the diamond heart-shaped brooch flashing over left her breast and a matching diamond bracelet. Obviously she would wear that brooch and bracelet even were she dressed in her usual uutfit: jodhpurs, boots, and denim shirt (and probably does). Her son Jethro is whatever the lanky, with-it teenager seems; he behaves like that too.
Victor Johnson wears neat, gray work-clothes. Hannah Judah wears a well-cut maid's uniform that shows off her full-figured Caribbean beauty.

Herbert Simonson sips a Perrier as though even that plain glass is one he holds unwillingly. Victoria Glasgow steadily refills her sherry from the crystal decanter, and smokes through a long, diamond-embossed Dunhill holder.

Maddelena Garnet is the well-dressed private-school girl, prepping for Finch College, say, or Miss Whatever's. Her Peck and Peck dress enhances her fresh, sulky beauty, though she is clearly a strange girl. She will wear another outfit in Act II.

Gideon Petrowsky is a well-fed, unathletic type who prefers to lie back in his armchair, feet stretched out, head back, eyes generally upward or inward, avoiding contact with others, though he hears everything and likes to control. Dolores, however, is not controllable — not by him, anyway. He is in touch with Power, and is not only pleased to serve it, but complacent as well. He is not unreasonable or arrogant; his moderation takes the Establishment form of smoothing over the daily outcroppings of rocks and hard places by setting them into larger, abstract contexts, as though the formulations of sociology might palliate existential reality. It is the weakness of his profession. When he lurches to his feet occasionally for snacks or a refill, he is awkward.

It is Christmas Eve. The year is 1968, when our world became a free fire zone.

This play is dedicated to our hungry ghosts. May we find ways to appease them, and may we permit them to keep us properly and justly, and for our own good.

Act I

DOLORES

. . . Well, because her father always wanted his Christmas tree. If he had to fly in from Zambia or Thailand or Paraguay . . . well, he just did. Couldn't explain it. Sticks his papers in his bag, stands up from whichever conference table, checks himself out, and flies home. A problem for him Never make it to the top, I said. *But why not?* he said. Tell it to the underdeveloped nations, I said — all right, Third World — tell it to your subsidized dictators and your smiling commissars and your kingpin druglords and your Establishment buddies, but — don't tell me. *What do you mean by that?* he said. I'm a woman, Jack. When you tell it to a woman, make sense, Jack. *Well, it's the symbol of peace,* he said, *and Christmas Day is universally understood as a day of peace, at least one day of peace . . . and besides, I like it,* he said. Dear Jack, I said, That's nonsense, you know. *Nonsense?* Look at me, Jack, look me in the eye and say that. And his mouth goes tight, and he puff-puffs on his pipe — but he can't look at me. *It's important,* he says. I don't believe in it, I said. *It is too important!* You're sentimental, I said, and what's worse, you're a card-carrying atheist. Grow up, will you! So we fought over it, every damn year we fought. Whose fault is that, his or mine?

MADDELENA

You didn't. Not really. Mummy, you exaggerate.

DOLORES

I exaggerate.

MADDELENA

Don't make a thing out of it. Mummy. Please.

DOLORES

I? I?

MADDELENA

Still, it was the only time I saw you and him —

DOLORES

— saw us making up. Right! For whose sake, ours? For god's sake, child. No, you're not betraying him. We fought. Fifteen years of fighting an undeclared war, right here, heart to heart, bogged down in that filthy marriage ditch. Oh we fought! Honey, they don't know what it's like, do they — how can you expect *them* to imagine what it's like . . . why, *they're* over thirty!

JETHRO

Don't underestimate us, Mrs. Garnet.

VICTORIA

Jethro, Don't provoke us.

JETHRO

Just because we've been oppressed by your regulations
all our life, doesn't mean we Don'tknow what a ripoff it
is! Man, watching you screw up all over the place and
bomb your way over the opposition, just because you
can buy mercenaries. Some day. . . .

GIDEON

When you get it together, like —

DOLORES

And his family was Orthodox, mind you. Descendants
of Hasidic Princes. Meditators, Mystics, Scholars, Lo-
gicians, Lens-makers, Diamond-cutters and Goldsmiths,
and whatallnot. Till yesterday their women wore wigs.
Till 1848, I mean. But then the Spirit left them, the
Spirit vanished. Where else but in The Promised Land!
They came for salvation, and they got — rich. Came
seeking freedom and found — slavery. Oh, they'd once
had that old-time Spirit. The Power, I mean — when
they'd had a tight fix on the ninety-nine names of the
Lord — they were homing in on the secret name of
God Himself. They had influence with the Holy Establishment: they were even allowed to approach as near
as the door to the room where you'll find the steps to
the feet on the legs of the Throne itself!

JETHRO

Bitchin'! So, what happened?

DOLORES

America. This dark and bloody ground. They broke out
of the sacred circle. This country gives you room for
maneuver. From mystics to manipulators. Gideon, you

ought to write a book on it. Call it *America Happened: A Case Study in Yesterday.*

GIDEON
It's been written. More than once. Today interests me more.

DOLORES
And I'd like to know about tomorrow. *That* concerns me. Nobody else seems to care about tomorrow, though.

JETHRO
Who? I mean, who had the Spirit. . . ?

DOLORES
You know what the Garnet money came out of?

HERBERT
I've wondered. But never asked.

DOLORES
Why not?

GIDEON
You don't ask.

DOLORES
Why the hell not.

GIDEON
Personal. You don't invade.

DOLORES
Money? Money's *personal?* Since when?

GIDEON

Private, I mean. You don't spy on a friend's resources.

DOLORES

Why the hell not!

HERBERT

Decency, for heaven's sake. You have to main'tain protocol. Not that Jack wouldn't have told me had I asked.

DOLORES

Would he? Gideon, you went to school with him. Bet *you* don't know.

Many details I wouldn't know. I don't trespass.

DOLORES

Since when is money a detail? Money is shit. Is shit a detail? Let me put you in the picture.

GIDEON

Don't break silence. Never broadcast. Standing orders. Main'tain secrecy. Safer that way. The enemy's always listening.

JETHRO

Too late! We're all in this now. Spill some blood. Yuk yuk.

GIDEON

Aren't you still a freshman, kid?

VICTORIA

Straight A's. Though you wouldn't think it, to hear him

DOLORES

Gideon, this may surprise you.

GIDEON

Not here, Dolores.

DOLORES

And astonish *you,* Herbert.

HERBERT

Not now, Dolores.

DOLORES

Always some other time, some other place. Keep it off
the record. You men just love to play your little classi-
fied data games. As though it's vital to our security. But
money is no secret: money is a matter of fact! If you
want real secrets, try living with a woman. You men
with your combination locks on your drawers full of
dossiers,. Do I have to spin you out some plot to keep
you suspended till midnight? What is this, a thriller?
No more plots! No more motel rooms! Out in the open!
Facts! I'll tell everything! Make you a bet — when I'm
through it'll all be a secret still! Why? Because who is
there to understand it?

HERBERT

I'm positive Jack wouldn't want his business affairs to
be exposed to —

GIDEON

You just aren't trained to grasp the intricacies of mod-
ern-day corporate combat.

DOLORES
Because I'm a woman.

GIDEON
Don't start *that* business. You could get yourself an MBA, and you still wouldn't know —

DOLORES
Are you ready? A mountain. The money came out of a mountain. One single solitary mountain. You don't believe? all right, I'll tell you. Doesn't matter now: it's merely history. Refills, Hannah, please. Jack's grandfather Moses wanted to retire to the hills. Felt he should go into the country to pray. Moses, Moses, his wife said, I beg you, Moses. Moses said, don't , woman, I must. . . . Bought himself some goats, so he could drink goat's milk and make yogurt and follow his goats around while he picked mushrooms for his barley soup and meditated on Maimonides and The Law. Some operator, a two-bit realtor, some Joe Miller with three teeth to his head and his longjohns hanging down over his socks — some smelly *schvintler*, he called him — sold that old man a mountain pasture, sold it for a song, naturally ... just one big stony pasture clear around, with water dripping off the mossy rocks. It was a mountain so stony, so barren, even goats could barely make a living off it. And what do you think?

MADDELENA
Oh, Mummy. That's impossible!

DOLORES
Doesn't sound like your chummy girlfriends' families, your investment bankers' daughters, at Miss

What'shername's boarding school, eh?

JETHRO

Man, I give up. It's gonna be heavy. Right?

DOLORES

Right, right. Trying to dig himself an outhouse in that pasture, that old man struck stone barely one foot down. Only that stone was marble: black granite. Solid, beautiful, and black. Enough marble for all the mausoleums and banks and executive suites the world will ever want to build. The hell, you say? And when Moses climbed over the mountain to dig his outhouse again on the other side, what do you think he found? Are you ready? Clay. A whole, sheer cliff of clay. Not for the kindergarteners to make their flower pots. Oh no. And not *just* enough kaolin to stop the runny bowels of poor, bleeding Humanity from now till Doomsday. Oh no. Better. *This* clay is composed of ten kinds of rare earths! And smack in the center of this clay pit there is something more: a pipe of ores running right down through the middle of the goddamned world! Ores of precious metals: molybdenum, manganese, palladium, who knows whatallelse. *(They are scoffing)*

JETHRO

Sounds like the right stuff to me.

DOLORES

Well, I don't put you on. If it weren't for reasons of what Gideon calls "national security and survival," I could tell you exactly where to go to find it. The Government of the United States has surrounded that hole in the ground with cyclone fences and razor wire and twenty-four-hour sentries and lights . . . the whole bit.

On *that* one we collect royalties. I mean, Jack's family does. They work that black marble quarry too, six days a week . . . his family does, I mean. I used to say to Jack, that old man with his white beard down to his lap must have been a sain't: God told him where to take his crap. God sent him out of the prison house of Europe and planted him in America. And then God took him to that mountain, and led him up that mountain, and God said, Moses? Moses Garnitschitzki! Dig your shithouse here! And so Moses did. If it *was* God.

VICTORIA
Some shithouse!

DOLORES
And Jack's father died organizing the hell out of that mountain. Protecting it, I mean. Joe had to fight off the whole damned world. Imagine what it took to hold that hill against Wall Street and Washington combined. But Joe did it. It was war, war all the way. Became a killer, like them. King of the Mountain, Joe Garnet was. And I married his son. His little Harvard lawyer son, Jack.

Mother, not tonight, please. It's not even a year.

DOLORES
Well, marry Jack I did. Hardly top secret, that! Now if I could just have married the old man — *there* was a crap-artist! That would've been something. But those children! They couldn't wait to get rid of him And he was too damn proud to take the Fifth Commandment against them. One fine Sabbath morning he turned his back on them to pray — and that was that. Family caught him and shipped him off to do his praying from

that year on in Jerusalem. Of course, it's where he wanted to be really. He's ninety-nine now, going on a hundred. Still praying. Wouldn't even go down into the shelter when the Jordanians shelled the Quarter. He'll make a hundred. I'd marry him right now. Tonight. If he'd only let me.

MADDELENA

Oh for god's sake. I only wanted a Christmas tree.

DOLORES

My poor Jack. The one thing Jack had, he had from his old man, Moses. Moses laughed. That was the true legacy. Jack had his royal laugh. They couldn't tie that up for twenty-five years with phony trusts and fancy mortgages in everyone else's name — but not his own woman's name. After all, it was merely a wife and daughter: two women. To them women aren't women. Women are incidentals, or worse, nuisances: contestants, enemies, strangers, aliens. Even old man Moses, who wouldn't pray with a woman, or even look at his wife in bed, even *he* treated his women better than that!

MADDELENA

If you don't stop this now —

DOLORES

And why did he? Because we have souls too. Women. Can you imagine that? Though Jack didn't laugh much. And always at the wrong thing. Nothing *I* said ever made him laugh. But then, who was *I* to him. Only his wife, only the damned woman who —

MADDELENA

Mother, if you don't stop it —

DOLORES

It may cost you your schooling, and a hell of a lot else, child! There is no Trust! Never mind. You've got your own battles ahead. You don't imagine this little penthouse roof over your head is funded by *Garnet* money, do you? Never mind. Still, that laugh of Jack's — that was a laugh you'd hear coming up straight from his grandfather, old man Moses' balls, like somewhere deep inside himself he was still a dancing rabbi — though he wasn't, you know, not at all, not anymore — and it was as if he could hear the angels of God shouting down to him from the four corners of the world, laughing and shouting for the sheer joy of being. *Halloo, Jack! We're still here! Dance, Jack, dance! (Her rich laughter)* . . . And somehow, Jack, oh dear, Jack grows up to wear J. Press shirts and ties, and three-piece suits. *And* he carries one of those green Harvard bags over his shoulder, twenty-five years after graduation still carrying his little Harvard ditty bag. . . .

GIDEON

Top of my class.

DOLORES

Thought you were tied for first?

GIDEON

Well, Jack edged me by half a point. Mind you, I never conceded. He always used to mention it though. When the President made me Chairman of his Special Task Force on Alienation and Human Resources, Jack was really sore. Called me up from Damascus, can you imagine, Damascus! Started in arguing about some Pass/Fail course he remembered on my transcript. . . .

DOLORES

. . . And then he dashed over as usual for one of his
damned trees! From Damascus. Jesus! How in just two
generations that family dwindled: from sain'tliness into
legal sociology!

GIDEON

Well I wouldn't put it that way. You have to recognize
the real world, how the world actually. . . .

DOLORES

Okay. Real world. Urbanology. Criminology. Finagle-
ology. How merely flabby that thinking is. Alienation.
Human Resources. Priorities and Targets. You men.

HERBERT

Don't you think you're down on Jack too hard. We do
have to try to solve society's problems, Dolores.

DOLORES

Don't tell me — I'll tell you! Fifteen years of my
goddamn life, ever since I was a blushing five-dollar,
court-house bride of twenty eloping with a rich and
guilty intellectual who was just off the plane from Juarez
— third time around for him — oh, busy busy busy!
Marrying on the run. I've watched that crowd wing
around this country, and go flapping from conference
to air-conditioned conference everywhere in the miserable world, advising and negotiating their heads off.
I've listened to them lecture at each other in their offi-
cial gobbledegook, and I've even rewritten their policy
and position papers assigned them by politicians who
throw them odd jobs out of Congressional petty cash, a
couple of magazines to publish and a few professor-

ships and committeeships where they can spend a day
a week mumbling more of that gobbledygook women
and children can never understand . . . even though our
lives depend on it. Our very lives! Commuting like con-
cert pianists all over the continents and playing the latest *ologies* Right and Left to sweating, militarized bu-
reaucrats, and for what? Who pays them any attention?
Not in the Pentagon nor at the White House, nor up
on the Hill, and certainly not down Wall Street. Fifteen
goddamn years I've observed you and your think-tank
strategists . . . and *he* tells *me* to recognize the real
world. . . .

GIDEON

Which demolishes my beach-head. I think I'll disen-
gage while I've still got a way to retreat from this,
this . . .

HERBERT

Quagmire . . . ?

DOLORES

Oh no, Gideon, I didn't mean you to . . . what am I
doing again . . . oh god, please, you know I didn't mean
to, Gideon. It's just this annual tree of Jack's. Is that so
nutty of me? I suppose they're not so bad, lit up. When
I was her age I used to dive into the packages. I scattered that entire oh-so-carefully-constructed pyramid
of offerings to the household neurosis, those rewards
and punishments all wrapped up in candy stripes, oh
my! How angry it made my brother and sister, you can
imagine, knowing *them,* Herbie — ha! Those two square-
cut guardians of the left hand and the right hand —
the parental laws. . . . Remind me to describe them
sometime in all their nifty detail, Victoria — and

Herbie's been their doctor since nursery school and thinks of them as highly successful people like himself, blahblahblah, and *he* is tops himself of course, he's *been* tops ever since he was in nursery school with them, Until now his left leg's in Physicians and Surgeons and his right leg on Mount Sinai —

HERBERT

Which puts me smack in Central Park. Without escort. At this hour. Christmas Eve. Tsk tsk. Especially. Unsafe. Belongs to them right now.

VICTORIA

But it's snowing like hell.

GIDEON

Interesting thing about urban facilities: their usage represents a constant laminar flow of social cross-sections. You can have baby-carriages and ball players and bicyclists and shoppers and joggers and gangs and guerrillas all simultaneously holding down the same territory. There is no borderline anymore.

DOLORES

And what about sweethearts? And lovers?

HERBERT

If you go out there be sure to carry a twenty-dollar note and be ready to hand it right over on demand. Don't hold back for a second.

GIDEON

Function of the clock. Our diurnal cityscape. It's only when one sub-group overlaps another on the same turf

that you tend to have some difficulties in accommodation.

DOLORES
Fatalities, I think you call them. To me, it's slaughter.

GIDEON
Yet the place is always full of people.

HERBERT
Fascinating. Nothing makes any difference.

GIDEON
Some recent studies I've seen charting sub-group inter-
faces, and it's an interesting problem, I mean, to corre-
late group perception and group expression of hostility
levels with changing social dynamics —

HERBERT
Rain, hail, snow, lightning and gloom of night makes
no difference. Someone's killed every hour. Somebody's
raped on the half-hour. They're breaking in, they're bur-
gling every thirty seconds. Someone's car is stolen every
twenty seconds. Each single minute of every hour all
day long, they rip somebody up. Mugging. Slugging.
Thugging.

DOLORES
I've never noticed. Have you, Maddelena?

VICTORIA
I got here yesterday. I'm only visiting. This morning
ten taxis, ten empty taxis! rattled past me. I shouted
and I waved. They saw me. They stared at me. And
they never even slowed down.

DOLORES

I don't have any trouble with taxis.

GIDEON

She runs right out into the street at them. So far, they've all stopped. She's terrific. She should have a medal. Silver Star.

VICTORIA

I wouldn't volunteer for that.

HERBERT

People are ambushed right in their shiny automatic elevators. Blood spatters the polished walls. Bodies are broken to pieces, apartments turned to a shambles. Empty garages, buildings going up in flame, burning in the sleet. And they wait for you in the shadows around the corner.

VICTORIA

Sounds like you're under siege.

DOLORES

Men are number freaks, Victoria. Give them a chart, oh, anything — birthrate per teenagers per shoe size or suicides per dollars per number of bathrooms — and they'll play with it for hours. You know. You're safe enough. Haven't I lived here all my life? Where else is there? And if there is somewhere else, we've been there.

VICTORIA

Could I be that blind?

DOLORES

What's to see. Don't let them spook you with their bloody numbers. There are worse things than numbers.

HERBERT

That's a matter of definition. I want to give her some bearings before she ventures out. That's all.

DOLORES

Some things you can't count.

HERBERT

That's a matter of definition.

DOLORES

Herbie, she knows where she's at: Nine Ninety-Nine Fifth Avenue. Not bad, as shelters go. Considering conditions. Considering morale. It's not Cambodia. It's not Beirut. Or Lhasa. Or Kabul. It's not even Rio. Some technical problems, supplies and scheduling, but don't let's make it out worse than it is. It isn't No Man's Land. After all. Things get blown up by the media. Keep things in perspective. At least. God knows, *I* manage to. Considering.

HERBERT

Say it was just a visitor's briefing, Dolores. So she can cope with the natives. The do's and the don't s.

DOLORES

Victoria's a professor. Treat her like a learnèd colleague, or you'll be cut down and chopped up before you know it.

HERBERT
Ah. Professor of what, may I ask?

VICTORIA
Semitics.

HERBERT
Ah?

VICTORIA
Assyriology, actually. Clay tablets they dig up. Cuneiform things.

HERBERT
Oh.

DOLORES
I used to dig myself in, I would tunnel under that collapsing pile of presents looking for the tiny ones. They were for me, tiny and flat. In those little boxes were colored tissues. Inside the tissues were marbled envelopes with deckled edges. In one envelope there'd be the Tiffany Certificate. That was pearls. In another, the Saks Certificate. Good for five hundred a month. And the other would be the Lord & Taylor Certificate, or Bergdorf's. It varied. You know. One time, my Uncle Jeremiah — you remember that crazy? my Uncle Jeremiah gave me an Abercrombie & Fitch, for Christ's sake. What's he expect me to do, go out and make a man of myself, me, after eight years of Dalton School? *(Her big, throaty laugh, which communicates her meanings as well as expressing them)* . . . I said, Unkie Jere, Jere my dear, what a beautiful Unkie you are, you

are . . . and what am I supposed to do with this? And he said, *For a year and a day, you will think of the way, and by using your mind you'll eventually find, on this island it's not so far, so far . . . so get your nose out of that Russian novel, it's not healthy, pick up your boots and saddle and spurs and do the Park around in the morning. You're fourteen, what? nearly fifteen, and you don't ride? You're supposed to be crazy for a stallion. If you're good, I'll buy you a stallion. How in hell will you ever learn to ride a man! Shit, Dodo!* Darling Jeremiah. Only one in our family who spoke English to me: shit, shit, and shit again! And was *he* ever cornered, my Unkie Jere! The pack zeroed in on him: before you could say, *Man your stations!* they'd bought him out, stripped him bare and retired him him! For life. Put him under intensive surveillance. Jeremiah, Jeremiah! He winked at me behind their backs. He said as they carried him out of the action, *They can't pin me down forever, I'll be out there fighting like hell before you even lose your cherry, Dodo!* And he was saner than all of them together. You know it! Just that his tactics were out of style. That's all. Never saw Jere again. He refused any defensive alliance with evil. He fought alone, his back to God. But — God wasn't at his back. My family nailed him to the wall. And Jack's people are a hundred times worse than mine! Herbie knows.

HERBERT
Nothing. Absolutely nothing.

DOLORES
I should've gone right down to Abercrombie. I should've cashed in crazy Unkie Jere's Certificate, not for a saddle, but for one of those Hemingway elephant guns, a

Mannlicher .405, say. And I should've used it, too! On myself.

MADDELENA
Mother. I'm sorry I asked for anything. *(Her habitual, ineffectual remonstrance)*

DOLORES
(Grinning) At least for the ivory, Maddalena. I'm sorry, dear. Don't worry, it's too late now: they've all gone yellow, see? But *you* should ride this Spring, honey. If ever Spring returns. Ever ever ever. Jesus, what is it with that goddamn tree!

MADDELENA
It's too big. Even for us, Mother. Can't you see? I'm sorry.

DOLORES
Can't I see. Kid comes down from school the very last minute — other girls got home a week ago, the stores have been so full of girls you'd think they'd been turned into relocation camps! She walks in whimpering, *Can't we have a tree like Daddy always buys. Wahwahwah.* Well of course it's a year now since the last one. All right, Jack, all right! She's your daughter too, so it's a bad time for her and a bad time for me, and a bad time for us all here. . . .

MADDELENA
Daddy loves me.

DOLORES
And *I* love you. We signed the same papers; we're in this together now, huh? . . . So it's a bad time for *him,*

too. Well, maybe worse for him. Maybe. I swear I don't know which is worse. Hell, I didn't mean that, Maddalena, did I. You know I didn't. It just comes out … *comme* ça. I'm all right. Really. I am. As though it matters. So I give her a hundred dollars and she goes down with Hannah and looks for the kind of tree her Daddy buys. Finds it on Lexington. One hundred and fifty bucks. So *That's* what the damn things cost! Jesus. And do you think they deliver? They never. Not in New York, they don't deliver. And Lex is on *our* side of the Park, Victoria. And do you suppose they're still there today? They are not. Hit and run. That gang packs its fake goddamn trees and fades away up in the jungle of Harlem, or over the river in the East Bronx, or out in Brooklyn somewhere, 'way beyond the goddamn security zone.

VICTORIA
I hope you reported them.

DOLORES
And I'm left with my kid all weepy. What do I do when she's turned into a homeless like that. Sure I report. I say to the authorities, We bought this hundred-fifty-buck tree, and blahblahblah, and now what. They say, Madam, a dozen ladies have been cheated in that precinct but not one seems to recall what they looked like. What are we, the Christmas Tree Bunco Squad? How do you expect us to find them? People rush down the last minute blindly shelling out their thirty shekels, and then they scramble back to their towers to start in with the old mumbo jumbo . . . so the children can remember something nice some day, once upon a time. When *was* that time anyway?

JOHNSON
(He has by now secured the tree upright. He is answering her last remark from the distance and over his shoulder, so to say) It's now or it's never, Mrs. Garnet.

DOLORES
Now is just as good as never. Never is now. *(Her big laugh)*

GIDEON
Who'd you talk to at Headquarters.

DOLORES
I know who to talk to, thank you. Haven't I had a life-time of you officials and you lawyers in and out of this house, thank you. Man called Adams. Asked him over tonight. Sounded single to me. What the hell, he's a man. At least. How many of that species are blowing round out there tonight? Not counting your muggers, sluggers, snipers, deserters, spies, and thieving merce-naries in blue uniforms. And not counting the enemy!

VICTORIA
If you don't count enemies, nothing doing. They're men too. Always in short supply.

JETHRO
She'll even draft the dead!

HERBERT
Those men? You women don't know what you're say-ing!

DOLORES

Love them. Want them. Need them. Herbert, show us a man, show us just *one* man?

GIDEON

I've recently been studying some figures on the distribution of bachelors, divorcées and widowers relative to population densities in this urban agglomeration, and it seems that, structurally speaking, the demographic —

DOLORES

One, Gideon. Just one.

HERBERT

Dr. Herbert Simonson reporting, Sir. Neurosurgeon, Sir. Ma'am. At your disposal, Sir! That is, Ma'am.

DOLORES

Heshie! Baby!

HERBERT

Dolores! *(Reproaching her for using that childhood nickname)*

DOLORES

Oh, crap, Heshie. And if Mr. ADAMS is free tonight, I'd like to know what's wrong with him too! . . . Did I hear the baby crying? Sssh. Is that little boy crying? Oh my god, he'll die tonight. In my house. Oh my god!

HERBERT

He's all right, Dolores.

DOLORES

Hannah! See if the child's breathing — quick! I couldn't stand it if that child died tonight. I couldn't stand another fatality, not now.

HERBERT

Stop that!
(Dolores holds up an admonirory hand and they all wait)

HANNAH

(Returning) He's asleep, Mrs. Garnet. Breathing heavy, but he's surely sound asleep.

DOLORES

Oh thank god.

VICTORIA

This tree's half the size of a Douglas. My Daddy'd be marking it for cutting in a couple of years.

HANNAH

Pardon me, Mrs. Glasgow, but you said . . . ?

VICTORIA

Not just this *one* tree, Hannah. My Daddy's got whole mountains of trees.

HANNAH

Christmas trees?

DOLORES

V.G., she's from Jamaica.

VICTORIA

Redwood. Fir. Daddy lumbers them. California. Oregon. Washington. Out there. Where I grew up. Wild country. Used to be tranquil: sky full of clouds, valleys with bear and elk and fish and Canada geese rising in clouds. Turkeys, mallards and swans. Almost gone now. Clear-cutting it to hell and gone.

DOLORES

What's gone, where? *(She's confused)*

VICTORIA

Timber, for one. After you exterminate the big trees those mountains seem half what they were. Slashed, gouged, gray and crummy slopes, full of stumps that stick up like stubble in your armpit. Soil turns to mud, slips down, drags boulders along, blocks the streams, makes marshes. Not much skin covering those hills: it's scarred and burned and broken by the tractors and avalanches. Like the Marines worked over them. You know. Peace is extinct. And down below, along the streams and roads, what they call settlements: whole towns of shacks and supermarkets. Noise, dust, motorcycles, car bodies smoldering. A whole culture of relocation camps. And my Daddy owns the mineral rights under all of it too.

HERBERT

Well, you still have San Francisco.

VICTORIA

Mess, Doctor, mess. Tourists assaulting the hills, overrunning the docks. Refugees from the lost American provinces, The Heartland! Pouring into a couple of square

miles of brand new slum, children drifting in from everywhere and out again, sick, undernourished, going
into hardcore corruption. Half the town's dying of the
needle and the fucking plague. Talk about Sodom! And
up in their offices in the towers sit the remittance men
in their Brooks Brothers suits: lawyers, accountants,
brokers, clipping clipping clipping coupons for their
clients. Clipping them for me! Nothing much else doing there, whatever reporters say. Same Chamber of
Commerce briefing handed out every year. Cable cars
to Gomorrah. You'll find better newspapers in Missis-
sippi or Alabama, I bet you. No such thing as San Francisco: blank streets. No trees. Big park, though, and
the usual slugging thugging on the half-hour. Dolores,
where'd you get this damn tree?

DOLORES
So I sent the kid out with Hannah again this morning
to grab anything they could dig up. They went over to
Broadway. Found the last tree, they said. Chopped it
down in the park, for all I know. So it's too big. Two
hundred bucks, plus twenty for trucking. Do all right
for us though. Mr. Johnson, you're very good to set it
up. You're on duty tonight, I hope. I'd be sorry to have
kept you if you're not. You know that.

JOHNSON
I know. I'm on the door. Glad to help out. Hannah
surely couldn't do this tree herself, could she now. And
cook dinner for you all too.

DOLORES
You are a considerate man. At least.

JOHNSON

I don't stand sentry till later.

DOLORES

Some people in this world are still considerate. Considering. You'll take care of him, Hannah?

HANNAH

(Under her breath) Till death do us part. *(Aloud)* Don't you worry about him, Mrs. Garnet. Leave him to me.

VICTORIA

That's a .38 Colt, Mr. Johnson. *(It's under his belt, on his left hip)*

JOHNSON

Um, why yes, believe it is. *(Looking down over his shoulder while securing the angel)*

DOLORES

Really? Whatever for.

MADDELENA

Mother. You know why. Stop it.

VICTORIA

Why should he be packing that? Here? Inside this building, I mean?

DOLORES

Victoria, it's New York. Streets are teeming. You heard them. Makes life vibrant. Keeps us stimulated. You know?

JOHNSON

It's for when I'm on, Ma'am, after 11 in the p.m. Gets a little quieter round about midnight. Not always. You know. But you won't hear too much up here, 'cause it's snowin' so hard? What racket they make summertime — it seems a slaughterhouse. Lively, I mean. That angel will stay up there good now, Mrs. Garnet. Tied him down tight. He safe up there. I like him. That's one *old* angel. Real old. Friend of old peoples. Now, you wouldn't noway find whittlin' like that no more. Angels is a lost tradition.

VICTORIA

(Putting on folding miniglasses) I don't quite see . . . ah, the angel . . . Baroque? German? Spanish? Can't be French? I don't quite see what, uh . . .

DOLORES

Gideon, you know Jack. He went trotting off the other year with what'shisname, that fail-safe expert? They were consulting with the Defense Intelligence Agency? That perfectly atrocious man with the one arm? That mathematician — oh, what *is* his name . . . ?

GIDEON

Actually, he's more of a statistician, though he calls himself a logician. I wouldn't call him that. You mean Arnold Dorfman. Why do you call him atrocious? Just because he's full of hush-hush business for the National Security Agency? He's harmless — actually quite the connoisseur of food and wine. There's a champagne he touts . . . what's it called . . . ? Very expensive. Almost a thousand dollars a case! He brought one bottle around when we signed the Aggression Limitation Protocol . . . ?

DOLORES

Perfectly atrocious man. He *would* be involved with a Doomsday Button, wouldn't he, with his shrivelled arm. Röderer Kristall, you mean. *His* favorite stuff.

GIDEON

Delicious champagne.

DOLORES

Well, he made Jack buy it for me, for me! That angel. And where did he find it? In Saigon! It's fake, Victoria, Taiwanese or Mexican, who knows how it got to Saigon. Baroque angel! You just can't see it from here. Dorfman sent us a case of Röderer Kristall. Memento of Salt I, Salt II, Salt to the end of the end of time! He should open up a Salt mine.

GIDEON

Arnold wouldn't buy a fake. It must be French. He's very bright. He's got the generals eating out of his hand. Would you prefer the generals to have their fingers on the button all by themselves, and *without* Arnold's fail-safe? Would you? Would you? *(To everybody. He's anxious to make this point)*

DOLORES

(Screams) Shit, Gideon, shit! And you know it. Some Clerk First Class could put the wrong tape on the air and the generals'll blow up the world tonight! Nobody pays any attention to Dorfman's Fail-Safe, *or* his angel! Fakes! Fakes!

GIDEON
Unlikely. Impossible.

DOLORES
As soon as he invented his famous Fail-Safe, it *became* possible. Probable. Likely! That's why I made sure to drink up his champagne right away. So we'd have had *something* before then at least.

JOHNSON
He's a real nice angel, Mrs. Garnet. *(To Victoria)* Of course, Ma'am, come summer time, you know, they're everywhere, day and night, and it gets to be more, uh, action down there. Right up front, you know, close to home. Like . . . ? *(To Maddalena)* Hand me those lights and things while I'm here, honey. I'll start from the top.

MADDELENA
Wind them on left to right, please, Mr. Johnson.

VICTORIA
No. Oh no.

DOLORES
She prefers things to run counter-clockwise, V.G. Against the sun or something, she says.

MADDELENA
Hush, Mother, Don't *say* such awful things. *(Naively grave)*

DOLORES
Against the moon, too, she says. Aquarius, isn't it?

MADDELENA
No, silly. Now just stop it.

DOLORES
Harmonize with the turning earth, she says. My pagan child, my hip Tibetan daughter. My mystical Maddalena. So much for Newton-Einstein-Marx-Freud and blahblahblah. . . .

JETHRO
Widdershins, like our guts.

DOLORES
See? Never know what these kids will come up with. It's a no-no here, with a no-no there: everywhere a no-no. Rituals. How to purify the lost soul on its way to nowhere. Thought *you* knew all about that stuff, V.G.

VICTORIA
Semitics isn't anthropology. For Semitics you have to be able to read. History, at least. And things out of the ground. Real objects. Besides, how do *you* know about the counter-clockwise rules. . . .

DOLORES
Oh, I read it in some newspaper or other of record. *(Flurry of sirens, whistles, far below, muffled, perhaps some yells, shots, etc)*

JOHNSON
(Winding busily, the children helping) That sort of thing, Ma'am. Not a bad time, actually, for some terroristical action. Peoples carrying presents. All dressed up. Be-

sides, The Man can't get around fast in that snow, now can he? Smash and grab. Easy pickin's.

HERBERT
No, That's an ambulance. And that's the doorman blowing for a taxi. Taxis are hard to get in snow too.

VICTORIA
But I thought I heard shooting —

DOLORES
They're dying out there. That's what is going down. Anybody's next. Herbie patches them up. War's good for Herbie. Gets to practice new techniques. No need to fly overseas for interesting human carnage: New York's the action: Herbie's right on the scene.

HERBIE
Matter of fact, Mrs. Glasgow, I *do* get fascinating materials from the automobiles. Don't need any of that other —

DOLORES
Slugging, mugging, ripping and blahblahblah.

VICTORIA
I knew a man once named Simonson. Nice guy. Genius type. Had to trap him into a clinch. Sweet guy. Vulnerable fella. Couldn't sit his horse worth a damn. Nor, as it turned out, a woman. That was in Idaho.

HERBERT
Sounds like my brother.

VICTORIA

George. It was V.G. and George. For a while. One whole
Spring. George and V.G. Then he broke my new
Arabian's leg, and I had to shoot him. I was angry as
hell. He was always thinking of something else. I cleared
out of there fast.

DOLORES

Mistake.

VICTORIA

Fit to be tied, I was. But then, he never answered my
letters. I wrote. Begged for peace. Even offered myself
as a hostage. Anything. He was so sweet. Practically a
virgin.

HERBERT

Physicist.

VICTORIA

Physics. Right, right. I called him my little platonic
Physicist. He didn't like that. Came up to here on me.
I stopped trying to make contact with him. Guess some
other female ambushed him. Scratch another prospect,
I told Daddy. Oh well, not every tactic works according to the book. Couldn't even get him to engage. Had
to give him up for lost. *Son cosas de la vida:* casualties of
love.

HERBERT

Dead.

VICTORIA

He had so much going for him I mean, after all, with a
little more practice he could have handled a horse right.
Dead? George? Oh, I don't believe you mean *my* George,
Dr. Simonson —

HERBERT

My brother George. Out of action. Killed.

JETHRO

Does he have to send you a telegram, Mother?

VICTORIA

I never heard anything about it!

JETHRO

So send it already, do. Stick a gold star on it. And address it: *To Our Lady of Luxuries.* You could even send it
C.O.D.

VICTORIA

Killed. Don't tell me that. George said, *I know what I'm
doing.* Well, pretty much. *Every risk's a calculated risk,*
George said. *Crash priority,* he said. Don't tell me he's
gone.

DOLORES

George gone? You never told me! Herbert!

HERBERT

No point in it, Dolores. *(Uncomfortable)* Guess I forgot.

DOLORES
Forgot! *Your own brother?* Just because Jack doesn't like me to know what *he's* getting into —

HERBERT
Happened when you were sick. Forget it, Dolores.

DOLORES
When the hell was I ever sick! I *never* get sick. Never took so much as an aspirin in my life. Not even vitamins. I'm not one of your walking wounded, Herbert. This town may have become one tremendous Emergency Ward — but the City Morgue hasn't tagged *my* toe! Not yet! At least.

GIDEON
They will. Law of Averages. I'd be more careful. Random crossfire. Murphy's coming round the bend. Driving 300 horses as he comes.

DOLORES
Shit on statistics. Now, Herbie. . . .

HERBERT
Ah, Dolores. . . . It was when you were in hospital.

DOLORES
(Blank) Oh? Oh?

GIDEON
(Pruriently eager) When was that? Was Jack still. . . .

VICTORIA

I mean, what the hell happened to George! Just like that? I could have been with him I could have helped, couldn't I. Why did I leave him. I'd have done anything for George. Nursed him even. My Daddy would've. . . .

JETHRO

Mother. Why get uptight now.

VICTORIA

Don't worry, J.P. It's nothing to do with you. You were off at Laurelwood that year. Daddy said, *A military academy will make Jethro stand straight like a man.* I shouldn't have listened to Daddy, I know. You're not Marine Corps material. But Daddy always got what he went after, because after all, big bucks talk. . . .

GIDEON

. . . and schmucks walk.

(Jethro, however, is motioning her to look at Dolores ,who is gazing down oddly at her breasts, which she has exposed, touching them musingly, exploratorily, as though they were bleeding and raw. She may be up and moving abstractedly about during Herbert's following terror speech)

VICTORIA

. . . and Daddy always wanted you to be a man first, if at all possible.

JETHRO

Mother! *(She has noticed Dolores, but refuses to acknowledge)*

VICTORIA

I visited you every single holiday that year, J.P., didn't
I? Because George was working — even on holidays.
Crash Priority means crashing through, he said. *We stop
for nothing.* I asked him, How could he make love if he
had to make war first? He only smiled that sweet Georgie
smile at me. No one ever smiled at me before like that.
I was . . . .It was. . . . And just like that, he's killed?

*(Jethro is not listening, fascinated by Dolores' behavior, which the others
all refuse to notice. Maddalena hands him more ornaments)*

HERBERT

Not exactly just like that.

VICTORIA

He was, what, 33?

HERBERT

33, going on 16 maybe.

VICTORIA

And I was, too. 30, 32. We were so ready for it. . . .   I
mean ready . . . even for love. . . .

HERBERT

One afternoon in the lab, oh just about this time of
year, the matter, uh, heated up. . . . Shouldn't happen. But it can. It did. He heard the bells. Everybody
heard them. Alarm bells ringing high and low. Too late.
Ringing. Sirens whooping outside, far away. It was all
over by then. Too late. They got it damped down. Got
him out. Too late. Bells. Ringing.

VICTORIA
He knew what he was doing. *It's under control.* He said.

HERBERT
Hands numb, he said. Fingers tingling. *(Maddalena, Jethro, Johnson are throwing tinsel over the tree, sowing silver snow, flashes of light)* His right hand had been in contact with the, uh, stuff. Swollen. Left hand starting to swell, stinging. Sixty minutes. Nauseated; retching; vomiting. Twenty-four hours. Violent spasms. It stops. He is shaking. Hiccups. Continuing hiccoughs — spasms of hiccoughs.

VICTORIA
George.

HERBERT
His arms are swollen. Legs numbed. Swelling spreads upward till the numbness stops. He feels pain. The pain spreads, the pain is soaking into him from the outside, squeezing him, pressing him into himself. He's short of breath: he tries to move, he feels fain't. Suddenly very weak. They pump him full of pain-killers in fancy combinations, everything they have. There's a limit, though. A man's not a horse! I mean, you can't kill a man just to stop his pain. Can you.

GIDEON
Well if it's my own brother, maybe I don't . . . .

HERBERT
If it's my own brother, maybe I should. Despite medicine.

VICTORIA

Oh George.

HERBERT

Still and all — more needs to be learned. It's territory that *must* be conquered, right? Right. A good sample case thrown right in our lap. On the sixth day, poisoning of his whole system develops. He's steadily worse. And worse is coming. By the tenth day, he has a sore on his tongue. Cramps in his belly. Enlargement of the liver, gall bladder, spleen. Inner organs swollen, bloated, engorged. Yet empty too. Mouth inflamed, thick, white membrane coating the tongue. Lips swollen, cracked, bleeding. Mouth full of sores. Diarrhea, yet the bowels are obstructed, paralyzed. Sores in the oral cavity becoming destructive ulcers.

VICTORIA

My Georgie.

HERBERT

Though it's not yet come to worst. Prolonged periods of mental confusion. We call to him. . . . We call to him. . . . But he's somewhere else: he's not himself anymore. His fingers have gone into dry gangrene by day twelve. The skin on his lower chest and abdomen is totally destroyed. The worst pain is in his groin. On the seventeenth day, the heart shows signs of inflammation. His swollen limbs are blistering fast, faster.

VICTORIA

Oh my god, his groin. Gangrene. Georgie! Georgie! My puddin' pie. *(She is weeping silently)*

HERBERT

You may well say so. On day nineteen his hair is falling out in swatches. He is irrational, hallucinating. Comatose. On the twenty-fourth day, we let the patient go. On Christmas Day. His hair is gone. Skin peeled away. What was once George Simonson, top clearance and a future, is just a suppurating body, a mass of foaming, bloody bubbles. The Nobel physicist is dead.

VICTORIA

My poor, poor Georgie.

GIDEON

Risk he took. High gain, high risk.

VICTORIA

What a strange thing to happen.

DOLORES

Each man's death is strange. Only the certificates all look the same. Each woman's death, too.

JETHRO

Man, what were they *doing?*

MADDELENA

Doing their thing. You know. Who cares.

VICTORIA

Well, he sure goofed. Jeeehusus!

HERBERT

My brother. George Simonson. . . . So, you knew him, Mrs. Glasgow?

VICTORIA

I? I?

HERBERT

In Idaho. You loved him?

JETHRO

Simonson's listed right between Number Three and Number Four. She was trying to kick the matrimony habit cold turkey. Squirming on her buns: jugs sweating, running like sweet tears. She needed something to kill her withdrawal cramps, like. He held her hand. He stroked her forehead. She's forgotten all that. Later she saddled him up and they went riding, too.

JOHNSON

I'll be getting these steps out of your way, Missus G.

DOLORES

Get yourself something to eat, Mr. Johnson. It's a holiday meal. *(He goes off to kitchen with Hannah, patting her haunch)*

MADDELENA

Mummy, it's a beautiful tree. Say it is. Most beautiful ever. As though it *could* be. Without him. Even though we've cut off its crown.

JETHRO

Ever see the bitchin' trees they throw in L.A.? Man, they're so weird you don't even have to dress them. Perfect cop-out: they sell you pre-fabbed trees.

GIDEON

How's that?

DOLORES

Four kids at home, and the man doesn't understand a word they say.

VICTORIA

That's what I like about Semitics, I guess. It's mostly clay tablets over four thousand years old. I can just about keep up with it: contracts, business accounts, military campaigns and reports, letters about property, flattery with tribute goods, sheep, wine, and the brisk trade in girls. And praying. Prayers, prayers, and yet more prayers. Talking to the dead all the time, they are. You'd think they were one big family, the quick and the dead.

DOLORES

We have much to say to the dead. And I guess they have a hell of a lot to tell us, too. But we're not listening, are we. They talk to us all the time. But who listens.

GIDEON

Sometimes I truly don't follow you, Dolores. If you believe we're still talking these days to non-existent persons. . . .

DOLORES

Even *I* don't listen to them. But I should. I talk to them. But I don't *listen*, do I. Never never. I should listen. I will. I will. I will listen to them. And so should you!

HERBERT

Now, Dolores.

DOLORES

We could make peace with them. Couldn't we. Peace
with them, at least. We could feed them a little something. Blood, for instance. How much do they want, or
need? What do you say, Gideon. How about putting
out a feeler. Let's open negotiations with the dead. Some
surplus food for the homeless dead. Cheap at the price.
Are you willing, Gideon? To meet them half way . . . ?

GIDEON

I? I? *(Terrified)*

JETHRO

You buy 'em white or pink or violet or silver or blue or
red or orange even. Some they spray with glitter pain't.
Psychedelic, man, so absolutely corrupt, it's just
bitchin'. Turns you on without any of this packaged
crap. Pure, freaked-out trees, man.

DOLORES

We're all going over to their side sooner or later anyway.
They win all the wars, don't they. So why not arrange a
non-aggression pact now, Gideon, while there's a little
time left…. Let's defect!

HERBERT

Later.

VICTORIA

Later, thanks.

GIDEON

Plenty of time to think about it, Dolores.

DOLORES

That's where you're wrong, Gideon. *Dead* wrong!

GIDEON

We're outnumbered, so there isn't any question about the end game. It's no contest from the start. That's understood, in a way. So why not leave them alone, Dolores. For the time being.

DOLORES

Go on, Gideon, run it out on your little charts.

MADDELENA

Oh wow. But I like these old things too, boxes and all.

DOLORES

Black?

JETHRO

Hit me again? Ma'am?

DOLORES

Do they have *black* trees?

JETHRO

I, uh, don't think I . . . uh, black. Gee, hey, no. How about that.

MADDELENA

Pink trees? They must be off the wall in L.A.

JETHRO

Well, man, they sort of get to you. Plastic forests lined up under the lights. And wow, you dig it, because that's where it's at. People driving golf balls till 2 a.m. and walking round in shorts and hair curlers, shopping for their trees, their mouths stuffed with tacos and frozen malts, and they're wiggin' their transistors and schlurpin' frostee cones, and it's all green, green grass all year and you get tired of that green-green, so a purple or silver tree in the window isn't *that* far out, right? It's just pure turned on, like everything else there. End of the world, man. DJ's call it *Soul* Angeles. And man, is Soul Angeles ever the city of peace — couple bottles of gasoline and they have had it! It'll burn right down. That's where it is there. You gotta be *cool* in *Soul* Angeles. Peace or else, man! Lost Angeles! Queens of Heaven! Last Angeles! I just dig it, man.

MADDELENA

I thought your Mom was in Boston.

JETHRO

Well, I was with my father. Stepfather. One of them, anyhow. You know. She sort of annulled him. Put him out of action last year.

MADDELENA

I read you.

JETHRO

Don't think you do, man. This was a shoot-out. Like, complicated. Now the one after him, Numero Quadro, that's one *I* groove. David. Man, that David Glasgow, he trips me out of my natural skull. A total bummer, from up front. Cat just raps me stoned. Like, pure speed he talks, without any of that middle-class, adulterated, bureaucratic, Establishment gunk you get around here. When *he* freaked himself out of it, no one even saw him go. That's how come she married him: she couldn't even read him in the first place. He is so far out you couldn't get farther outer with four hundred-watt amps blasting on sitars like crazy. Man, his head scene is, just, oh wow, bitchin'. . . .

VICTORIA

What are you telling her, Jethro.

JETHRO

Who-what-where, Ma'am.

VICTORIA

I can hear David's hang-up talk. When did you see David, Jethro.

JETHRO

He's in San Quentin. How could I see him. So cool it, Lady.

VICTORIA

If only I could.

HERBERT

Is there a convict in the family?

JETHRO

My foster-foster-foster father. They got him on a bummer.

MADDELENA

Whyn't he cop a plea?

JETHRO

Politics. He's on the list.

HERBERT

What list, may I ask?

JETHRO

Oh man, what list, he says. *Which* list, you mean. They *all* got a little list, you know?

HERBERT

That's one I must have missed.

DOLORES

V.G.'s a set of statistics all by herself. You should feed her into next year's Gross National Product.

GIDEON

(Snorting) I'll need some more indicators to index.

VICTORIA

David's no *man*. David is a freakola! Took one trip too many. David said, *I am going to explore the territory within. I am going unarmed, in peace. Explore my soul. My mission: Enlightenment for all!* Daddy offered him ten mountains, all prime timber. Daddy offered him half-shares in his new tree-cutter. You ought to see my Daddy's new tree-cutter: it fells a hundred-year old tree, delimbs it, tops it, cuts it into even lengths and stacks them . . . all in one minute, eliminating eight men, just like that! But, *no* thank you, not for David. Could he see himself in his own future with Daddy's tree-cutter? *Nooo*. But Daddy said he saw something in David. You don't think he'd give half-shares in his new tree-cutter, if he didn't see something. I don't know what. His *mind* was his future, David said. *What* mind, if you please! There's nothing at all there now. It's jelly. Future! I gave him his future — like handing him a million dollars, prime rate, without collateral or security: a certificate wrapped up in a neat little Christmas package. But what does Señor Nirvana say? *You think you can colonize me, Victoria? Think you can exploit my spirit and enslave my soul, you, with your linear thinking, Victoria?* Like a little boy. Jesus, *that* was my *husband?* Acid freakola. I can read cuneiform and hieroglyph; I can tell you what the hungry ghosts should be given to eat; but I sure couldn't read him. Mess. Only thing to do for him was lobotomize him — he's dropped all the pills and mainlined all the crystals and smoked whatever was next. And I *should* have signed the permission papers. But I got all weepy at the last minute. Woman's pity. Big mistake.

DOLORES

No peasant can afford pity. She has to sign on the line. But gentelmen and ladies, now, they merely weep their crocodile tears. They wallow in moral luxury.

GIDEON

I read a study last week about Western New Guinea matriarchy, and it seems those women use their men merely for —

VICTORIA

You should have seen how my Daddy wanted to tear him apart. Not bad enough, David wrecks Daddy's new jet, flying across Mexico stacked with guns, but then the narcos from Interpol said he had his damned nerve stashing all that other stuff, when the Government wanted him to keep the smuggling clean. *David* has to go use the CIA for *his* cover, when they're using him for theirs! And they — well, never mind. Too late. *How many games you think you can play when you're only an amateur?* Daddy asks him. Judge says, *If the Prosecution will agree to blahblahblah, and if Daddy's insurance will drop the charges on the plane blahblahblah, then he will quash the blahblahblah. . . .* You know the way it goes. We got him off *that* one. But then he turns right around, and he —

GIDEON

Sounds like a loser to me.

VICTORIA

Doesn't he just. I think so.

GIDEON

Out of touch. Negative. Sinking. Position confused. We have no use for them if they try to play their own little game on the side. Without our authorization. There are *some* rules. Rules.

JETHRO

Oh no, man.

GIDEON

Out of sight. Typical loser. Shits where he eats.

JETHRO

No, no, man.

VICTORIA
Daddy says —

GIDEON
Well, has he any options, I mean. Hasn't he dropped out, compromised his friends, blown his cover. I'd consider him totaled. I'd cancel him I would.

VICTORIA
Well, that's just what we did.

JETHRO
Wrong, man. He dropped *himself* out, he *cancelled* himself. There's a difference, man. He's free now. No more Establishment bull. Washington sucks.

GIDEON
No one remembers a loser. Except a sentimentalist. Don't be stupid, son. Our game's different from the games your peer groups play. Go pin up your rock posters elsewhere.

DOLORES
It's called Seek and Destroy. Use any and all means.

JETHRO
Peace, brother. Peace to your soul.

VICTORIA
Daddy's thinking of settling ten million dollars on *you*, Jethro. Ten entire millions. Now you listen to me, darling: if David's loose out there, if David's coming after me, I want to know about it. What if I died? What if David came in here out of that storm like a thief in the

night, what if he tried to. . . . Oh, you don't know the
real David, Gideon, if you imagine he wouldn't get that
money out of Jethro. He's not *that* far gone he can't use
money for one of his so-called revolutions. He'd make
himself Jethro's executor! You think that's funny, Jethro.
But it's money money money! *Real* money. I'd be dead
and he'd control the hell out of you, *and* with Daddy's
resources! You want to be subjected by some creepola
like David?

JETHRO

Bugs you more than me, lady.

VICTORIA

My Daddy fought like a hero for his money. You don't
think they made him Fire Commissioner of San Francisco for love! No, for merit . . . and donations. Merit,
too. And he was barely 25 at the time! You wouldn't
know how to massacre your competitors all your life
the way Daddy has. You and your cushy trust fund.
You with your plastic card for any bank machine in the
world! You may laugh when I say ten million dollars,
but just you try to —

JETHRO

Christ, tune me out tonight. (*Throws the last of his tinsel, and goes to stare out the window, taking his guitar and
plucking it with stylized moodiness now and then*)

VICTORIA

Jethro. Honey.

(*Eleanor Steiner enters, fur-coated, fur-hatted, sparkling chicly
with cold, loaded down with gifts she dumps unceremoni-
ously at the foot of the tree, stepping back to admire it, per-*

forming, and relishing the admiration she gets from the men.
She is gay, ditsy-seeming, with a lecherous cast to her eyes; yet
also a bit cold in her expression, as are the other two women.
There may be occasional warm laughter from the kitchen
where Hannah and Mr. Johnson are having a good time)

ELEANOR

Helloooo, everybody. Sorry I'm late. It's just glorious weather, isn't it. Wild. Chicago-style, but better: it ain't . . . Chicago! How's Bobby.

DOLORES

He'll live. We hope.

ELEANOR

What is she saying, people.

DOLORES

I'll be back after lunch, she said.

ELEANOR

So I did. Got pinned down unexpectedly. Surrounded. That's how it is, you know. Can't help that, can I.

DOLORES

Leaving me to hold the fort.

ELEANOR

It's only . . . what? Nine-ish?

DOLORES

Yes, well. Lenny, he ran that little fever right on up to 105. We had to call a doctor. Got his temperature down. Hannah did. Tubbed him and rubbed him

ELEANOR

She's a jewel.

DOLORES

Hannah's got things to do here besides nursing. But he'll make it. Took an awful beating though. It's not *just* a cough, Lenny.

ELEANOR

You're putting me on. Dolores, Don't joke. What did the Doctor tell you. Darling, don't ruin my day.

DOLORES

Think I'm a defeatist? Ask him yourself. Dr. Simonson, old family friend. Herbie, Eleanor Steiner. *The* Eleanor. You know: Jack's first great love? First of many, uh, great loves. You know?

HERBERT

The Eleanor? Ah.

ELEANOR

Love? Oh, well, love. So, how is Bobby. Let me have it.

HERBERT

He'll recover. *(Medical pause)* Shot a megadose of polycillin into him. Difficult patient. Fever usually slows that type down. Has he ever . . . thrown convulsions? Been in shock? Turned blue?

ELEANOR

What are you trying to tell me. This isn't a diplomatic conference. Put me in the picture.

DOLORES

Lenny, why not try to assess your position realistically.
That kid's going to have to live under siege conditions
the rest of his life. Like the rest of us. There are no
trade-offs.

ELEANOR

News to me. Doctor, I wish you'd say just what —

DOLORES

Don't act stupid, Lenny. I'm talking about survival. He's
got the rest of this century to get through, right? That's
hardly news. He's got an acute asthma. How can you
park him in a crowded, damp movie all afternoon while
you dash off around town on one of your expeditions,
or whatever you expose yourself to out there. . . .

ELEANOR

You're talking hysterical rot. Pulling some psycho-ploy
on me. I won't have it, not from you, Dolores. That
child will be a free man some day. Specialist told me
last week he'd had some allergic episode. That is all.
Something in the woodwork: my aunt's house is falling
apart with dry fungus. We've been out of there only
three days. Don't try to panic me with one of your atroc-
ity stories.

DOLORES

Dear Lenny, That is no allergy. He will live under a
regime of terror. I should know an attack when I see
one. At his age I was practically a basket case. Do you
know we could have lost your kid — like that! If not for
Herbie. You can't locate a good medico in this area today: they're all furloughed out for rest and

recreation . . . the Bahamas, Aspen, Palm Springs, Bora
Bora . . . who knows where in hell the jerks take cover
when there's a bronchial assault on this town. We have
to hold on without them. Unless you want to chance
the Emergency Ward somewhere. So, where were you
screwing around today. And who with, for a change.

ELEANOR
Who says asthma.

HERBERT
I do. But I'm a neurosurgeon, Mrs. Steiner.

ELEANOR
Eleanor.

HERBERT
I took strong, uh, countermeasures. In case the lungs
were suffering stress. These attacks tend to build up in
waves. Mustn't lose your head. Eleanor.

ELEANOR
I? I?

HERBERT
I mean, Bobby's not a total casualty yet.

GIDEON
I think maybe I should be calling in at home.

DOLORES
Do you good for a change. Is she trimming her tree all
alone?

GIDEON

I, uh, trimmed it yesterday. Look, Dolores, it is axiomatic that one never fights on two fronts. So don't you provoke an incident with me too.

DOLORES

But dearest, *you* are *my* only front.

GIDEON

What about me?

DOLORES

What *about* you.

GIDEON

I'll use your phone.

DOLORES

Take it in my bedroom. You know where that is. Use Operation Quick Brown Fox.

HERBERT

You know, Dolores is quite perceptive in her prognosis of the diagnostic picture.

ELEANOR

An attack? Was it an attack?

HERBERT

Bobby needs rest.

ELEANOR

(Beginning to accept it) An attack.

HERBERT

We don'twant an invasion of the lungs. The boy should be evacuated tomorrow. He needs rest. This zone's really, uh, much too active for him.

ELEANOR

Tomorrow? To Minneapolis? You've got to be kidding. Come on, Doctor Simonson.

HERBERT

Herbert. Theoretically. He should, I mean. But . . . *(Shrugs)*

ELEANOR

All right. I stand advised. Now, Dolores, I don't read you. What's *your* strategy.

DOLORES

You need better intelligence, Lenny. I was merely probing. You're very defensive, you know.

ELEANOR

Actually, I ran into an old friend. Sort of a friend. Said it would come along as escort. You don't mind?

DOLORES

Only if it's a man. There's a shortage. Unbalance of powers. As long as it's a man.

ELEANOR

That I don't know. Yet. Said it knew you. Intimately. Part of your economy by now, it said. What can *that* mean?

DOLORES

Only a few know me. *That* intimately. So?

ELEANOR

Henry Franklin. Is it a man?

DOLORES

(Her big laugh) Oh god, how . . . funny!

VICTORIA

Friend or enemy? *(Pronounced more like "enema")*

DOLORES

Neither. *It* is neutral.

VICTORIA

No man's neutral. Not even if he has the whole island to himself.

DOLORES

My lawyer. Suing the Garnet conglomerate. For Christ's sake, Lenny, what do you mean old friend of *yours*?

ELEANOR

He's admired me from the first. Collected me, I mean. Makes him a friendly, no? Now he's sitting on a fortune in Caseys. Ten or twelve pieces, the first three Queens. *But only the first three,* I reminded him. *Are there more,* he said. You'd better believe it, Mr. Franklin, I said. *Henry,* he said. How his eyes slitted. You should have seen his tongue wetting his lips. Neutral — a lawyer? Neutral — a man? Come off that, D.G. Like a weapons maker — That's how neutral Henry Franklin is! *Where're you staying,* he said. I'm holed up at Dolores Garnet's, I said, till the shelling slacks off, I said. My ex's lawyers are laying down one hell of barrage out there. *Ah,* he said, then he'd be glad to come up. Thinks he's pursuing more of my pieces. *I have no kings,* I said. *Might I commission one,* he said. *Oh?* I said, *Just like that? You think it's just like that you can be kinged? Well, it's my money,* he says, and blahblahblah. So I arranged for him to come up tonight —

DOLORES

No, it's Jack's money. It should be *my* money. So far I haven't tripped over half the safe-boxes Jack put his things in! Can you imagine the man's not keeping code book on it all? I suppose when I find them, they'll be booby-trapped some way and blow me and my debts and my life to smithereens. And Henry Franklin, my advocate, my counsel in court, will strip me naked after I'm dead.

VICTORIA

With a friend like that to defend you, you don't *need* an enemy.

DOLORES

Why V.G., you have the cutest folksy sayings. Did you pick up that one in Semitics, too?

ELEANOR

Some day soon enough he'll find he has a fortune in Caseys, I told him. When Caseys are on top of the market. In the event you're wondering how I found Franklin out there today, Dolores, my dealer brought us together. He was wandering round the Gallery in a daze. Battle fatigue, maybe? We sat him down to rest. He began talking, and we couldn't stop him

DOLORES

I don't like loose lips.

ELEANOR

He didn't give away any vital statistics. Don't worry.

DOLORES

I do worry. I don't sleep for worrying.

ELEANOR

One always needs a convoy. Not safe to travel alone.

DOLORES

We are never alone.

VICTORIA

When I do Semitics, I feel I'm with lots of company, though they've been dead four thousand years. But when I think of David plotting against me out there, I feel unarmed, vulnerable to sudden attack. Quite alone.

DOLORES

Or else maybe we're always alone, hah?

ELEANOR

What arms does he carry usually? I like to know my options.

DOLORES

Ask Gideon. He's up on the state of the art. Gideon, what are the latest developments in assault tactics? In the, uh, highly mobile field of mature, unattached, masculine marauders, sexual skirmishers, raiders and terrorists? What weapons have you guys got to use against us now, Gideon.

GIDEON

Who, we? *We?*

DOLORES

Top-secret, hah?

HERBERT

Arent you Eleanor *Steiner?*

ELEANOR

I fight under my own flag: Casey. Steiner's just one operational cover I picked up some years ago: valid for one baby boy. Hostage to life and fortune, as they say. I'm surfacing again now as Casey. If I can get the other side to accept my terms. It's hard to maneuver if you let names get in the way of tactics.

DOLORES

Steiner wasn't so bad.

ELEANOR

Steiner was hell. My former accountant husband, Doctor, with half Chicago in his sweaty fist. He behaved like an invisible security chief, a commissar. Steiner wasn't for real. Anyway, Steiner is dead.

HERBERT

I'm sorry.

ELEANOR

That's all right. Real problem's dividing the loot. Casey doesn't want Steiner, but Steiner wants the Caseys.

HERBERT
I thought you said he was dead . . . ?

ELEANOR
When a woman decides a man's dead, he's dead. And by then he already stinks to high heaven. Yet we never seem to let go till it starts coming apart in our hands like wet plaster. Classic female behavior. But Eleanor Casey is now learning new ways of thinking about the unthinkable.

HERBERT
Ah, you've separated.

DOLORES
Cutting her losses.

ELEANOR
Steiner's just a shit actually.

VICTORIA
Aren't they, though.

ELEANOR
I'm ten years older, see? Lost my youth all tangled up with a lousy pair of pants.

VICTORIA
That's not unthinkable.

DOLORES
That's veryday life. And death.

ELEANOR

What's unthinkable is that any minute another pair of pants will come trotting down the path, and I'll be waiting there behind my tree just ready and aching to —

DOLORES

Unzip him. Reckless woman. So another decade of hell commences.

VICTORIA

I don't wait *that* long to shuck them. Soon's I feel it hurting . . . here . . . I cut them loose.

ELEANOR

Meanwhile, it's war. Steiner's out there howling in the dark somewhere over Chicago, or over the Hudson, who knows? Legal maneuvers. And I'm supposed to walk into his trap with Bobby? *Eleanor,* my staff tells me, *appease* him. Some staff. They would give Paris away. So I've just plain run off. Retreated. Bobby's half his, of course: those allergies are Steiner allergies. I never had a rash till I married Steiner. Not to ask what it is, Herbert. Hives are for my shrink's eyes only. Anyway, when I saw my position was untenable, I withdrew. Didn't want to lose my hair too. Now I am a refugee. Soon to be a displaced person.

VICTORIA

I had four of them. None of them did me any good either.

ELEANOR

Husbands, Victoria? Jesus!

VICTORIA

Shrinks.

DOLORES

And husbands.

VICTORIA

Them too. If you *must* do a body count. But one was only some weekend sortie. Anyway, they don't mix.

DOLORES

Women. husbands. Shrinks. They certainly don't mix. Every man's hand lifted against every other man's . . . and against every woman's too. Unstable detente at best. No balance of powers in married life. all you can do is stay mobilized . . . and ready to give it up.

ELEANOR

For what? It doesn't change even then.

GIDEON

You are really very dark, gloomy women.

JETHRO

Bad scene, man, huh!

GIDEON

Do you know what you're saying, son?

HERBERT

On the other hand, the problems are there to begin with. Don't you think? Even before there are incidents? Don't you think? Before there are, uh, outbreaks.

DOLORES
Herbie, honey mine, are *you* ever lucky you have nerves of steel. Is it your training, or are you simply insensitive to our human-all-too-human condition?

HERBERT
And what is that?

DOLORES
Marriage. Men. Women. And shrinks.

HERBERT
Oh I'm pretty sensitive. I think.

VICTORIA
Prove it, Doctor.

HERBERT
Would I take up a position I couldn't hold?

ELEANOR
Put out a feeler.

VICTORIA
Show yourself.

ELEANOR
What side are you on. *(To Dolores)*

DOLORES
You're provoking him, girls. Don't. I know him. He'll retaliate. I know him.

GIDEON
You can always parley for a truce.

DOLORES
You stay out of this one, Gideon.

GIDEON
Just offering to mediate. Private talks. Old-fashioned
diplomacy.

DOLORES

Herbert's got nothing but overkill — *he's* never even
been married!

VICTORIA
We're dug in. Shoot, Doctor.

ELEANOR
Three . . . two . . . one . . . and . . .

HERBERT
Well — I am writing a book.

ELEANOR
(Laughing) Oh oh oh.

DOLORES
Better be a block-buster full of buggers and soulless
bitches. What's it called, *SECRETS OF THE TERMI-
NAL WARD? Or, EVERYTHING YOU ALWAYS
WANTED TO KNOW ABOUT DEATH BUT WERE
AFRAID TO ASK?*

VICTORIA

What's it about, Doctor.

HERBERT

It's Herbert.

VICTORIA

Herbert? Herbert?

DOLORES

V.G., you damn female fool! Don't you know by now
when to sit tight! Now you've exposed us. He'll chop
our flanks to shreds. Make tartar steak out of us.

HERBERT

Should interest you. Actually.

VICTORIA

Don't read fiction.

DOLORES

Late, oh, too late! Refills, everybody! Hannah, ice for
the martinis! Cheese, shrimps, olives, nuts, dips, spread,
anything, Hannah. Where's the paté ? Damn her, she's
probably gone downstairs to help him on with his uniform. Some women never do learn! Do you know that
girl had herself three babies by a man I had to buy off
just to leave her alone? I mean I had to beat him off
first, and then fight two trials to get him committed?
*(She can be laying out the ice and hors d'ouevres while she
gives the following speech and efficiently distributes snacks)*
When they found out he was crazy, they threw him out
of the Muslims. Shit. You think any of those insurgents
or guerilla gangs would trust him? He was well over

thirty anyway. Worse yet, he respected us, the Garnets.
In his own way, he even respected women. Not like
some men. You know, the guys who get cramps at the
sight of a woman and skip out to the john with diarrhea as soon as you open your robe. You know the type.

GIDEON

Dolores.

DOLORES

Ah, what the hell do I know about you, Gideon. Now
you're a city planner too. Even busier than Jack. Are *you*
going to pollute your model cities with people, *real*
people, hah?

GIDEON

Did I ever —

DOLORES

Telling story, people, telling story! So he comes in here
after her with a gun. *Look out!* he's yelling, *Hyer cum de
Jedge! Hyer cum de Jedge!* I stood at the door to her room,
and he says, *Mrs. Garnet, I'm saving you, God wants you!*
And I say, What for, Mr. Judah, to go on living like a
slave under the Garnet Monopoly? I want to be free,
Mr. Judah, I want to be my own woman — and so does
Hannah. So you just get out of here, and blahblahblah.
You know. And he says, *I'd sure hate to let my chief down
if I hurt you, honey! My chief, he wants you alive, honey.*
What the hell are you talking about, Mr. Judah! And he
says, *But I tell you one thing, I'm going to get me a good fat
piece of jellycide out of that witch's ass, I'm going to send her
on back to her real home, that obeah witch, with her black
tadpoles and snakes and roosters, send her home out of this
mess here, because I got my marchin' orders, Mr. Garnet,*

you hear? And there's but the one way to bring peace and harmony again in this world and the lion layin' down with the lamb, and Adam husband with Eve without no dragon to guide them, and I have found that way to the peaceable kingdom, if one more witch, the last witch, if that obeah woman of mine just be chopped up to little pieces, and I will eat her heart, I tell you. . . . Maybe I am only the one little man, but de holy spirit do declare me innocent no matter what you folks'll say, and so there be just one final solution for her. . . . Did you ever? And then he fires that damn .38 pistol at my head. There's the hole . . . up there.

VICTORIA

Sounds just like my recent ex! That is David Glasgow running amok.

DOLORES

And, if you please, my dear Jack stands there all the while smoking his pipe. Taking notes. Another case for the files: There's a real disciplined thinker for you. What could I do, the man's crazed. Always *was* a crazy.

ELEANOR

Which man. Jack or Judah?

VICTORIA

My David would say, Depends on the size of your bag.

DOLORES

And Hannah Judah hiding behind that door, who's come up from Jamaica to be my servant and clean up our mess day and night, when back home she ran a little agency and was a person of some dignity, and has to enter slavery in our bathrooms and kitchen just to get a

visa for this country. . . . Hannah's simply another item
for Jack's social science graph describing the current figures on Upward Mobility for Immigrant Minorities.

GIDEON

Too bad. Of course, population pressures generate wors-
ening inner-city conditions, tending to aggravate whatever purely personal problems —

DOLORES

Shit, Gideon. The truth of the matter, as always, is:
The last shall be last, and the first first. Forever and
Amen. For mine is the kingdom, not thine. Period. And
she loved him, she says. She still pities him, even now.
I walked right up to him with that .38 still smoking,
and he jabs it against me, here — (She shows her breasts
quite unself-consciously) — and I say, Shoot! Go on, give
it to me in my heart, Solomon Judah! You don't want
that woman to live, but I tell you she's my sister, I say.
Kill her, kill me, it's the same thing! Well, he couldn't
look me in the eyes even then. Jabs me here, the muzzle
is burning hot, and I had a purple rose that big for
three weeks.

GIDEON

He might have pulled the trigger.

DOLORES

Solomon Judah's no killer: he's a disorganized man. Or
so Jack called him. Disorganized! I took his weapon
from him, easy as that. He wept. I ask you, What does
it take to look a woman in the eyes? You men! Jack
never did. And now Hannah thinks Jack Garnet and
Victor Johnson subdued him! Shit, I take that pistol
from his hand and walk him to the ambulance. Which

is more than Jack can do. That man Judah was never anything but a killed. He wrote me letters till he died. I've saved them. They're fine letters. They'll make a book. Call it: *TESTAMENT OF JUDAH. (Dolores goes to a sideboard and takes out a packet of envelopes wrapped with a black ribbon and holds it shaking it at them as she orates in a semi-ironic tone)* They're like prayers. Black prayers, of course. Black souls on the march. Black souls walking to victory on that high road paved with black souls. Black souls under fire, oppressed, beaten, denied, destroyed and refined into fire, into black electricity. He's good, that crazy Solomon Judah. Black souls like bombs, like hand grenades, like land mines, like bullets and shrapnel slivers and bottles of gasoline. Black souls like death and destruction. God Almighty! Black souls exploding at you and at me, blinding us, leaving us in darkness, leaving us to grope in utter blackness, too. *JUDAH'S BIBLE,* I call it. Handbook of the Black Insurrection. Oh, it'll sell. Way love letters used to sell. We'll all be a-studyin' and a-quotin' from *JUDAH'S BIBLE* one day. See? Judah may be dead, but Judah's just beginning to live. You have to die if you want to live, huh? Think of all the black and dead souls, huh? Black and dying souls, huh? How many, Lord! And how long, O Lord! How long! My god! Oh, but that poor, demented man could scribble one hell of a letter!

HERBERT
Come down off that, Dolores.

GIDEON
You'd better pray we can contain it. Violence only meets with more violence. Besides, it's Christmas Eve, Dolores.

DOLORES

(Laughing hugely, enjoying their anxiety) You don't even know what I'm talking about. You tune out, Gideon, when I talk. You sure tune out, don't you. Some urbanologist you are! One of these days you'll see, though. I hope to god you will hear.

JETHRO

Let us pray for that, man.

DOLORES

You think it's race, or politics or class-stratification or economics. We're not on the same wavelength, Gideon. You're a sheer materialist, a regular Russian burocrat, Washington to New York to Boston shuttle-style. Computerized Machiavelli!

JETHRO

Groovy.

GIDEON

God, how I *do* love you, Dolores. Let me only count the ways.

HERBERT

Actually, my book's on æsthetics.

ELEANOR

Holy Mary and Joseph!

VICTORIA

What's wrong, Casey?

ELEANOR

Boringest subject men ever invented.

VICTORIA

There's Mrs. Langer, though.

ELEANOR

Indeed yes.

HERBERT

Mrs. Langer? The Vienna Pastry Shop Mrs. Langer?

VICTORIA

She's written all these books. . . .

HERBERT

Actually I've been thinking it over for twenty years, ever since I finished my residency in neurosurgery. I've finally written it. Uh, what does Mrs. What'shername say?

VICTORIA

Shapes, forms, how we see them. You know.

ELEANOR

I look at you, and you look at me, blahblahblah . . .

DOLORES

What do I see, and what do you see, blahblahblah. . . .

VICTORIA

You know, Êæsthetics?

HERBERT

Pure waste of time. Looking isn't seeing.

VICTORIA

What   about   Plato-Aristotle-Kant-Locke-
blahblahblah. . . .

HERBERT

Who? Who? Wrong track. Whatever they said. You have
got to begin at the very beginning, if you want to think.
You can't look it up in the philosophy of the past. That's
all dead. You begin here and now. With the correct
definition. Right?

DOLORES

Are we to take it that the correct definition is *your* final
solution, Herbert? Now that you've disposed of all the
others? *(She's threatening him, but he's too self-absorbed to
heed her mockery)*

HERBERT

No no no. I say two things only. I explain them on Page
1, and I therefore have the answer even before I start.
The rest is merely illustration and example. That's all
there is to it. So simple, no one's even thought of it. It
will wipe out all other ideas on the subject! You see, I
knew my goal from the start, and I proceeded with
simple logic. Wasn't easy. Been fighting my way through
the jungle for twenty years: even with my hands ex-
ploring an open living brain on the table before me,
I've groped towards it through such terrible shadows of
thought. It was so dark everywhere. Now I'm solidly
entrenched in the obvious truth. I'll overrun your posi-

tion, I'll crush your defenses. I'll slaughter your philosophers! Mrs Langer, too.

VICTORIA
(Recoiling as though actually alarmed) Oh my.

ELEANOR
A regular Genghis Kahn. He'll annihilate Êæsthetics.

DOLORES
Our good, kind family doctor. Who'd have thought.

HERBERT
What? Well, I start with the evolution of man. Got that?
Animal point of view. Start with that, you're on the
only correct road. Right? Right!

ELEANOR
Are you. Evolution of man. That's news to me. And
woman?

HERBERT
Man includes woman. Of course.

ELEANOR
He does, does he. I think of it as Eve-olution.

DOLORES
I've always thought woman includes man.

HERBERT
(The mild fanatic is vexed) Arghh! Don't play word
games with me now, Dolores. Mrs. Glasgow, I was
saying, wasn't I, that…?

VICTORIA
Victoria. *(Overbearing him, as if sensually)*

HERBERT
...that man, Victoria, *includes* woman. Generically, at least. We're all together in this. Homo sapiens, see? Now what is your most basic animal behavior?

VICTORIA
(Absentmindedly caressing his arm) Wait, don't tell me.

ELEANOR
Hunger? *(She turns tigress, hands clawing)* Growrrr!

DOLORES
Getting them born. Burying them.

HERBERT
I said, animal behavior.

ELEANOR
Oh crap, Herbert. I surrender. Sock it to me.

HERBERT
Think now. Movement? Yes, of course. But — *why* movement? Why any movement at all?

JETHRO
Buddha doesn't move.

ELEANOR
I give up! I confess everything. Where do I sign. I don't want to read it, just let me sign on the line. Take my mug shot, put me on trial, and beat me to death. I am

the enemy of the animal classes. I make art that doesn't
move.

DOLORES

Counter-revolutionary broads of the world, unite!

HERBERT

Tsk. You are avoiding me. Why movement? Tell me,
why?

VICTORIA, ELEANOR, DOLORES

We, representing all free and bereaved women of the
world at this moment in Man's history, united heart
and soul, *and* in the longings of our loins, we desire
you to speak, O, most dearly beloved, our Doctor
Herbert Simonson!

HERBERT

(Unfazed, undeterred) If you'll permit me. Ladies. What
gnaws deeper than hunger? What excites your little heart
and sets it beating faster than even the contractions of
your uterus? What drives you even more than your in-
vincible female curiosity to open a locked door, or your
swollen, aching breasts in the presence of the desired
male? Tell me, what makes you animals move at all?
Well? Silence? Come come.

VICTORIA, ELEANOR, DOLORES

We're not coming for you, O Doctor dear!

HERBERT

Gideon?

GIDEON

Not my field, Dolores. I deal with social structures. I've no expertise with the personal.

JETHRO

(Pleading) Karma, man, That's what. You move up or down, through good or evil. Man, that's the Karma. You move because you're paying it off, paying it off, paying it off! Otherwise, man, you don't move at all! You're in The Buddhahood … and you don't move at all.

HERBERT

Tell me, people, *what* is this boy saying?

JETHRO

Music moves. Only music. Nothing else. It's all just your illusion.

MADDLENA

Right, right!

HERBERT

Well, ladies?

VICTORIA, ELEANOR, DOLORES

Well, Doctor?

HERBERT

You don't see it? I'll tell you. *It's . . . fear.*

VICTORIA, ELEANOR, DOLORES

Oh? Oh?

HERBERT

Fear alone moves us. We are born in fear, we breathe, we live each moment by and through fear. Fear is our fundamental emotion.

VICTORIA, ELEANOR, DOLORES

(Laughing) Herbie!

HERBERT

And our fundamental emotion is fear. You just stop and think about that. Even when you laugh, you're relieving your fear. Think about *that,* now.

JETHRO

(Moaning) Oh no, man. You got a head like a Mosler Safe. Man, if they ever blew your mind, there'd be nothing inside but a mess of wires and steel gunk and broken glass.

DOLORES

Herbie, do you know what you're talking about?

HERBERT

Argument's unbeatable. It's fear. Fear lives in each cell of our body. In the nucleus of the cell, fear burns like a small, white flame. Fear is twisted in the coils of the genes themselves, the molecules are tied by knots of fear. . . .

VICTORIA

Ah, ah, ah. *(As though being caressed)*

HERBERT

. . . and everything follows from that. Our life is fear, and fear alone is our life. I shall make the first revolution in æsthetics — *and* the last. After me, nothing more will can be said.

JETHRO

Peace, man, peace.

HERBERT

Why do we thrill at killing, at tragedy, at the idea of death, and the idea of dying? Why do we need it?

VICTORIA

The thought of it! *(She is half-swooning)*

VICTORIA, ELEANOR, DOLORES

Do we? Do we?

HERBERT

And *that,* ladies and gentlemen, is my final solution.

VICTORIA, ELEANOR, DOLORES

Is it? Is it?

HERBERT

I'll overthrow your æsthetics forever!

JETHRO

Hey, man! Beauty. What about beauty?

VICTORIA, ELEANOR, DOLORES

Beauty! *(Laughing irrepressibly)*

HERBERT

Beauty? Beauty? (*The chimes of the door sound. Dolores dashes out, returns with Henry Franklin, who with Hannah's assistance is toting some immense Christmas packages. Hannah takes his hat, coat, scarf, galoshes. Dolores embraces him affectionately, and holds on to his arm protectively, even possessively, until he is forced to extricate himself. He is elegant and conservatively dressed. Holds himself well. Is used to being listened to*)

FRANKLIN

Hellooo, everybody. How goes it in the tower, high above massacre and storm? Dolores, Don't let them get past your outer perimeter. Art of self-defense means hanging loose, and — attacking. Attack, attack, attack.

DOLORES

Not to worry, dear. I'll ask you to lay down some covering fire if it gets too tight.

FRANKLIN

A Marine is always prepared! Merry Christmas! Is that the password?

MADDALENA

Who knows, anymore. (*Depressed, petulant*)

DOLORES

I gather you've met Eleanor Steiner, in one way or the other? This is Victoria Glasgow, *Professor* Glasgow, I mean; and this is her only son and heir, Jethro Pritchett. Doctor Simonson you've always known, of course. He's a reliable ally, though on whose side I have yet to figure out.

FRANKLIN

Herbert. You have been ministering to these diseased minds, I hope.

DOLORES

Herbie's trying to blitzkrieg us with some frightful old notions.

HERBERT

I? I?

FRANKLIN

An offensive? On Christmas Eve?

ELEANOR

Philosophy! Æsthetics yet!

DOLORES

More like hellfire preaching. He announces that it's been Judgment Day ever since time began. He thinks we are no different from the first bacterium! Just a bunch of genes trembling in their chromosomes. How's that for a deep freeze? As if time had never marched on! *(She moves towards the grandfather clock and stops it by holding the pendulum and casually stroking it)* If it will ease your mind, Herbie, I'll stop it for you tonight. There, Doctor, how does that feel?

HERBERT

(Upset, but hiding it) Tonight? Don't be ridiculous.

MADDELENA

(Alarmed) Mother, don't make it worse for me. I'm scared. *(She has a tremor in her limbs that she suppresses by*

holding on to herself) You're wrecking things again.

HANNAH
(Passing near behind Dolores, and starting the pendulum again, holding her arm and gently moving her away) You don't want to do that, Mrs. Garnet. I'm telling you true, Ma'am, and I know!

DOLORES
(Continuing as though nothing had happened) So let's call a general cease fire now. Truce, Herbie, hah? ...And this is Gideon Petrowsky, our other wise man. Gideons' become a Special Presidential Taskforcemaster these days, something to do with money, what's called ethics these days....

FRANKLIN
I've read about your Commission. Good luck.

GIDEON
Don't believe everything you read.

FRANKLIN
Who does?

DOLORES
Only a blizzard could ground Gideon. Which way were you flying, I forget. Home to family and hearth, or home to the White House basement? Oh, these crisis managers, Henry, a life of computers and shredders. How they sacrifice their comforts for us! How they desert their homes and loved nes and lovers here and there, and all for our nation taken as a whole. Not only that, but he to think about unthinkables all the time. On order. From the

President. Look how worn out the poor man is. Take his pulse, Doctor.

GIDEON
That bad I hope I don't look.

FRANKLIN
Nonsense. A Crisis Manager *thrives* on the unthinkable. Crime and Crisis may never harm him, but peace and good will can break his bones.

GIDEON
Ive even been accused by people who should know better than to write it in the *TIMES*, of actually mobilizing catastrophes, even settin up situations that could destroy us all … just to keep it up, just so I could stay in office —

FRANKLIN
You mean, get it up?

JETHRO
Oh, wow.

FRANKLIN
Excuse me, Maddalena, I didn't see you there. This is for you, you know.

MADDALENA
Mr. Franklin, you didn't have to bring such a big whatever it is.

FRANKLIN
It's nothing. Call it . . . gratitude?

DOLORES

For what?

FRANKLIN

For all that I am today. To you, Dolores, I owe something.

DOLORES

He means he's suing the Garnets for me, good people.
And all I give him is an IOU. How long can I main'tain
him? Imagine the overhead on a man like this!

VICTORIA

I know it to the dollar. You can write most of it off.

FRANKLIN

It's promising to be a long, hard campaign. Just what I
like.

DOLORES

Contingency — on a 100 million dollars, say? At five
hundred per hour. And he thinks it could go on forever.
The Garnets are tough. They'll fight to the end.

FRANKLIN

No, they'll settle. If you're not *too* careless, Dolores.

DOLORES

You mean with *him*? But Gideon doesn't allow us to
discuss our human lives, let alone live them, not even
though we sit here under fire. You need his permission
to laugh, not to mention, well. . . . But — does he let
us in on *his* thing? Ah no — *he's* the professional at
social salvation. That's what Harvard does to some men.

One look at him, and you know it's not a laughing matter. Besides, the Garnets have been family to him since he was that high. So they know it can't be love, not with *him*. *(Her laughter)* I just think I sort of —

FRANKLIN

— Want him?

DOLORES

Or maybe just need him. Who's to say anything about need, real need. Question is, Need for what?

FRANKLIN

Security.

ELEANOR

Ransom.

VICTORIA

Trophy.

FRANKLIN

Nostalgia. You remember something about trousers from long ago.

DOLORES

(Laughs) Unthinkable: he's still married!

FRANKLIN

You girls *are* quite something.

HERBERT

Undisciplined.

ELEANOR

Unconventional.

GIDEON

Unchivalrous.

VICTORIA

Below the belt.

DOLORES

Merciless.

ELEANOR

Pitiless.

VICTORIA

Ruthless.

FRANKLIN

Excuse me, Gideon. Interrogation. I need some orientation on this field. Where am I? I mean, where the hell are ours?

GIDEON

I'm okay. It's going over my head. They haven't got the range. So far.

FRANKLIN

Maddelena, as the counsel on retainer here, I think I may legally advise you. Open it now, if you like. Merry Christmas won't suffer.

MADDELENA

I don't like to. It's not time yet.

FRANKLIN
It will never be. I should know. Go on, don't be afraid.
It's just a toy, actually.

*(She begins unwrapping the complicated parcel, which has
parcels inside, styrofoam packing, etc. Jethro helps. Door chimes
again. Hannah goes out, returns hesitantly, unsure what to
show on her face)*

HANNAH
Mrs. Garnet, it's a young . . . man. Says he's from the
District Attorney's Office? Should I. . . .

DOLORES
Adams.

HANNAH
B'lieve that's what he *says*.

DOLORES
(Busy with unpacking) Oh Hannah, don't be so. . . .
Bring him through. He's my guest. It's nothing to do
with you. Remember? You're okay, remember?

HANNAH
I remember. But I don't like this here now. . . .

DOLORES
For God's sake, Hannah, let me fight my own campaigns.

*(She's still absorbed in the dismantling of the gift, which is
coming into view as flashy equipment: complete with VCR,
video camera, wires, et. They pass pieces of it around, ad-*

*miring the elements. ADAMS enters, a simply-dressed, neatly
stylish, black man, handsome and self-confident, pleasant,
yet carrying his poised authority with him from the D.A.'s
Office. Briefly, he gives the great living room with its now
resplendent tree and all that an appreciative look of ap-
praisal. Pursing his lips to whistle with pleasure and admiration)*

DOLORES

I'm over here, Mr. Adams. We started early.

ADAMS

Mrs. Garnet?

DOLORES

(Emerging from the group) I'm Dolores Garnet.

ADAMS

I see you got your tree after all….

DOLORES

No, no. That's not the original one. It was the last
one left on the West Side. And we've had to mutilate
it to et it up here. It has no crown, but — will have
to do for us, don't you think.

ADAMS

Quite a tree.

DOLORES

Do you like it really? Wil it make this Christmas
joyful for us? You never know in advance, do you.
People count on the tree so much. I hate to hang my

hopes on it…. Yet what els is there, after all. So here
we are. Yes?

ADAMS

Just beautiful. *(He is admiring more than the tree alone)*

DOLORES

Hannah, give this man a drink. I know you don't
drink, and you won't bother us, blahblahblah, but
you're off-duty tonight I trust….

ADAMS

The D.A.'s Office is never of duty. But I'd be de-
lighted to have a drink with you.

DOLORES

Wassail! Wassail! I'm dolores, Mr. D.A. Right?
Hannah, he's way behind us, so give a double-double
of whatever. Everybody, this is Mr. D.A. —

ADAMS

It's Adams.

DOLORES

— and he's come all the way up from Foley Square to
help us solve The Mystery of the Missing Merry
Christmas Tree. Meanwhile, he's welcom to join us
for dinner, too. Cops can be handy to have around.
Right, ladies?

(Everyone says Hellooo! over their shoulders)

So what has the Third Wise Man brought us? What's it
supposed to do? Do you know, Mr. D.A.'s Office?

ADAMS

Adams. VCR. Camcorder. Nice.

FRANKLIN

Top of the line. Mini-movie studio. Maybe we should use it right now. I sense . . . difficulty in the air. It is the annual uptight hour in our lives. We are somehow . . . haunted. We know not why, but we're bored . . . somehow restless?

GIDEON

Frankly, I'm hungry.

FRANKLIN

Yes, the animals are pacing. We need, we need, and there is no satisfying our need in a hungry, famished world. Dolores never eats, I know; but we are mortals merely. You can't act on a full belly, however; so let's just shoot now and review the consequences later. Unsound legal advice. But in real life we do it all the time, don't we. Anyhow, we're among friends and loved ones. Right? Right!

DOLORES

Hannah, is dinner ready?

HANNAH

Roast's just getting itself ready to be born, Mrs..Garnet. Five minutes till delivery.

FRANKLIN

Good. Let's see how this contraption works. Maybe we'll find ourselves in it. On the big screen. all right,

Maddalena?

MADDALENA
Nothing's ever for children. Whatever you think you're giving us, we get nothing really.

JETHRO
Amen! Amen!

DOLORES
That's the line going down these days, people. Why do we have children? In order to deprive them. To abuse them. Next thing, you'll say, to eat them alive.

ADAMS
She has something there.

ELEANOR
That is one hell of an expensive gift, if you ask me.

DOLORES
Mere bagatelle. We could have got her a speedboat or something. Anyhow, there's plenty where that came from. Franklin will pick up your next sculpture, Lenny. For cash. And then some.

ELEANOR
Bitch.

DOLORES
Cunt.

VICTORIA
David once ran a short wave station from our cellar, and before he was through buying his equipment I was out

a hundred thousand dollars. Daddy was just fit to be
— and blahblahblah. When it was over, that high-pow-
ered stuff was a dead loss to me. That was the least of it.
You know. And the noise David brought in! Media
maniacs: the whole world talking like crazy. Voices dron-
ing all over the place. He had it rigged so you'd hear
them everywhere, even in the john. He wanted to satu-
rate us with voices. Voices, voices! I was in the tub one
night — really, I kid you not — when all of a sudden
there was this screechy yowling, and David came in
with his face like a zombie, and he says, *I've contacted
them. It's them!* Who? *Them,* he says, *them!* At that point,
I knew he was —

JETHRO
Mother, it was the invasion starting. Dig?

VICTORIA
Invasion, hell. There won't be any more invasions,
Daddy says. David was starting his trip — out of this
world, J.P. Gagaville.

GIDEON
Guerrillas, yes, coups, yes — but, invasions? Not anymore. That's in the past. Romantic pamphlets. Posters.
Wallpaper. Graffitti. Even hi-tech can't hope to hold its
ground. The lesson's been learned.

DOLORES
After there's no ground left to hold!

JETHRO
I mean, it was Kali. It was Siva. The Messenger!

HERBERT

Who?

VICTORIA

Now you stop that nonsense, J.P. Honestly. I have enough with my Semitic demons, and *they're* dead these five thousand years.

JETHRO

Says who.

MADDELENA

How do you know.

ADAMS

Harlem voodoo stuff.

MADDELENA

(To Jethro) They just don't know anything. And they don't *want* to know anything. *(To Franklim)* How do we do this thing?

FRANKLIN

HERBERT, can you handle this rig? Gdeon??

GIDEON

I don't know from gadgets. My assistants do all that.

DOLORES

Henry, for twenty years he has had assistant professors to lug his suitcases, to fetch him from airports, even bring him drinks. His orderlies. They're glad to do it.

What an opportunity for graft — I mean, grants. He hands out grants.

GIDEON

After all, what does it cost me? Look, for the price of a load of bombs, a young man can do some interesting research for eighteen months.

ELEANOR

Gideon, you're on the defensive. Doesn't become you. Hold your line.

VICTORIA

She's got a point.

DOLORES

Shit.

ADAMS

I can do it. Just hand me that camera. *(They unpack it according to his directions)*

VICTORIA

Do we need light?

FRANKLIN

We can always use more light. Now, what shall we shoot — some sonofabitch interview? Our social situation as sitcom? A hard-hitting, high-fashion newscast? A space trek? Or cops and the slaughter of the innocents? Or a wicked, dog-in-the-manger commercial, or just downhome Merry Champagne Christmas? Shall it be family fare, film fun? Or X-rated for intimate friends?

Soft porn? Hardcore? What haven't we seen a thousand times before?

DOLORES

Shoot us we *are*!

ELEANOR

Only as we are?

VICTORIA

Just as *we* are?

DOLORES

As we are. Let us hang it all right out. See what we can see.

GIDEON

And champagne!

JETHRO

Shouldn't you be shooting, man?

ADAMS

I'll get you, don't worry.

HERBERT

A true documentary?

FRANKLIN

For the record.

DOLORES

Truth? I'll believe it when I see it.

FRANKLIN

I think we'll pass, yes. Safe enough, from the legal point of view. Friends, dinner, hour of quiet and hope amidst the fever and struggle and . . .

ELEANOR

. . . all the blahblahblah.
(Sounds of disturbances from far below outside, storm-muffled, blasts, whistles, etc)

MADDELENA

Music might help us along.

ALL

Yes, music!

VICTORIA

Sing something, darling. Doesn't matter what, as long as it moves. Bach, Mozart. Whatever?

JETHRO

Yeah, I'll give you something cool and holy-like.

FRANKLIN

We'll have a solemn procession. Peaceful, joined in a love feast. Goy and Jew and black and white together. Integration. Maddelena, lead us. Shouldn't the child lead us? Eleanor, would you and Mrs. Glasgow —

VICTORIA

Victoria.

FRANKLIN

Would you join me, Victoria — on my right, thank
you? Dolores, you may come last, as our Queen of the
Night, with the good doctor and your task force master. Adams, you're in control. I rely completely on your
skill. Capture us as we are. But use your judgment, too.

ADAMS

Don't worry. I'm the man.

FRANKLIN

Maddelena, begin, won't you. Lead us, lead us kindly
on. Jethro, play as the spirit moves you, right?

JETHRO

Right on.

ADAMS

There you go now.

*(Jethro sings "Radiation." The procession will wind right to left around
the tree, with whatever choreography seems imaginative and appropri-
ate. Hannah will enter and move after Dolores, with a Jamaican dance)*

[JETHRO'S SONG]

"Radiation"

Not one star shining tonight,
The planets are lost out in space,
But the darkness is filled with light,
And the light shines from your face.

What is it that glows in this room,

What is it that drives out the gloom,
And brings us together in peace,
And holds us together like doom?

It's radiation, sisters and brothers,
Radiation, enemies and lovers,
Radiation . . . Radiation. . . . Radiation. . . .

DOLORES

Marvelous, simply marvelous! Jethro, you're lovely. *(She embraces him)* Aren't we wonderful? Aren't we beautiful? Aren't we happy? After all? Oh yes, we are, we are. I'm so glad you're all here with me tonight. Even though you'll never understand. *(She is laughing and weeping at once)* . . . Is that Bobby crying? Sssh. Listen.

ELEANOR

No.

VICTORIA

It's down there. Outside. In that other world.

HERBERT

Bobby's sedated.

HANNAH

Mrs. Garnet, dinner is ready now.

DOLORES

Oh, I wish Jack were here after all!

MADDELENA

Mummy. how can you!

DOLORES

No, dearest, I truly wish he could see us, how happy we all are, even in this fire storm. And you won't even open your mouth all year long, Maddalena. Not even to say I love you. With all the shit that's flying through the world, I don't blame you. But here we are, happy for just this little, little while. Aren't we happy? Aren't we?

ADAMS

That's enough. *(Stops shooting)* You can go in now, folks. Right, Mrs. Garnet?

DOLORES

Right, right! I'm glad you all followed your star and came to *me* tonight. Thank you so much!

(Jethro hums "Radiation," following them in to dinner)

*   *   *

Act II

The company returns from the dinner table, some with demitasse in hand. They are lighting up, cigarettes, pipes, Gideon perhaps with a cigar. ADAMS shoots them coming in and settling down. When he finishes, he will fiddle with the camcorder, extracting tape and loading it to the VCR preparatory to playback. At the far end of the room, a huge TV monitor now faces the audience. Hannah has been emptying ashtrays, setting pillows straight, moving furniture for viewing, But, practically speaking, to make room for the action to come. She will also carry in a great ice bucket with a jeroboam of R^derer Kristall. She will go out for a platter of cakes and a cart of liqueurs, from which brandy, port, etc., are poured. Jethro strum the refrain of ìChicken Delight.î Maddelena is seated by the tree in a lotus-position, ìmeditating.î She wears a harlequin pantsuit, black and white diamonds. DOLORES' guests, replete, are calm, contemplative. They will occasionally go to gaze out at the violent storm whose muffled gusts rattle the double-paned windows. (

THE MEN
Wonderful meal, Dolores! Wonderful. Yes. Terrific! Never ate anything like it. Even at the White House? Even at the White House! *Never* at the White House! Never anywhere. Even if it's my last meal, I'm satisfied.

DOLORES
Praise Hannah.

THE MEN

Hallelujah, Hannah! Hannah, Hallelujah! Food for the soul. Once in a lifetime! A Christmas feast to be remembered!

HERBERT

Cholesterol count in the millions.

GIDEON

Who's counting.

HERBERT

It's a slaughter of the innocents. Kills you sooner or later.

FRANKLIN

Make an exception for suckling pig, Doctor, once a year at least?

GIDEON

Baby pig? Once in a lifetime's enough. Little too sweet, though. I didn't see any apple.

ADAMS

Got to be sweet.

FRANKLIN

I had a piece.

DOLORES

We all had a piece of the apple. Each of us did. I saw to that.

GIDEON

I was in Borneo last year on a stopover, and they dropped
me into a head-hunting banquet. Strictly hush-hush.
You know, it tasted just like that dinner we just had. . . .

ADAMS

You mean you ate human being?

FRANKLIN

Surprised, Adams?

GIDEON

It was just roast meat.

ADAMS

(Still stunned) You ate a human being!

GIDEON

When in Rome. . . . No choice, really. As the U.S.
Government representative. . . .

ADAMS

But you *know* better! You can't sit down with cannibals
and just dip into the fleshpot.

FRANKLIN

He's taken on his friend Jack Garnet's job in life. He's a
relativist.

JETHRO

What does that mean?

FRANKLIN

Doing what comes natural.

GIDEON
I was their guest. It was expected of me.

ADAMS
Jesus X. Keerist. Some things have been forbidden for ages!

DOLORES
Listen! Isn't that — ? *(Jethro strums a few chords of "Chicken Delight," louder this time)*

ELEANOR
No.

DOLORES
But that's a child. Crying.

ELEANOR
Bobby's asleep.

DOLORES
I thought I heard. . . . No, listen.

JETHRO
Now for some more holiday music, folks. This my latest number. I call it "Chicken Delight."

[JETHRO'S SONG]

"Chicken Delight"

Like, you kill me,
— and it isn't enough!
And I kill you,
— and it isn't enough!

And we all kill each other —
the father and the mother,
and the sister and the brother —
— and it isn't enough!

And everyone's a stranger
with a pistol in his fist,
and trippin' out on danger
like some teenage nihilist!

'Cause the smoke's getting' thicker,
and it's coverin' the skies,
we're coughin and we're sicker
while we tell each other lies —
though we're dying with each breath!

Ya! Ya! Ya!

Still we tell each other lies —
'Cause we hate ourselves to death!
I can see it in your eyes!
that we hate ourselves to death . . .

Ya! Ya! Ya!

'Cause we only get one thrill
as we're rollin down that hill,
and everyone's a corpse alone
like a goddamn wailin' evil stone
rollin' down alone, alone!

Ya! Ya! Ya . . . !
She's a-squeezin' on that trigger!
He's a-slashin' with that knife!

They're a-stompin' everybody
that shows a sign of life! or love!
Any sign of life or love!

O Christ! O Christ! O Christ!

We'll just murder anybody
that speaks one word of love:
So never look at nobody!
Never speak that word of love!

'Cause there's one kick left in life,
and we only get one thrill,
to remind us of our life —
and it's — kill, kill, kill!

Ya! Ya!Ya!
Kill! Kill! Kill . . . !

DOLORES

That *is* a child. Crying.

VICTORIA

I heard nothing. But then, we never hear someone else's
child.

JETHRO

You never hear, period.

DOLORES

Maddelena, see if he's — *(Maddelena doesn't respond)*

ELEANOR

I'm Bobby's mother. If I say the child's asleep, Dolores, the child's asleep.

HERBERT

I gave him enough to put *you* away for twelve hours, Dolores.

DOLORES

It was there. And here. Just now. A child. *(Her hand-to-her-bared-breast gesture)* I'm not hearing things. Am I? *(They look at her, genuinely concerned)* It *is* crying! Oh, come on, good people. Listen, and you may hear. Maddelena? *(Maddelena barely twitches her shoulder.*

FRANKLIN

We have it on maternal testimony. You saw him, Eleanor.

ELEANOR

I? I?

FRANKLIN

Medical evidence, then. Overwhelming. Conclusive. At this eleventh hour, what more is needed? Anyone?

JETHRO

Judas Priest! Pontius Pilate. That's what *you* need!

FRANKLIN

Go back to your manger in the stable, kid.

JETHRO

Oh, man?

FRANKLIN

I'll render a verdict, if I may. Considered judgment, rather. And we can wash our hands of it and have our moment of peace. At least. What more can be done? Wherefore, Bobby Steiner was asleep; whereas, he sleeps yet; moreover, will go on asleep. Consensus: the child's sleeping. Case dismissed.

ELEANOR

Thanks, Your Honor.

DOLORES

Drumhead court. Tell it to the Marines. Better a firing squad with no nonsense. Anyone got a blindfold? At least let me have a last smoke, for the love of god! *(Franklin gallantly flicks his lighter for her, as she looks him in the face with a strange expression)* You're the last one to speak, Henry Franklin. Liz was sleeping too.

FRANKLIN

Dolores.

DOLORES

Or so you said. And she's still sleeping.

FRANKLIN

Listen to me, my darling: That's a no-no.

DOLORES

Fast asleep: on the good ship *ANDREA DORIA.* Bottom of the wild Atlantic. In the deep, soft ooze, her bones covered with little shells and barnacles. Hermit crabs peeping from her eyes. How very pretty.

JETHRO
(Soft whistle) Whew-eee. *(Strums some bars of Ariel's Ditty, "Full Fathom Five," etc.)*

DOLORES
You *might* have gone to see if Liz was asleep, Henry. But you did not. Or did you? And now I am not allowed even to suggest that someone should reconnoiter down my own hallway to see to that child. Henry, life is very cheap these days.

FRANKLIN
Thanks. You have no idea what you're saying, do you, Dolores.

ELEANOR
I *told* you, darling. You're *hearing* things.

VICTORIA
It's just the wind, and nothing more. People, this is not the time to. . . .

DOLORES
(Contrite, though unsubdued; just warier of them) . . . What it comes down to. I hear things. Once upon a midnight dreary. . . . Sure. Right in my own home, the small voice of the child cries, unnoticed, unheard. The bitch-mother is deaf. The terror-doctor, deaf. Even these hip, with-it kids here, deaf. *Am* I hearing things? Good people, you have that certain look. . . . and it says, *Dolores* is the crazy. Okay okay. So you've got better information.

FRANKLIN

No appeal from facts. As I should know. But when I forget my facts, I may rest assured Dolores Garnet is there to set me straight. Oh, I can count on Dolores! Right? Right!

ADAMS

Mrs. Garnet, they're your friends.

GIDEON

You can trust us.

DOLORES

You? You? *(Her laughter)*

GIDEON

We're all with you, Dolores. And *for* you. Remember that. We admire you, believe it or not, we really do admire and, uh — love you. Why else would we be here tonight? We could just as well have gone home. . . . After all, it's Christmas Eve.

DOLORES

You should be home in Boston — or Washington or Warsaw or Bermuda or wherever your military-academic love feast is being handsomely catered this time. . . .

GIDEON

Berlin, actually. But, next year — in Jerusalem! *(Herbert laughs)*

DOLORES

Don't crap me, you sociologist, you! You're merely grounded. There's a blizzard tonight.

GIDEON

Actually . . . I came to see you, Dolores. Remember?

DOLORES

Darling, I'm sorry. Really truly and blahblahblah. I shouldn't get you mixed up with Jack, should I. Or with David or Adam or Norman or George or Marvin or Pat or Henry or. . . .

GIDEON

We knew how you'd be feeling. We came to help. Stay with us. Try, Dolores. Makes sense, doesn't it. Dolores?

DOLORES

What does! Nothing makes sense. Admit it, for god's sake.

GIDEON

Calm. Calm. Be reasonable. Or . . . beautiful. Be an angel. You know how.

HERBERT

You can, Dolores. If you try. It's a small thing to ask. Be brave. Strong. Don't give in to it, don't. Brave? Brave now? Dolores?

DOLORES

Give in to what? *(Sweetest of smiles)*

HERBERT

Oh hell.

DOLORES

(Talking about Herbie to the others) Look who's talking! A man without imagination. Without nerves even. Great doctor, though. The best. But, did you ever once in your whole life tell anyone the truth. Herbie?

HERBERT

What do you mean.

DOLORES

Did you?

HERBERT

All right. I've told a lie a day. A hundred thousand lies. So what.

DOLORES

Ummm.

HERBERT

What am I supposed to do. It's a matter of life and death. Death, usually.

DOLORES

Precisely. Life . . . and . . . death. See, ladies? *(She is suddenly feverishly gay)* Lawyer like Henry, that's a man you pay to lie *for* you. Gideon, god bless him, doesn't even know what lying is — he just makes up new *ologies* to fit his research budget. You'd have to dry up Health, Education *and* Welfare, with its billions of dollars and millions of men, before *he'd* see where truth lies hidden. And by then it'd be dead, down the tubes and gobbled up by the eels! But our Doctor Herbie — he's your

barefaced, professional liar. Lies with a straight face. Gets
paid for it, too. Right?

HERBERT

Woman in the office this morning. Lovely woman. Your
age, Dolores. Now, I *know* what she's got, but I say,
*Those headaches are nothing. A little eyestrain, a little hy-
pertension. It's metabolic. Hormonal. Take these pills.* You
know, sugar and spice. Should I hold her by the hands
and look sweetly into her eyes, and tell her that in eight
weeks she'll be unconscious? That before Spring returns,
she'll be dead and gone. Is *that* what you want?

DOLORES

Life is a terminal case.

ELEANOR

I want Spring to come back. For us all. My wish, good
people. It's Christmas Eve.

DOLORES

If ever I get *that* kind of headache, Herbert Simonson . . .

HERBERT

Which, god forbid!

DOLORES

. . . and you don't issue me a communiqué as to what
sort of "migraine" it actually is, so help me god . . .
*(She moves fast to a drawer and pulls out the .38 revolver
she had described in Act 1)* . . . See this? I'll call me a
taxi, if it's the last day of my life I'll call me a taxi, I'll
storm your office, and blow your goddamned lying head
off.

HERBERT
Thanks a lot, Dolores.

FRANKLIN
Hang in here with us. We need you, Dolores. Don't desert your own party now. We'll all back you. Really. I know how you feel.

DOLORES
You? You? People, can you imagine how they live up there, these Henry Franklin corporate counsel types! Fifty storeys up, triplex palaces, Louis Quinze furnishings, wine cellars, Persian carpets like oil sheikhs, walnut libraries, "missing" Goyas and "lost" Vermeers, Renoirs and Braques, de Koonings and Pollocks and Stellas, and Caros and Hepworths and Lipschitzes . . . little bonuses that get racked up by their platinum contracts. . . . While down below. . . .

FRANKLIN
. . . While down below, it's all going to pieces. City's not the same anymore. You can see that. I look out those windows of mine as the sun collapses down there over the river. It's gold, then it's black, that river. And out of the dim chasm below, the hopeful little office lights are climbing up. How far it is to the bottom down there. How far. . . . The city's changed. I don't know. From one month to the next, skyscrapers, towers, terraces and all. Avenues altered, erased. all of it . . . gone!

GIDEON
Growth problems. Building the 21st Century.

FRANKLIN

We send the freshman lawyers out one afternoon every week, pro bono, to take care of their souls, for housing and prisoners and ghetto defence. Pro bono makes them feel better about their 150-thousand-a- year entry-level salary. But I want — to get hold of things. And I can't . The city seems to have grown . . . transparent. How? All that stone and concrete, marble and glass, those cars and trucks and busses and trains and masses of men all moiling down there in that meat-grinder . . . that *phantasmagoria!* And I — I go; I go down; I go down — into that steel and stench; and I walk. In the city. And it's — transparent! As if, as if I were not there. Or as if all those things were not there. And I am strolling. Alone. Hatless. Through the silence. I am naked in the wilderness. Rock. Sand. No trees. Before the beginning. Or after the end. No trees. Nothing. I am the only one. Only I. I alone. . . .

ELEANOR

Told you I found him wandering around at my dealer's.

VICTORIA

The man's in shock.

ELEANOR

He'll have to stay here with us.

DOLORES

He just doesn't want to venture into that howling, frozen swamp of a city. Capital of the world, and you're all scared. Charlie Citizen's infiltrated every district. Elevator's booby trapped. You can't tell Charlie from your own gooks; and your own side's just shitless soldiers. How pathetic. Three such Wise Men taking shelter from the storm with the crazy woman, you know, that Dolores Garnet, in her stable high above Fifth Avenue. And *she* hears a child crying just as we're getting our desserts. Towards midnight, a sick child crying out of nowhere. Is the little bastard an orphan, trapped under the wreckage of our lives? Mr Deputy District Attorney Adams, judging by the cut of you, I'd say you're a married man, right?

ADAMS

Samuel.

DOLORES

Make it Sam, right?

ADAMS

Right, right.

DOLORES

Married, yes?

ADAMS

Don't ask me to take a polygraph.

DOLORES

Oh, for Chrissake! What *is* the password into a man's mind! I see we need a formal arraignment. Are you now or have you ever been . . . married, or whatever.

ADAMS

Was.

DOLORES

But not now?

VICTORIA

You should be. Sam.

ADAMS

That's a personal option.

DOLORES

In theory.

VICTORIA

Most of us should be. Some time. In theory.

ELEANOR

At least.

DOLORES

Not too much, though. Or too often. Then it's just Game Theory.

ELEANOR

Within reason.

VICTORIA

Yes. And no. If you could just hang one of him in the bedroom closet and take it out every a day for a good screw.

ELEANOR

Anyway, we've had it. We're all on the casualty list. Veterans. No more.

DOLORES

Never again?

VICTORIA
Thank god. Grown up at last.

DOLORES
As much as we'll ever be.

ELEANOR
And don't count on those strangers on the other side of Generation Gulch over there — they're enemies. *(Indicating Jethro and Maddelena)*

JETHRO
No way!

DOLORES
(Laughing) Gideon's the only one here who's *still* married. And he hasn't slept with his wife for a year, he says. How's *that* for a squad of mature heterosexuals! See us on a stage and who'd ever believe it!

ELEANOR
Anyone over thirty would.

DOLORES
God, nowadays even the Gays put on a better show. At least they *sleep* with somebody!

GIDEON
Dolores. . . .

HERBERT
In the end it kills them .

ADAMS

Addicts mostly. They don't make such a fuss. They're
dying anyway. You name it, they swallow it.

HERBERT

Depraved.

GIDEON

Displaced persons.

MADDELENA

(Without looking up) Homeless.

JETHRO

Refugees.

GIDEON:

Can you count on that kind to hold up under attack.
Undependable.

DOLORES

Can we count on *you*? What's the difference? You and
your buddies have been shooting your way up and down
the Establishment's corridors for years, and you're still
at it. Let them change the names on those revolving
doors all they like. Anyway you're alive, and I guess
even an urbanologist has to have a sex life. Even a professor.

FRANKLIN

This morning I saw our Presidential Counsel trying to
cross the Avenue of the Americas against the light with
a girl two heads taller and thirty years younger. Furi-
ously happy, he looked, leading her by the elbow, and

grinning like a raw grunt through sleet and slush. She followed him meekly on her long white legs like a dream, ash-blonde hair down to there and sparkling with snow crystals. I wished I was in his galoshes, with a piece of prize loot like that in hand. Try *that* in Red Square.

DOLORES

Oh, screw Red Square. Try it in Washington! They'll make you a headline! But this is New York! Who cares? *(No one hears her)*

VICTORIA

(Very close to him, purring) Sam, why not marry again? I mean, your children shouldn't have to live like orphans.

ADAMS

Who said whatever about children.

VICTORIA

I'm sorry. Couldn't you have children? You look like you could have children. At least.

ELEANOR

Spared them their lives, right? Left them out there un-born. In the blank of limbo. But they're still there, Sam Adams, still waiting to come in. They are very patient. Empty outlines waiting for you to call them. Call your little children in unto you. Dolores hears them. They are crying for you.

DOLORES

(Vaguely) No. No. I don't think I hear *them*.

JETHRO
(Cackling to himself) Oh man, what did I tell you! Off the wall persons! Right off that wall! *(No one listens to him*

ADAMS
(Laughing) My black babies. My little, low-IQ black babies. Bred for slavery, and born to be massacred in this smoky, stony jungle. I do love their strong and docile souls and their enduring hard little heads. And they want me!

ELEANOR
I hear them too. Like my sculptures, I mean. They call out to me to bring them into existence, long before I make them.

ADAMS
Well I wouldn't bring a solitary one of them here into this world! First-degree genocide. You could put me on Death Row for the rest of my life first. Mary felt the same. We quarreled all the time. Over nothing. Couldn't even negotiate over the breakfast table. You know.

VICTORIA
Ever try bed?

ADAMS
Argue in bed with a chick like Mary? Only made her laugh. Uh uh. So we agreed to fight our own wars apart. You know. Conflict of interests?

VICTORIA
She's beautiful. Like you. Right?

ADAMS

High fashion. Jets here and there. You know. Washing-
ton one week. Consulting. One week London-Paree-
Rrrrrrromma. Consulting. Malibu and Acapulco and
Puerto Vallarta, you know, and a week back up in
Harlem to touch home base. Consulting!

VICTORIA

She must be very beautiful.

ADAMS

Now, well she's in with a movie crowd. Kinkies. Grass,
speed, acid, snow, smack and crack, you name it! Cos-
tumes, you know, heavy stuff. Monks and nuns, robes.
Gang-bangs, chains, whips, all colors and all sexes. For
all I know, she's snuffed by now. Out of the picture.

DOLORES

Heard your voice on the phone, and *knew* you were a
man. One of the few surviving. Let me kiss you.

ADAMS

No point in marriage when your soul's turning to red-
jelly shit.

DOLORES

Oh, let me kiss you. I was going to anyway.

ADAMS

No point in it. Is there. *(She kisses him tenderly, intimately. A display of tenderness, not of bitchery. No one pays
the least attention)*

DOLORES

My own dear urbanologist thinks I'm a mad bitch.

GIDEON

I? I?

DOLORES

Because, to be myself, I need . . . love.

ADAM

You complimenting me for being your fantasy darkie, Mrs. Garnet?

DOLORES

Dolores.

ADAMS

For being as miserable up here as on the street?

DOLORES

Same difference.

ADAMS

My reward for not blowing my brains out?

DOLORES

Dolores.

ADAMS

That's all I get?

DOLORES

Think about it.

FRANKLIN

Be a man, Adams. Take it while it's hot.

ADAMS

A Purple Heart. Just for me. Golly gee. Thanks . . .
Dolores.

*(More noise from outside, wind gusting, faint shouts,
whistles, the sound of a helicopter passing almost through
the room.*

DOLORES

What's that, now. Not what I heard before. Lenny, go
look at your baby. Please.

ELEANOR

For the last time! He's four years old. And asleep.

DOLORES

Something's there. I hear it. Crying. Tell me. People?

FRANKLIN

Show time! Adams, plug it all in and get that contraption going. Dolores, sit down. Take some brandy. With
me. Come on, now?

DOLORES

You know I won't touch it, Henry.

FRANKLIN

Do you good now and then. Are we ready? Sound?
Lights? Et ceteras? Is everybody here now? Is everybody
happy? Adams, get going, dammit.

(The grandfather clock whirs, preparing to strike 12. They freeze. Then it starts, slow, sonorous. Dolores leaps up and goes for it)

DOLORES

Christ, we're not through with this evening yet!

MADDELENA

(Sits up sharply, awakening) Mother! You mustn't!

DOLORES

(To the clock, to no one, to them all) Quiet, you! I'll fix you.

MADDELENA

Don't tamper with it, Mother! It's not time!

DOLORES

What do you mean, "It's not time"! I know whatever the hell I'm doing. It's time, all right.

THE MEN

It's time? Time? What's time? *(She opens the case and stops the pendulum. Silence. She turns, dazed, controls herself with a shiver. She is steady, but also disturbed)*

DOLORES

It's just that we all need more time. Don't you see?

MADDELENA

That does it! So now we have none left at all. *(She withdraws into herself again)*

(FRANKLIN holds out a brandy glass, and Dolores takes it, mechanically. He gestures to Adams again. Lights fade, playing of the tape begins. We hear Jethro's guitar, unnatu-

rally loud on the sound track, and the tape of the procession is played. However, we don't see the scene as it actually took place: another will be used, pre-edited. First, a slow pan over each person's face, offering a series of close-up portraits, Until we realize we are seeing more persons in it than were actually in the room. At first the additional people may be fuzzed out of focus, but there is no doubt they are there. They will show up at the first scanning of the principals. Must be done for maximum visibility and effect. Responses of surprise by the characters onstage. Perhaps the portraits may be busts, naked like Roman portrait busts, bare to the shoulders: marmoreal, potent, living statues)

FRANKLIN
What in hell. Herbert . . . ?

HERBERT
Yes. I see. But! Well. . . .

ADAMS
(Notices nothing, since after all they are not his *ghosts)*
Now there you are coming back after dessert, I think? Not bad.

JETHRO
Either There's hash in this fruitcake or, man, I'm just dorking out. Hey, V.G.!

MADDELENA
Mother, what are you doing! *(She's not looked up)* Stop it. Please.

DOLORES
Yes, it is! It is! It is! Yes! *(As though to herself)*

*(As the procession approaches the camera, there are defi-
nitely others visible. And we will see them materialize in the
flesh one by one, as well as on screen. They are the Hungry
Ghosts: Solomon Judah, Liz Franklin, George Simonson,
Jack Garnet, David Glasgow. They may drift into place in
slow motion, but turn substantial in normal time, materi-
alizing when it is their cue to interact with the living in the
room. Till then their marks are unlit)*

SOLOMON JUDAH
*(Beginning with a low, long humming, a rapt keening to
himself on the Blues note)* Ummmmm. Ummmmm.
Hongry. Ummmmmmummm. I'm hongry.

GIDEON
Who the hell's that! Dolores?

DOLORES
(Taking it for granted) Told you about him Were you
even listening? Do you ever listen? *That* is Solomon
Judah.

GIDEON
Who asked *him* in here!

JUDAH
Hush, you! Don't *need* no invite.

GIDEON
What the hell does he want !

JUDAH
Nor no damn permission neither. *(Spoken like the
drunken old field hand)*

GIDEON

Chrissake, Dolores. *(Makes a token move towards Judah, But is repulsed by the man's gesture of disdain)*

JUDAH

You shut up your mouth, you atheist cannibal Jew. Hear? Wipe that baby pigslops off of your chin before I comes and taken your head off and chops you kosher guts and fries me a mess of trayfeh fetts. Ahhhh! And take you eyes and you ears and you tongue and take you heart for horsedovers, and stews you liver and lights for soup, and roasts you red meat and bones like a general welfare meal. Then for a encore fracassee, I takes you balls and slices you little weeny fat dick and makes me sweets fritters all in whiskey butter — oh my, oh my! and then I gon' sleep me a whole jellybelly week in an' 'nother week out. And I will, too! 'Cause I's hongry!

GIDEON

Who let this man in here!

JUDAH

Mister Solomons Judah to you. Now and forever after. Don't you try me, I says! Now then. Where is she, hah?

HANNAH

Right here, Judah.

JUDAH

Where, honey? Oh honey, where you at? *(He seems to be blind, looking vaguely in the wrong direction, as though she were invisible to him)* Come closer here now, honey. Won't you?

HANNAH

Judah, you know I can't, not ever. For why? You's a bloody, brutal kind of man, honey.

JUDAH

Thass all over. Thass over now.

HANNAH

Nothing changes. Never. It's too late. What you want from me.

JUDAH

Hannah, I want. . . . I want, Hannah. . . .

HANNAH

Come too late! You done missed your meal! Only scraps left. Want them leftovers, Judah? Want some old gristley bones and burnt rinds to chew on? You cain't eat that truck? I'd've saved some apart if just you'd've said you's comin' home tonight. But then, you never did say, and you never will. Mind, I always do save some my sweetness for you. Not never no scraps neither.

JUDAH

Comin' home? I *been* here, and I been *here!* Lot of good it done me. Never got no more than their cold trash. Ever since the fust beginning of the beginning. Woman, I am starved!

HANNAH

Too late! Savage! Too late!

JUDAH

Talkin' at you. Hannah. You hear me now! I am talkin' at you.

HANNAH

You, talk? You always yellin' and preachin' and poundin' the four walls. You not talkin'. Uh uh. Fightin' me and fightin' everybody. Always fightin'. And who you ever hurt, Solomons Judah, who? You own self, you hurt! No one but you own poor self.

JUDAH

Yah. Yah. Man don't fight hisself, he ain't no man at-all!

HANNAH

Only trouble is, you lost!

JUDAH

Yah. So. I lost. Never no chance, no way. But, honey woman — you got to respect the defeated too! You jus' got to. Defeated is a honor, too!

HANNAH

I? I?

JUDAH

And now, Hannah —

HANNAH

Stay right where you at. You jus' stay there. Forever. I don' want you. . . .

JUDAH

HANNAH, honey. . . . *(Slides into his Blues. Jethro picks up soft obbligato: bottleneck, lowdown, funky)*

SOLOMON JUDAH'S BLUES

I'm gon' leave muh prison,
    Gon' come up for a meal,
  Gon' ta leave muh midnight prison,
      And I'm comin' for my meal,
I'm hongry, yes I'm so hongry for you, baby,
      Can't say anythin' I feel.

HANNAH
Never did sing before. What's got into him!

JETHRO
Man says he's hungry.

HANNAH
Never could sing before. What's he after!

MADDELENA
Feed him We ought to feed him

GIDEON
Before he hurts somebody.

ADAMS
(Detached) Takes more than food. Oh I reckon he'll kill again.

DOLORES

Frightened, Adams? It's just your own shadow.

ADAMS

I suppose you're not? He'll come after you first.

DOLORES

(Her big laugh is her only response. Judah picks up on it)

JUDAH

They put muh haid where muh ass was,
Tied my arms round my spine,
Stuck my heart in my belly,
Tore my good two legs outta line. . . .
And if I dint have my eyes swole bloody,
I'd get around myself jus' fine.
Yes, Lord! if my two eyes warn't all swole up,
Two eyes swole up so bloody,
You know I'd get along jus' fine.

HANNAH

Don' look at *me*? *They* done it to you, Judah!

GIDEON

I doubt that. Lots of changes have been made. Sweeping reforms in penal theory and practice. Short term intensive rehabilitation treatment. Take my Commission's recent Report to the President. Consult pages 525 through 603.

HERBERT

Whole new spectrum of tranquilizers. Conditioning therapy. Even your violent maniac, even your totally schizoid patient, I mean, like him . . .

FRANKLIN

No saying what he could have done to society. That sort of fellow attacks innocent persons. It's in his eyes.

VICTORIA

I have seen that look in a man's eye. I even married that look. Almost killed me, too. But — what is it?

ADAMS

They imagine most of it. Inflict it on themselves. They expect to be pitied. I know them. Jesus. You could give your whole life over to them and still you'd end up nowhere. Saturday night specials. Winos, Junkies, welfare bums. Homeless now. Crack and needles.

JUDAH

When I come on cryin' for my dinner,
*   Wid my mouth open like the sky,*
When I come on cryin' for my dinner,
*   You gon' have to stuff the world in,*
Baby baby baby, you know the reason why:
*   You jus' gon' have ta feed me, 'fore I die. . . .*

But if you know me not when you see me, baby,
*   You lost your one and only true friend,*
'Cause if you denies me when you sees me, baby,
*   Then your world done reached the end,*
*   Your whole damn world come to its end. . . .*

JETHRO

That is laying it on them. I hear you. Man, do I hear you. It's like, well. . . .

JUDAH

Don' have to say it, But oh, don' you know,
   I don' have to say it, but baby baby baby
Now don' you jus' know
I's the man you's waitin' for,
   Man you's needin', man you's prayin' for,
So don' you say you dint hear it,
   Loud and clear, long, long time ago. . . .

JETHRO

Yeah. . . .

VICTORIA

For talking like that, they suspended you, J.P., and that
mob of nutsos, *students* you call them. I would have
expelled you, all of you! For that, I blame David.

JETHRO

Not for *talking*, V.G. They Don't suspend you for talking. And they Don't expel you anymore. We got our
rights. They busted our heads with gas. They kick ass.
They don't *listen*, V.G.

GIDEON

Neither do you. We try to reason with you, and we try
to tell you. . . .

JETHRO

We heard that bullshit for years already!

GIDEON

(Mildly) Facts. Just plain facts.

MADDELENA

(Sweetly awake) I think facts change from day to day. Don't you? The question is, What do they tell us?

GIDEON

(At a loss; it's a novel question to him) Uh. Could be.

MADDELENA

And they add up, day by day. In twenty years, everything's changed. You don't see it, do you. But I think that quantity changes quality. Don't you know that law?

GIDEON

(Surprised and irritated) But the point is . . .

HANNAH

Honey, Judah, I think of you and I think. all the time. But you know it's no good. I don't know why. Man and wife, and nothing ever any good in it. I don't understand. I never will.

JUDAH

Oh baby I'm gon' leave that prison,
Gon' come up for my meal,
Gone leave that dead man's prison,
And come up for my meal —

And if you can't feed me, baby,
Your whole damn life ain't real,
You cain't treat me right, baby,
Your whole damn life's not real,
No, no, no, your whole damn life, baby,
Jus' ain't never gon' be real. . . .

(Solomon Judah subsides little by little, curled into a dark, catatonic ball off to one corner, his eyes gleaming, watching the rest. He has done his work as the first ghost messenger)

LIZ
(Becoming gradually visible) And I should know. Oh, should I know!

FRANKLIN
I won't discuss it. Not here. Not now.

LIZ
You don't like to show what a sharp lawyer you are, Henry. But when it comes to smarts, you've got them, all right.

FRANKLIN
What do you mean.

LIZ
Oyez! Oyez! Oyez! This is an adversary proceeding. Defend yourself, Henry Franklin!

FRANKLIN
No contest, Liz.

LIZ
Shall we take a body count?

FRANKLIN
You win, you win.

LIZ
Can we talk? In open court?

FRANKLIN

I won't give you a hearing.

LIZ

Court of last resort?

FRANKLIN

No, Liz, no. A thousand times no!

LIZ

I want to talk. What harm in it. Come on, Henry. Talk.
Let's. You and I.

FRANKLIN

I can't . I'm so alone.

LIZ

You have me.

FRANKLIN

I never had you!

LIZ

Not even then?

FRANKLIN

Just what are you getting at, Liz? I warn you: I'll hold
you in contempt.

LIZ

All right. Truce, kiddo? *Nil obstat*, Mr. Franklin?

FRANKLIN

Oh Liz, Liz.

LIZ

Good people, he doesn't trust me. Shall we adjourn to Judge's chambers?

FRANKLIN

What do you *want!*

LIZ

Let's us confer in private. Chamber of horrors, Henry.

FRANKLIN

But we can't just act as though anything is possible —

LIZ

The man's forgotten. Already. So soon.

FRANKLIN

What do you *want* from me!

LIZ

You won't get away with it!

FRANKLIN

Case was settled. Long, long ago. Who remembers? Statute of limitations, Liz!

LIZ

I don't give up. Do you hear me! I don't ! Never ever.

FRANKLIN

Whenever that was. I forget. Long, long ago. Settled for good.

LIZ

Never!

FRANKLIN

It cannot be reopened, Liz. It's been, oh, years and years, Liz. At least.

LIZ

As long as things are like this, I won't give up, Henry. I'll fight you. I'll fight everyone with you. I'll never give up.

FRANKLIN

I can't go on with it. Forget it.

LIZ

I'll petition for another round of talks. Appeals to a higher court. Arbitration!

FRANKLIN

Let it drop. I *won't* fight, Liz.

LIZ

For another hearing. And another and another. Till you drop. And you *shall* hear me!

FRANKLIN

Please. Dismiss it from your mind.

LIZ

I'll sue, I'll sue and sue , Henry. You'll never get out of this one alive. Don't you dare put in for dismissal of charges! Not on me!

FRANKLIN

It's over. I'm simply not in it with you anymore, Liz.
Can't you understand?

LIZ

Not in it! How dare you!

FRANKLIN

Neither are you. Even if they write a book about it.

LIZ

Never. Never never never! I will be heard.

FRANKLIN

All right. What do you want from me.

LIZ

What do I want from him? he says. What do I want! I
want an explanation. At least.

FRANKLIN

Case closed. No venue in this District. Go somewhere
else.

LIZ

He doesn't listen, people. He still won't hear me.

FRANKLIN

Can't review it. No appeals. Period!

LIZ

Once more. Darling. Let's. Something. Just once more.
Maybe I didn't understand. Darling?

FRANKLIN

Don't you dare pull that on me. You should know better, you with *your* IQ! This is ridiculous.

LIZ

Just listen to him, good people.

FRANKLIN

Besides, who's to judge. Tell me that. Who could judge?

LIZ

Ladies and gentleman of the jury. Thirteen years of marriage. Two lovely daughters growing up. Someday to become women. And he's still unable to acknowledge my existence. People!

FRANKLIN

God damn you black and blue!

LIZ

Town house on Park Avenue. Country place in Connecticut, 160 acres, drained at the south end — no beavers. Lily pond with 3 bronze Queens by that rising young sculptor, Eleanor Casey. How lovely they are in all the passing seasons, that patina growing over everything, rusty green, like old money money money! Shack in the Virgin Islands, and a 60-foot ketch to get there with. Fat corporate retainers just flowing in all the time! And a wife written up in *Vogue*, the Sunday Times society page, *with* photos. Too classy for People mag, though. Even too classy for the Cape and all that new Mafia money. How lovely she is, is Liz Franklin! Yes, and she writes novels too, and blahblahblah. It's lovely and it's

tidy-tidy and it's lovey-loving and so remarkably
blahblahblah. . . .

FRANKLIN

You crazy cunt.

LIZ

You left me. Henry Franklin! You left me there!

FRANKLIN

Oh Jesus God.

LIZ

Got him now. Don't deny it. Hah! Comes the crunch,
and oh oh oh! What a scene, and he loses his nerve in
the countdown. *(She laughs)* Left me . . . and my lovely
girls. Just growing into women.

FRANKLIN

Sophy. Pearl. They never got over it.

LIZ

People! *What do you mean?* he says. *Can't talk here,* he
says! Good people!

FRANKLIN

All right.

LIZ

I ask you.

FRANKLIN

If we must.

LIZ

Well, thank you. Ready my deposition, Your Dishonor?

FRANKLIN

What do you want from me.

LIZ

Me to know. You to find out.

FRANKLIN

The bitch will drive me to the wall.

LIZ

And up against that wall too, you motherfucker!

FRANKLIN

Liz, Liz!

LIZ

We should pity *him*? Yet look at *me*. What do you see.
Look!

FRANKLIN

(Not really looking) Well, ah. . . .

LIZ

Exhibit A: Liz Franklin.

FRANKLIN

Well, yes. What I expected.

LIZ

Good good! A beginning. At least.

FRANKLIN

Again?

LIZ

Got to start somewhere.

FRANKLIN

But why here?

LIZ

And why not.

FRANKLIN

Why now.

LIZ

Why the hell not!

FRANKLIN

My god.

LIZ

Here *and* now. I have waited so long. To begin. The facts.

FRANKLIN

If we could just make an end of it. Here, and now, I'd give you my *nolo contendere.* In writing.

LIZ

Never!

FRANKLIN

What I suspected. Oh dear, dear god!

LIZ

Too late! Look closely now. Try to remember now. *(As she talks on she disrobes. By the end of this scenelet her body will be revealed to us in a bloody peignoir. When it falls away, we see her woman's body, broken, crushed)* Fifty thousand dollars. Beautiful clothes. A whole new Balenciaga wardrobe. Second honeymoon. Madrid. Or third, fourth, whatever. Two weeks in the fitting room during the siesta every long afternoon. Mornings in the Prado. What was Henry Franklin doing? I dunno. Initialing contracts for bomber bases, I guess. Or hiring ten thousand extras for the Battle of Carthage or Waterloo or the Siege of Troy. Which scenario was it that time, bombers, yes? Refinery? Fuel depots? Cut-rate in Madrid, and strategic. But I was stripping most of the loot from him at Balenciaga's. Week on Costa del Sol and on to Gibraltar. I don't like to fly, so we board a new ship, maiden voyage. Not mine, though. I have my two daughters with me. Trophies from my own maiden voyage years and years ago. Fast trip, but you never reach shore again, do you? So here I am, last night out, standing in my nightgown, with a whole new trousseau for the whole new season of life — we're still at peace on this trip. I am, at least — give a girl 50 thousand bucks' worth of Balenciaga, and you'll appease her, you guys . . . long enough for a 30-day cease-fire, say? — and I am humming to myself, all my valises and trunks open, I am counting out my honey. . . . And where's Henry the Ninth? where is he at 23:00 hours? Up in the lounge, drinking men and money? When along comes a black ship to smash in her bows! *(Hysteria barely under control)* Right there on a quiet, foggy night in the empty Atlantic, the prow of that damn Swede crashes through! Right through the wall of my cabin, right down the middle of my cabin, right between our beds, and carries me off through the corridor and through the elevator, my god! the empty elevator shaft, and presses me flat against the wall like you'd crush a cigarette. And there I am, Henry. And the siren's whooping and the gongs gonging and the feet of the crew clomping along, *Mamma mia! Mamma mia!* and the Doria's tilting, tilting . . . all night long . . . and every rat goes sliding with them into the sea, taking all the boats, and yelling away in the night and fog. But — no one cares to come for me. La Doria, La Doria! *Finita, la storia!*

FRANKLIN

I cared. I came, Liz.

LIZ

Not enough! You heard me there in that shaft.

FRANKLIN

Liz, I still *see* you in that shaft.

LIZ

Pinned on my back against the shaft by that ten thousand tons of ghastly Swedish steel, bleeding from my ears and my mouth and my eyes, bleeding from every hole in my poor body . . . and you stand there, ax in hand like some rookie fireman. . . .

FRANKLIN

 . . . and I try to chop away at that fifty feet of goddamn Swedish steel . . . !

LIZ

When all I ask of you is one swift blow to the head! Why don't you kill *me*, Henry?

FRANKLIN

Is that what you mean? Is that what you want!

LIZ

Why can't you end it for us, Henry. That blinding pain! I feel it, Henry, here, here, here! Why can't you take pity on me. At least.

FRANKLIN

Kill you?

LIZ

Mercy, Henry! Have you have no mercy in you!

FRANKLIN

(Stunned) I? I?

LIZ

Ladies, before you judge him, you should know this: after ten years with his left hand in my twat and the other at my throat, ten years squeezing the best I have out of me till my boobs were bursting with blood, you yellow, sadistic, torturing bastard, you coward, you! you stand there in the door of that elevator shaft, and you. . . . Look at me!

FRANKLIN

Ship's tilting. It's dark. Suddenly quiet. Awful. The Swede backs away. She tears herself out — that grinding and scraping of steel on steel . . . like being inside an avalanche in a mine. . . .

LIZ

. . . and you leave me there in that dark elevator shaft, pinned to the wall in a puddle of bones like a bag of bloody garbage. Alive. And you. . . .

FRANKLIN

All right. I can't stand it anymore. I run.

LIZ

Ax in hand, you run away.

FRANKLIN

But you're quiet. You are dead, I think. Maybe, you must be, you have to be —

LIZ

No I am not. I never was. Call that loyalty? Call that love? Look at me.

FRANKLIN

I can't hear you. Can't see you anymore.

LIZ

Throwing your wife alive to the sharks? Ah, what a frenzy of sharks feeding !

FRANKLIN

You are dead!

LIZ

Look at me, I say. Coward! You traitor, Henry Franklin. Ladies and gentlemen, the Prosecution rests.

FRANKLIN

Persecution, you mean.

LIZ

I hope you get life! Forever and ever!

FRANKLIN

You'll never prove your case.

LIZ

Give it up!

FRANKLIN

What?

LIZ

Surrender yourself!

FRANKLIN

I will, I do appeal. Liz!

LIZ

Liz? Liz? Don't expect a pardon from me! And so, goddamn you to hell.

FRANKLIN

But, good people. . . .

GEORGE SIMONSON

. . . We're all good people. We wouldn't be here, if we weren't g-g-good p-p-people. *(A stammerer, George is)* But then something h-h-happened to us. We d-d-didn't do it, d-d-did we. Ac-ac-accident, is all.

(George Simonson wears his long white lab coat. His feet are naked in hospital slippers. He is made up in the terminal looks of his own liquefaction. He will be taking off his lab coat and we will see his hospital gown, and then he will peel off pieces of his body as he talks. No one heeds him, except Maddelena, who stares fixedly, blankly, in his direction with horror, her legs trembling, her hands trying to lift to point at him, terrified and failing)

DOLORES
What do you think of therapy, Herbert? *(Indicating the girl)* Should I treat her. Can it actually help?

HERBERT
Depends.

GEORGE
F-f-feel someone, they said. L-L-Love someone, they said. At least.

HERBERT
Calculated risk. Sometimes worse than surgical intervention. Like transplanting a heart. And you need more than faith.

GEORGE
I wanted to go to the stars. That's all I w-w-wanted.

HERBERT
Medicine. Even science. You never know. Of course nowadays these young people do have problems.

GEORGE
I dreamed of finding new galaxies. Everywhere. Even n-n-nearby right at hand. Shining through all the wreck-

age and d-d-dust of the universe. Shining. all that l-l-light! And we all l-l-live in this . . . this d-d-darkness.

HERBERT
We need more knowledge. The human enterprise. Exploration. Their future, after all.

GEORGE
Live down here in the dark. D-D-Dark in the midst of all that l-l-light. *(He holds up a radiant cube of "the material")* Even inside a m-m-mere lump of m-m-matter, there are stars, invisible stars. Sh-sh-shining!

HERBERT
But it's dangerous, of course. You never know. My BROTHER George, for instance.

GEORGE
And st-st-stars inside the stars! I wanted to know. I w-w-wanted. At least.

HERBERT
He'd started analysis about that time. Was making progress in his therapy, I think. But then . . . that accident.

DOLORES
And he never loved anyone at all.

VICTORIA
I think I could have loved him

HERBERT
Never had time to. Loved his work. He was making some progress, I think.

GEORGE

Alpha rays. B-B-Beta rays. G-G-Gamma rays.

HERBERT

Then, without his even knowing it, he died. Just like that! Absorbed by his work.

GEORGE

But it was all an ac-ac-accident!

HERBERT

Never had the slightest chance.

GEORGE

Ga-ga-gamma rays!

DOLORES

Pity.

VICTORIA

I began to love him Even after he killed my horse. At least I began. A little. At least.

HERBERT

Nothing to be done. And he had nothing more to say. Not to anyone.

GEORGE

Ga-ga-gamma rays. And, alpha, and beta, and ga-ga-gamma! Gamma! Gamma! Gamma! *(He fades into a flash of blinding light)*

JACK GARNET

I do, though. Lots. To say.

MADDELENA

(Speaking slowly, tranced. Does she even see him at first?) I knew you would come. For me, Daddy. At least. That's why we have the tree. For you, Daddy.

JACK

And lots. I never did get to say some things.

DOLORES

Aha!

JACK

Need to say. I. . . . *(He wavers. A strong speaker, pedantic and exact, yet also always wavering, as though confused, not really knowing what he means or sure of what others mean)*

DOLORES

Oho! *(She jeers, but she is never quite that certain with him, either)*

JACK

Give me a sign, Dolores.

DOLORES

(Suddenly exhausted) Tired of talk. No more talk. Can't hear you. Anymore.

JACK

(Perky) Fine tree, Maddelena. Where did you find such a beauty left standing in this zone?

MADDELENA

It was the last one, Daddy!

DOLORES

Long story. Tired. Tired.

MADDELENA

Why don'tyou ever call me your Maddy? Talk to me, to me. At least.

JACK

Sweetie . . . I can't . . . reach you. Your mother's broken off all contact. It's always a state of emergency. She's jamming me. Can't get through to you.

DOLORES

I? Jamming? I?

JACK

Belligerency footing. Martial law pending. Oh, yes, she is definitely a hostile. War, war! Her whole family: they are hostile to me. She won't make peace, ever. Keeps me on the defensive. Mobilized. We could never observe a cease fire. Violations every day. Shelling, shelling.

DOLORES

From both sides. Oh, Jack!

JACK

Capitulation. What she wants. Unconditional surrender. Peace without honor. Submission. I had hoped *you* might mediate. At least.

DOLORES

Jack, Jack.

JACK

Never loved me!

MADDELENA

Daddy. I'm here. I love you.

JACK

Never. Now, when I need to come in from the cold to talk, to say . . . oh, lots of things. Because I had no time actually. Never was time. What was I doing! Fighting out there. Enemies everywhere! Here too! Infiltrated.

DOLORES

Jack!

JACK

What was wrong with this . . . this. . . . Even here in my home at least — no sanctuary for me.

DOLORES

Jack Garnet!

JACK

Good people, tell me. With all my might I was doing good. Wasn't I doing good all along, doing right? For the world. For people. At least.

DOLORES

Wrong! Never ever. all wrong. Ask Gideon. He should know. Gideon, for god's sake, send him a signal. You were buddies. At least.

GIDEON

I? Dolores. You want me to call in fire on my own position? Keep your Silver Star. I don't want your Bronze Medal of Valor. Bleeding hearts, all of you! I'm wised up.

DOLORES

See? He's another. What good can he do, when he does it all wrong, from here! *(Showing her heart, baring her breast and pointing to her heart, in that gesture of the Jesus of iconography)* My heroes!

JACK

How could you do that to me. How could you. We are man and wife, Dolores.

DOLORES

You came swimming back up out of the ether, Jack. And you had that silly nurse by the crotch, that nurse with her tight little, white little, mini-skirted ass, and you were making a date for lunch.

JACK

Who told you that!

DOLORES

Stroking her hot little ass like you'd known her a whole week. At least.

JACK

She told you. Didn't she. You sisters sure stick together, Don't you.

DOLORES

Oh, shit, Jack! I was sitting by your bedside like a good wife when you woke up.

JACK

Well, I wasn't conscious. Coming out of anesthesia. I really Don't remember.

DOLORES

Your crummy little hernia, Jack. Private nurses for the lecherous boy. Who did you think you were, the President? Well, she was the last one. I never kept a body count, but she was the last one. I missed the others.

JACK

Others? Others?

DOLORES

You just had to score off the females of the world, poor things. Couldn't help it, could you. Picked off whatever cunt came creeping down the jungle path into your sights .

JACK

That was just banging, Dolores.

DOLORES

Just banging, says he. And good people, I am supposed to watch him booby-trapping himself? Whatever for dear god! At 38, ladies, at 38 that man has himself a massive coronary that no one even hears for a week because it's tearing at the back of his heart. Though I hear it, all right. His whole Garnet tribe thinks he's overworked, stressed out because of Dolores, or he's got the

flu and he's anxious about his crazy wife, Dolores, and
he's got five books to finish writing, five books all con-
tracted and paid for in advance . . . but he is not writing them. Because . . . ? Because he is worried worried
worried! What will the Senate sub-committee say if he
is not there for the conference on the Progress of Crime,
or the Hearing on the Air-conditioning of Underground
Movements, or testifying on Women and Defensive al-
liances for the Promotion of Voluntary Death Controls,
and blahblahblah. . . . Okay? But — I *hear* that coronary. I *see* that coronary in the man's gray face. Panic!
He's in a real panic.

JACK

I? I?

DOLORES

Now he wants life. *Now* he thinks of living, just as he is
about to become a number! Put Jack Garnet in the files,
put him on the waiting list for a new heart, add him to
the computer's program for that zigzagging dot on the
cross-index of ventricular occlusions and their vicissi-
tudes by race, age, occupation, height, weight, and
number of years of education. Okay? Too late, Jack!

JACK

How you hated me.

DOLORES

Has Jack Garnet written a single note for any of those
five books? He doesn't even know what these books are
about! I made up the five titles for him I wrote them
down myself on those contracts for him You don't have
to be tied for first place in the Harvard School of Law
for that, Jack! Such a panic that man's in. What do you

think he does to make his peace with the super powers of Life and Death? Are you ready, good people? He goes right ahead doing *good* all around the world, just to keep the Garnets' philanthropic, public service flag flying . . . and preserving our way of life here and abroad, as well as incidentally preserving the Garnet bucks too. But *I* know he's panicked. That is why he is flitting from Washington to Tokyo to New Delhi to Istanbul to Paris to Rio and beyond, drinking Röderer Kristall champagne with what'shisname, that Fail Safe engineer at the Pentagon: and eating, drinking, smoking, and just banging away at every mercenary little twat that sings out, Wuv me! Wuv me up! What's it supposed to prove, that you're a man? Shit, Jack.

JACK

And how you still must hate me.

DOLORES

I? I?

JACK

You really only loved Pierre. Not me. Pierre always. And when Pierre drove his Ferrari into that tree at 150 miles an hour, you flew to Bordeaux to pick up the pieces. You buried him, and you cried with his mother and his sisters, and then you screwed his brother in Biarritz — a whole goddamned month of condolences for Pierre. Oh, unlucky Pierre. Happy Ricardo, though. A month in the sack Ricardo has with my wife Dolores. And what are they doing? Crying and fucking, and fucking and crying! And I'm supposed to lie plugged into my hospital bed for that! I? I? Oh no! For Pierre *and* his brother, too?

DOLORES

(Her big laughter) That was just banging.

JACK

What was so great about Pierre.

DOLORES

You wouldn't understand.

JACK

That's how you took care of me. Sure, sure. Fine, woman, just fine. From year to year to year, you thought only of Pierre. A wine merchant! A Catholic millionaire! And a Communist, too!

DOLORES

You couldn't understand.

JACK

What do you mean by that?

DOLORES

Jack, I married *you*. I had *your* daughter, Jack. I followed you to the cemetery. Which is more than Mother Garnet did for you, or your sister, or your brother! I buried you while Mother Garnet goes off on her cruise in the Caribbean. She had her tickets already, and one couldn't really expect her to change her plans just for her own son's funeral, blahblahblah. But you — you put everything away in a dozen different banks from Texas to L.A. to Zurich, for all I know. And you forgot to leave an inventory of stocks and bonds, and you *never even put our names in your Will, Jack!* And what a crummy will it is. And you a lawyer, first in your Class at Harvard

School of Law. And what a lovely time I am having now. If the Garnets don't drink it all dry, Henry Franklin will suck up the dregs.

JACK

Franklin's a hell of a good man for Probate Court work.

Dolores.
But the Will, Jack!

JACK
Well, I was never into Wills and Trusts.

DOLORES
What!

JACK
So I forgot. I meant to look it up. I got involved with that pipeline, and there was that tanker spill. They were sabotaging us! It was an international crisis.

DOLORES
You forgot?! They were sabotaging us? Who, us?

JACK
Their guerrillas. Fanatics. Another month, and we would have lost our hold on them. . . .

DOLORES
Too busy for years after a major coronary! Oh Jack, get out of that argument. You'll step on one of your own anti-personnel landmines yet. Give that strategy up. It's too late. Fifteen years of war, war, war. You won't

make it, Jack. Your heart knows it — but you don't know your own heart.

JACK

You never loved me, Dolores.

DOLORES

Oh, love, love.

JACK

Yes! What I mean. Love!

DOLORES

People! Good people. I lie awake at night. Towards daylight I say to myself, I say, *If I could only just get my hands on Jack Garnet again. I would. . . . I would. . . .*

JACK

Here I am. I'm waiting.

DOLORES

I'd. . . kill you!

JACK

Me? Me?

DOLORES

Kill you! Yes, kill you!

JACK

Hear that? People!

DOLORES

You got away. Bastard. Oh, you just got away from me.

JACK

I? I did?

DOLORES

Thinking of your own sweet self, as always. Hit and run. Woman-killer! You just went and checked yourself out.

JACK

I don't understand. My darling. DeeDee!

DOLORES

And you will never understand. Your whole existence was wrong. And I didn't see it till now. I stalemated my poor life with you. But now I know: I will never make peace with you!

JACK

But we can't go on like this forever. We have to arrange a settlement. Now.

DOLORES

Peace now, huh? He wants peace now! Listen, Jack: my lawyers are talking to your lawyers. Okay?

JACK

But DoDo, I *am* talking to you! Listen for once, goddamn you.

DOLORES

And I can't quite see how I can offer you any conditions you'd be willing to initial.

JACK

Dolores, communiqué? I want . . . to come . . .
home . . . to you. Any terms you name. To be. Here.
With you. At least.

DOLORES

No.

JACK

Any terms you name. Just let me be! Dolores!

DOLORES

Never.

JACK

Let me come. Give me your breast. Take pity.

DOLORES

Never! *(Scornfully, she opens her robe)*

JACK

I want. . . . I need. . . . You. Dolores! At least!

DOLORES

Drop dead. *(Her big laugh is full of contempt)*

DAVID GLASGOW

Yeah yeah. This looks the place to crash. *(Gesturing to
invisible companions)* Come on. It's cool. God, but I am
strung Out. You better believe it. Yeahyeahyeah! *(Yelps
wildly, like a drunken Pole)*

VICTORIA
Devil! No you don't ! Not here!

DAVID
Nobody home. 'S cool. Nobody here at all, man. Nobody but us heads. Us vipers. Fiends. Freaks. Monsters.
Humongous shit, man. *(Cackles)* I vote we come on in
here. 'S okay, peoples. We're home. Home at last!

VICTORIA
I warn you, Spook! *(She is a big cat, rearing back, spit-
ting)*

DAVID
(Still talking to his unseen companions) Sisters! Brothers!
We will let it all hang out here. The entire basket of
worms. At least. Ball, ball, and ball. No clothes here to
hide the truth. No more hassles. Free bread. It is the
ultimate. Peel, peel, peel. Let us remove our skins! Home
at last. See? Take out their batteries, and they just stop
dead. Goombye, all you plastical people! Peace, peace
at last. After what I have been through? Life. Man, oh
man!

VICTORIA
I forbid you!

DAVID
Oooooooo, but they messed in my skull. all in pieces,
like they broke down my Porsch engine and laid it out
on the bench and went away and never came back from
lunch and left me to get the shit all together again —
without a single friggin' tool in the whole friggin' shop!
What a ripoff! Goddamn!

VICTORIA
David Glasgow!

DAVID
Yes, Ma'am? *(Innocent-voice mockery)*

VICTORIA
They put you down for ten and life. So how did you get out?

DAVID
Stone walls do not the prison make. Come again, Ma'am?

VICTORIA
How did you get here!

DAVID
Y'all still in you li'l ol' box, lady? Ax me another, Ma'am. Come on. Gimme five! Tscha!

VICTORIA
Stop that mountain man put-on.

DAVID
Wise up, V.G. At least.

VICTORIA
Why are you here now?

DAVID
Come again, V.G.

VICTORIA
What do you want, David.

DAVID
Once more, bitch. Pretty please.

VICTORIA
I ask you for the last time, What do you want here!

DAVID
What do I want. Nothing. Just a little boomboom. Start praying while I get my clothes off. Man, it's so hot in here! Because you can't hide that Babylonian cunt from me now! You got old, cold Babylonian spells around it, V.G. I can smell them spells. But for once, I am going to burn on through and reach your witchy, frozen heart. *(Yelps like a wild dog)* Are you ready? *(Pig snuffling sounds)*

VICTORIA
(Unfrightened) You weary me, David. Just where are you coming from this time.

DAVID
(Abruptly fading in his power and volume.) Man, that is one nowhere trip, V.G.! You guys gotta help me. At least. *(Addresses the other shadow people, and the people in the room, as well as the audience by implication)* This is one castrating broad. And like, zap! all a man's manna-baraka-spunk shrivels up inside him, and his aura, like, shrinks to zilch? when she unleashes that cold-cock, evil, Babylonian cunt spell at you! That is one freezing bottomless crevasse you got there, V.G. There lie the peckers of many brave men, and husbands too, yes! all junked at the bottom of Victoria's gap, and she's still

crunching away at them down there. *(Another howling yelp)* You better believe it. And I am down there too. Help! Help! *(Zany laughter, desperate laughter, as he strips his clothes off and circles Victoria warily, stroking his pudendum aggressively, balls-hoicking. Victoria, on guard in a semi-crouch, turns on her heels, at bay, her left hand guarding her solar plexus, her right arm out warding him off, her middle finger pointed at him like an Australian aborigine's pointing bone)* You minerals! Vegetables! Animals! Listen up — I have brought the sublime poop for all you folks out there. Dig this now: I am slipping the real, actual, fucking apocalypse shit to you! Like, man, it is war! Are you ready?

VICTORIA

David, don't. I beg you.

DAVID

If I could just . . . V.G. . . . . But I can't now. Tell you what it's like.

VICTORIA

Take what you want, and go, Spook! *(She sinks down, rolls over. Through his next utterance, she writhes in slow-motion, slowly jerking herself as in a dream orgasm. It comes slow and hard to her. In the end she subsides)*

DAVID

I am here to tell you. I see war, war to the end! War against the earth, war against the mountains of the earth, against the rivers and the seas, war against the clouds and the trees, against the insects and the birds and the beasts. War! War against the moon, and all the planets! — war against the sun, and all the stars in space . . . War! I bring you war, war everlasting!

VICTORIA

Ahhhhh. . . .

DAVID

I tell it like it is, man. I kid you not.

(Maddelena and Jethro join in his song)

LIVING SOUL LAMENT

There's a million men on my right hand,
                and a million on my left,
        There's a million men above me,
                And a million underneath.
And it's dark and it's quiet, and it's warm and it's damp,
And we're lyin' still like lumber, still and breathing . . .
        But not one in all those millions will ever speak a
        word,
        No, not one in all those millions will ever speak a
        word:

        For our lips are shut forever,
        And our tongues are down our throats,
        And our eyes are wide as rat holes
        Eyes black and filled with nothing,
        Filled with nothing but the dark —
Oh god, oh god! not a word from all these millions in the dark!
        For we're resting and we're sighing,
        And we're waiting for an end,
                Waiting for the end to come.

And we're stacked up on each other
        Under pressure in the dark,
                Till our bones crack through each other,

And we fuse and join like lovers,
  Rotting slowly hard together in the dark.
Like clay and mud we're fusing, fusing in the dark,
And our flesh and bones are turning into shit.
While we're waiting here and thinking,
Oh god! how hard we're thinking in the dark . . .

And man, it's one tremendous thought,
  A thought that sounds like prayer: God! oh god,
oh god!
Coming bubbling, bursting up like prayer, Oh,
God!
    Don't you hear it all the time?
    Saying, We're here! We're here!
    Whispering day and night together,
    We're here, we're here, we're all down here!
Whispering forever, We're all down here, oh god!
we're here!
    While the earth revolves around us:
    Sliding, cracking, heaving, groaning,
    Folding up like boiling mush —
    Continents and oceans grinding,
        Grinding everyone to slush!

The waters far above us,
  And the mountains pressing down,
  And rains of fire blowing, blowing burning
sparks that fall,
    Falling fires falling through the stone and dark-
ness
    Till we burn with life and death —
But we cannot move a muscle
Not a twinge can cross our face,
    For we're lying packed here thinking:
        This is such an awful place!

Thinking one, silent, roaring thought:
This is sure an awful place! God! oh god, oh god!
But — we thank you for this place!
We thank you, thank you, thank you,
God!
We sure do thank you for this place!

Since there's neither hell nor heaven,
But the world is all there is,
And it has to start and finish like a thing,
A thing like you, a thing like me —
And it seems to have no purpose, like a thing —
A thing like you and me, oh god!
But to bring us into being,
And then to leave us here!
With our thoughts that never stop,
Like consciousness, like prayer!
So we lie here stuck together,
Calling out, Oh God! oh god! oh god!
If you listen hard and long,
If you listen carefully,
You will hear us calling out, God! Oh god, oh
god!

And you know it's where you'll be:
Packed in shit and garbage
With everything that's been,
Every thing That's ever been!
And waiting for the others, God, oh god!
And thinking thinking thinking:
We're here, oh God! forever!
Packed in shit and garbage
With everything thing that's ever been!
We're here, oh God! forever!
We're here, we're here, we're here!

DAVID

And that, V.G., is what it's like. Truly. I kid you not.
See you laaaater. . . . *(Fades out)*

*(Dolores and Eleanor lift Victoria to the couch. Maddelena
and Jethro have retreated to a corner, she huddled against
him, both averting their faces. Herbert examines Victoria's
staring, iconic and rigid unconsciousness, shakes his head,
noncommittally, takes the black bag Hannah has brought
in and holds out to him, and gives her a shot, which immediately relaxes her into a deep sleep. Henry Franklin
already has his overcoat on. People move in a blurred way,
slightly out of synch with one another and with time, as it
were)*

ELEANOR

Going, Henry? Leaving us here defenseless, as you see.

FRANKLIN

You are no more defenceless than the dead. But we can't
really stick together, can we. We are essentially going to
go it alone.

ADAMS

I don't think I can stand any more of this action myself.
(Putting on his coat too)

GIDEON

Pulling out and leaving me to guard the fort. Thanks,
men.

HERBERT

What about me. You can't leave me here.

FRANKLIN

Can you minister to a mind diseased?

HERBERT

I can put it to sleep. At least.

FRANKLIN

Then, Doctor, you do just that.

HERBERT

It helps. At least.

DOLORES

Hannah, these boys are crying in the dark. They are thinking of deserting. Let them go.

(Hannah sets the pendulum going again. The clock resumes and finishes striking twelve. They all move about normally once more, as though waking from a century of sleep)

FRANKLIN

Well, now, it's Christmas Day after all! The one day we have. Let's call for a cease fire. At least.

HERBERT

Dolores, does she have a history of epilepsy?

GIDEON

I could use a nightcap.

FRANKLIN

Let's have it at my place. You can doss down in the guest room.

GIDEON

Yes, I'll need some sleep. At least.

ADAMS

I'm glad you have your tree, Mrs. Garnet. At least.

HERBERT

(Gets up abruptly, having decided not to be left behind) It's too bad. But I have a few serious patients this morning to look in on. Might have to operate. Even if it's Christmas Day.

DOLORES

(She and eleanor stand facing each other across the sofa over the prone body of Victoria) Terminals, Herbie? Taking heroic measures, Herbie? Aren't you afraid they might come back to haunt you?

HERBERT

Well, we have to do something!

DOLORES

Our men are deserting.

ELEANOR

They won't get far. They'll get picked off one by one. Women are always out there, hunting down strays and stragglers. They'll run into some ambush or other, the cowards.

DOLORES

Will we miss them, Casey?

ELEANOR

We'll miss them.

DOLORES

Does it matter?

ELEANOR

It matters. But since our rescue mission has failed
us. . . .

DOLORES

It's history now. But we can make it without them.
Therefore let us start our day of peace, our one day of
peace, here and now: women and children first, women
and children, alone, and together. At least.

ELEANOR

At least.

THE ANNIVERSARY

a "Passion Play"

LIBRETTO
FOR AN
OPERA IN TWO ACTS

Music composed by Ned Rorem

Persons

FRANK SINGER: A vigorous, intelligent, and still young man: what but the rising executive?

[Baritone]

ELLEN SINGER: His wife, who after seven years of marriage senses the vacuum before her and comes to understand that not even candor and love will sustain her. Mature, intelligent: doomed. A trace of apprehension is revealed by her makeup, in the haggard touch about the eyes.

[Soprano]

At opening, Frank and Ellen Singer seem the ideal, upscale American couple of the corporate world. Frank is in formal attire: blue silk, red tartan cummerbund, a large white chrysanthemum in his lapel. Ellen's dress, a pure and passionate color, such as turquoise, expresses a woman who has attained a hard-won beauty by preserving a look of fragile, or delicate, reserve and reticence. Cosmopolitan provincials, in fact, like most people of their kind. Personifications of the New World's Best, they also reveal the shallow yet fathomless mystery of contemporary life.

MASTER OF CEREMONIES: Owner and manager of the COOL WATERS. Also a performer there. Powerful; sinister. He wears an elegant cutaway of original design: its color seems a Plutonian black, although Under different lights it appears to be phosphorescent — pale blue, pale violet, pale red — and at the end of the play it is seamed with running, cobalt fire. He carries an ebony cane emblematic of his office and powers.

[Bass]

MISTRESS OF CEREMONIES: His consort. Chanteuse. An imposing figure: a Hera. She wears an extraordinary red gown. Though regal, it is hellishly, and libidinously, red (though not a cheap "hot"). Let it be a sheath of glossy fire enclosing her from the waist down as if she were a full-blown, infernal flower; let it expose as much of her from the waist up as is indecently possible (perhaps styled like the ancient Minoan gown). Shoes to match. Let her have red nails, redder mouth: subdued flames. Her hair, too, is done in a fantastic red. Perhaps a Medusan wig, as much coiffure as she can carry. No earrings, no necklace: she is a queen, not a courtesan. She may, however, wear arm-bracelets, thin gold serpents. She may wear rings on her index and middle fingers; these must not be outré, But sapphires and rubies of indubitable consequence.

[Contralto/Mezzo-Soprano]

HEAD WAITER: The Maitre d'Hote provides occasional abstract narration, singing from obscurity or from an inconspicuous angle. He serves specialties: a tray of exotic, foaming glasses, etc. He is also the Announcer in the TV-studio of Act II.

[Tenor]

HOMONCULUS: A Man-Creature who is constructed Out of heterogeneous parts by the M.C. in Act I. When he comes alive, he will be dressed in simple evening clothes of a dusty, dull fabric. In Act II, he appears to sing The Riddle, and again in the Epilogue. He is made to look like an albino or else a man in a black and white negative.

[Counter-Tenor]

CLOAKROOM GIRL: The Snake-Arms of Act I. The Golden Serpent-Sylph of the Epilogue.

[Dancer, non-singing]

COUPLES: Chorus of singers and dancers in evening dress, paired at tables in the COOL WATERS. Also, wearing street clothes, the audience of simpletons in the TV-studio of Act II. In the nightclub, the singers are seated in obscurity so that when they give voice their remoteness is somewhat startling: like most choruses, they are people and/or ghosts, as you like.

PIANIST: A silent, faceless, diabolically-skilled performer who accompanies and improvises at the COOL WATERS. The same at the luminous "console" in the TV-studio.

Act I

The Place and the Time

Cool Waters, an ultrachic nightclub in consuming Manhattan. Its walls seem merely thickenings in the black air, reticulated by chrome and fire. Elegant and luxurious appointments: tables and chairs, for instance, are rather Platonic ideas of themselves; also, they may suggest the garden of summer as it might be remembered during the long winter's night of the north. Tables will be occupied at right. At rear, a small indication of the entrance, a foyer from the street, containing, just visible, a cloakroom from whence a pair of slender arms reach out intermittently for hats and cloaks: naked arms shimmering with golden scales, writhing delicately about the Headwaiter when he loiters next to them. At left stage, a small, transparent dance floor, with flaming beneath it, behind which, at left, the Exit to the management's "Office" glows with fires reflected from a lower level. At left center, a diminutive entrance from which service by the Headwaiter issues: liquors swirling and steaming. Halfway down, left, a baby grand piano, luminescent, the blue of flame tips, whose keyboard is turned so as to show the player head-on. His face, masked with thin rubber, is horribly expressionless, a no-face, non-commital — in contrast to his music. In the curve of the piano, a floor microphone (functionless so far as sound is concerned). We gaze into an abyssal space.

Darkness. Curtain is down. From behind it, choral cries, vocables. As the curtain disappears, darkness continues. The Mistress of Ceremonies gradually spotlighted where she leans languor-

ously against the piano. Some couples continue to dance somnambulistically in shadow. Her song takes us into the terrible heart of
this place: it seems as if we have died.

New Year's Eve.

CURTAIN OPEN

MIST. OF C.: HER TORCH SONG.

> When mind and body knew no pain,
> The sun shone warm on love's long hours:
> Now falls the black and winter rain
> On this isle of shining towers.
>
> In the dark the world is turning,
> And the years dim like old desires;
> Full of light, the stars are burning:
> Far through cold space, eternal fires.
>
> The city will rise proud and bright,
> Stone and steel cannot feel sorrow;
> But love is born and dies each night: [*]
> What of you and me tomorrow?
>
> The black rain falls
> The world is turning
> In the darkness
> Stars are burning
>
> Stone and steel
> Cannot know pain
> But love is born
> And dies in pain

What of you?
What of me?

(*) A man at the front table, fascinated by the song, is oblivious of his partner, who taps his arm. She turns, seeking help, and her glance falls on a figure silhouetted at the "Office" door: i.e., the M.C.'s. Hypnotically fixed, she rises moves upstage through the dancers and halts before the M.C. As though shucking an ear of corn, he rips her dress down in one motion and leaves her standing there naked. He gestures authoritatively, and she moves, tranced, through the Exit. He slips in after her.

By the close of the Mist. of C.'s song, [cf. directions in piano-vocal score], the man to whom she had directed the last line of her song stands uncertainly to leave. As he goes out at the front, Frank and Ellen enter. The Snake-Armsî assists them in removing their wraps. The Headwaiter escorts them to their seats at the just-vacated table, all the while singing about them, although they are quite insensible to his words.

HEADWAITER:

I see them everywhere,
I'd know them anywhere:
The man you'd like to be,
Our hero from the start:
Handsome, clever, and free
(No stronger than his heart).   [mocking gestures]
And the woman, what is she?
She'll always play her part: [puzzled, querying gesture]
Her life's the mystery
(As secret as her heart).

If he seems anyone,
She is anyone, too.

Take pity, everyone:
Their story concerns you!

After he disappears into the wing, the M.C. appears in his place. Frank and Ellen look up as he addresses them. Evidently he knows all about them. They are not surprised, however, by his materialization, nor startled by his particular knowledge. Such bored sophisticates they are.

M.C.:
Good evening.

FRANK, ELLEN:
Good evening.

M.C.:
Mister and Mrs. — [he mind reads] Singer, I believe?

FRANK:
Why yes, that's so.

ELLEN:
How did you know?

M.C.:
My talent, I could say, [shrugs] for names.
A useful gift, since [shrug] I play games.
For example, — now let me think [he mind reads] —
Frank and Ellen? I'll bet your drink.

ELLEN:
Is there something else you've learned?
I like secrets...where I'm concerned.

[From the outset, this is a bold flirtation by *double entendre*.]

M.C.:

> Nothing I say will surprise you.
> Whatever I know, you know too.

ELLEN:

> I'm not sure I know what *you* do.
> If you'll tell me, then *I'll* tell you.

FRANK:

> What point learning what we know?   [skeptical]
> Why not tell us what we don't ?

CHORUS:

> If he seems anyone,
> She is anyone, too.

M.C.:

> What you do know, you ought to know.
> [scornful, mysterious]
> You won't know what you Don'tknow.

CHORUS:

> Take pity, everyone!

FRANK:

> I Don'tthink I want to hear.

M.C.:

> Why not?

FRANK:

> I don'tthink I want to hear.

ELLEN:

> But I think *I* want to hear. [ignoring Frank, cajoling M.C.]

M.C.:
No, *he* doesn't want to hear.

FRANK:
I *don't* .

M.C.:
Yes, But she *does* want to hear.

ELLEN:
I *do*.

M.C.:
Why not?   [casual, sardonic, he mind reads]
Frank — loves — you.
You — love — Frank.

ELLEN:
That's true.

FRANK:
Why not?

M.C.:
And — you've been married seven years.

FRANK:
That's true.

M.C.:
Yes, seven long and happy years.

ELLEN:
Why not?

M.C.:
And have you *any* cause for tears?

ELLEN:
There is no reason we should.   [to herself]

FRANK:
What is the reason we should?   [to himself]

M.C.
You're sure you have no cause for tears? [skeptical, pressing
them]

FRANK:
I guess we've been as happy as we could. [to himself]

ELLEN:
Have we been as happy as we could?

M.C.:
Why not?

FRANK:
But *have* we?

ELLEN:
Haven't we?

M.C.:
Why not? [demanding]

FRANK:
Why not? [asking]

ELLEN:
Why not?   [doubting]

CHORUS:
Why not?

In sudden quiet, Frank and Ellen stare at one another across their table, as though meeting for the first time after having known each other so long: as though seeking the future in one another's face. Lighting condenses upon them,* and we hear the Headwaiter from somewhere in the back expressing their unconscious thought:

HEAD WAITER:
After so long, we meet again.
Again, for the first time.
How new your face — how unfamiliar.
 And how empty!
Who are you? Who am I?
Are we strangers?
I am frightened.

[*Optional Business. *Ellen nervously opens her purse, rummages in it and takes out a large compact. She scrutinizes her face in its mirror, is startled by what she sees. She brushes at her cheek, taps at her lips. She looks up hard at Frank, who cannot meet her gaze. Frank fumbles cigarettes out of his pocket, holds the case out to her. She takes one, and leans trembling to him for a light; holds his wrist as though supplicating; looks again into his blank expression.*]

CHORUS echoes softly as the M.C., who had frozen in darkness, breaks into their now anxious reverie, dispelling it by resuming his magisterial banter. Lighting intensifies.

M.C.:
Tonight, say goodbye to — [announcing]

FRANK:
Seven. [takes off his boutonniere, gives it to Ellen]

M.C.:
— heaven.
Goodbye to —   [aside, ominous]

FRANK:
Seven!   [aside, sadly]

M.C.:
— *heaven!*
Tonight, we celebrate —

ELLEN:
Eight.   [she puts the flower to her lips]

M.C.:
— your fate. [impulsively, Ellen passes the flower to him]

—

FRANK:
Then, give us —   [with forced exuberance]

M.C.:
— Champagne! [he guesses easily] Ice like diamonds
Glittering in the silver bucket.

*M.C. snaps his fingers, and the Mist. of C. appears beside them,
holding the same flower, mysteriously acquired. At the same moment, a jeroboam of champagne appears near the table.*

FRANK:

Champagne!   [astonished]
M.C.:
    And give us crystal glasses
    Bubbling, brimming with palest gold!

[Suggested business: as the M.C. produces four glasses, the Mist.
of C. puts the flower to her lips as Ellen had done, and then inserts
it between her breasts, where it suddenly sparkles with tears. Frank
looks at Ellen, who is gazing at the M.C.; then looks at his flower,
from whence his eyes move up to the Mist. of C.'s, where they lock
for a precious instant, before the situation is broken by toasting.]

Frank and Ellen rise for the Quartet, during which it is obvious
that the M.C. drinks to Ellen, while his consort drinks to Frank.

QUARTET:

FRANK & ELLEN:
    Let us recall our happiness: [warmly]
    Our seven years of married bliss.

M.C. & MIST. OF C.:
    Let them forget their happiness: [coldly]
    Those vanished years of "married bliss."

FRANK:
    Your smile in the morning,
    Your bright, singing form,
    Your breast warm as sunlight
    After the night's cold storm....

M.C. & MIST. OF C.:
    But when that sunlight goes,
    Your voice is colder,
    Silence in your wild heart —

Your night grows older.

M.C. & MIST. OF C.:
> Face to face in the dark
> You lie joined as one,
> Hearing the naked truth
> Together, alone,
> Alone together.

ELLEN:
> Though There's noon and evening
> You are you all day

FRANK AND ELLEN:
> So sweet, so rich our lives,
> To live in love this way.

> *They all drink.*

FRANK AND ELLEN, M.C. & MIST. OF C.:
> It would be misery and torment
> Were we parted at this moment.
> Could anything be worse?
> Not blindness, nor lost health
> Nor flesh that feels like brass,
> Even the shock of death!   [to their new lovers]:
> Yet we must conceal our torment
> As we stand apart this moment.

> [Each to himself, to the other, all to their new lovers]:

> Could anything be worse?
> Better flesh like brass,
> Be tter blind or sick,
> When will this dead life pass?

They all drink again. Then toast in common.

FRANK:
   I have no future without you! [clinks with Mist. of C.]

M.C.:
   There is no future without love!   [clinks with Ellen]

MIST. OF C.:
   Whatever comes, it's you I love!   [clinks with Frank]

ELLEN:
   Love never happens without you! [clinks with M.C.]

They all drink a last toast.

Lights down. M.C. and Mist. of C. vanish. Frank and Ellen rise and dance casually as the piano rambles in mocking sentimentality. Vaguely, at rear, the Headwaiter is outlined. Again he sings their thoughts. Other couples walk-dance past them, a crowd with no direction.

HEADWAITER: [from the dark]
   Down the cold streets of stone and glass
   Among silent staring faces
   Our way has led us from the past
   Into these dark, fearful places
   From which no one returns the same
   And everything is lost in flames
   From which nothing can be recovered
   And what we are shall be discovered

CHORUS: [Men]
   Mornings we theorized
   What the days should bring;

Evenings we realized
We had done nothing.

CHORUS: [Women]
    What else could I offer
    But to be his friend?
    I rejoiced and suffered
    As he sought his end.

HEADWAITER & CHORUS:
    But then we lost our way:
    [Walkers freeze in several attitudes]
    Where it is, no one can say.

CHORUS: [women]
    If he'd believed in me
      How brilliant his life!

HEADWAITER:
    Children of the City!
    Who will take pity?

[Chorus fades, disconsolate, into dark]

Gentle spot on Frank and Ellen seated again unobtrusively, holding hands across their table. As the spat blows up between them, the light changes to a greater intensity than before the toasting commenced.

ELLEN: [coy, teasing]
    Frank.

FRANK: [a tardy response]
    Ellen.

ELLEN: Frank?

FRANK:
  Ell en ?

ELLEN:
  Seven years. Was it a long time?

FRANK:
  They were a long time.

At this moment, Ellen, unconscious of her behavior, takes her hair down in one motion, pulls off her jewelry (earrings, rings, necklace, wristwatch, bracelet), and sets the things on the table before her as though they were burning hot. This action takes place during the following lines. Frank does not react.

ELLEN:
  Yet gone so fast. I'm afraid.

FRANK:
  Why should you be afraid?

ELLEN: ⸱ [abruptly]
  Frank, dear, I want to hear you say
  "Ellen, I love you,"
  As if, tonight, those words were new.

FRANK:
  Yes, of course, Ellen.

ELLEN:
  That's not what I mean.

FRANK:

Does this convince you?

He leans across and pecks her cheek. Sitting back, he unconsciously scoops her jewelry to him and pockets it item by item during the next lines. She watches his hands.

ELLEN: [shocked]
You won't!

FRANK:
Won't what?

ELLEN:
Say you love me.

FRANK: [acceding, reluctant]
I love you.

ELLEN:
Frank, you're lying.

FRANK: [flustered]
Ellen, I love you!

She deals him a violent slap. Then buries her face in her hands.

FRANK: [remonstrating, taking her wrists]
You're crying! Ellen!

Lights down abruptly. Sharp spot on Mist. of C. at her microphone, a great foaming champagne glass beside her on the piano. As she introduces his act, the M.C. is visible as a tall, faintly luminous shadow. He stands before a sarcophagus, draped in blue-black velvet. She walks among the guests, rudely touching those parts of the body she names.

MIST. OF C.:
> Ladies and Gentlemen! My friends!
> The time's come as an old year ends
> To groan for your human miseries:
> Headache and backache and heartache,
> Your rotten teeth, your graying hair,
> That swollen gut, those fatty thighs,
> The curving spine and bleary eyes,
> Your hips and waist, your arch and arm,
> Coughs and creases, ulcers and corns,
> Bloated and bloody, shrunken and cracked:
> Yesterday, young. Old, tomorrow.

> *Returning to the piano, she drinks deep.*

> But why moan, friends? Friends, why sorrow?
> And why remember what you've done?

> *She walks about again, glass in hand, her back to the audience.*

> You promised father to be strong
> And promised mother to be kind
> You promised sister to be true
> And promised brother to be good

She suddenly dashes her glass to the floor, whirls wonderfully round to the footlights, and addresses the theater audience directly.

But stabbed your best friend in the back

CHORUS:
> Where else?

MIST. OF C.:
    Precisely!
    — And smashed your sweetheart's open face

CHORUS:
    What else?

MIST. OF C.:
    Exactly!
    — You changed your mind to suit the bed

CHORUS:
    Why else?!

MIST. OF C.:
    Naturally
    — And sold yourself to keep the job

CHORUS:
    How else?

MIST. OF C.:
    Certainly!

She turns round again to the Chorus.

    Oh friends, although you've lived by crime,
    You found success too hard a climb,
    And lost your way before your time,
    And sank into the world's black slime.

CHORUS:
    What have we done? Where have we gone?
    Our time is done! OUr hope is gone!

MIST. OF C.:

> There's no reason for your fears:
> While you live you still have years!
> Go on, go on! The world has space:
> You're bound to find that happy place!
> Go on! go on!

CHORUS:

> O, Lady! Tell us where?
> Where is that springtime day?
> Now, before we despair
> Show us the secret way!

MIST. OF C.:

> Just weep one small tear from each eye
> And sigh one miserable sigh.
> If you want life, you still have time.
> Friends, drink! Forget your ancient sins!
> Drink! Drink and laugh! Our show begins!

The Chorus laughs, happy now, relieved. From the shadows an echoing bellow of benign laughter, a little too rich. What is the joke? Who's it on?

MIST. OF C.:

> And who laughs most?
> None but our host!

Spotlight away from Mist. of C., onto the M.C.. He now wears the magician's silk cape, and a top hat which he removes and sweeps across his knees as he bows, gracious and condescending. He stands before the long table covered with drapery. He smiles, and flourishes his cane.

M.C.:

> You shudder when I take
> My cane? My cane's — a snake!

The cane becomes a live boa constrictor in his hands. He offers it jestingly to his audience, which shrinks back. He laughs as before, but more sardonically.

MIST. OF CER.:

> They've seen through illusions.   [reproving and inciting]
> They're bored by illusions.
> Show them what they came for.
> Down here what counts is truth.

M.C.:

> Where shall I start,   [bantering]
> The head or heart?

He stops the Headwaiter, who was pouring champagne at an adjacent table, and turns him about to face the audience.

M.C.:

> Here I find a human being
> Made of blood, guts, bones, meat, skin.
> Or so it seems. But knowing's seeing.
> I wonder what I'll find in him?

He takes the Headwaiter by the bow tie; yanks down. Sawdust cascades out; the Headwaiter collapses, like a Punctured balloon, into the floor — empty clothes. The M.C. laughs again. Demoniac. Then he assembles a man. He picks up various body parts from behind the table. Beginning with the legs, he mounts a torso, arms, and head. When he has finished we will see an innocuous creature (the sections of its clothing are not joined, not having been sewn).

Here I have some feet,
Legs to match. Quite neat.
Trunk for them to join,
Just so, at the groin,
Hands — to arms — to chest:
    All seems for the best.
Yet the thing is dead
While it lacks a head!

He finishes by screwing the head to the neck bone, and makes a few passes, first of entreaty, then of command.

Rise, rise up, my boy!
Go, and seek your joy.
You've legs that can walk,
A tongue that will talk,
    Eyes shall see, hands take,
Brain know — heart break.

The newborn Homunculus looks about.

HOMONCULUS:
    I, I, I, I! I am! I think! I think I am!

M.C.:
    So! I do not deceive:
    Believe what you believe.

HOMONCULUS:
    I am, I think! I think! I am! [pained bewilderment of awakening]

M.C.:
    Let's call you Adam! Where's your Eve? [somberly amused]

HOMONCULUS:
> Still, why do I feel so bereaved?
> Is there something I've not received?
> Or something lost I can't retrieve?
> How can I know what I've not perceived?

M.C.:
> Go! Search! Find! Take! Enjoy! [commanding like a wizard]
> Lose! Grieve....

Happy applause from the Chorus. The Homonculus turns quite round about, spots Snake Arms in their cloakroom at the rear; runs to them; is embraced; pulled into their darkness., he disappears. They have "danced" him into their hold. The M.C. takes up the spot again. Now he is somber.

> That's enough for simple tricks.
> If you thought that was magic,
> Let me try some mathematics,
> Formulating what is tragic.

> A while ago these two were one.
> But one of them will now be two.
> The other one one-half: alone.
> Stay there, Frank! Ellen, I want you!

As the M.C. points, a spot picks up Frank, who freezes as he was, bored by the whole thing, quite self-absorbed. On 'you!' he points at Ellen, and the spot burns on her, cooling on Frank. She smiles delicately. She rises and glides rapt to him, like a woman going to her pleasure. The M.C. whips the drapery from his table, revealing a crude pine box on trestles. With a gallant gesture, he picks Ellen up and lays her out in the coffin. She reposes there, smiling, expect-

ant, peaceful. The M.C. speaks confidingly, pattering like the conventional magician.

M.C.:
>   Now, your attention, please! The box is real.
>   And the lady's real too. What do you feel?

On "feel" he begins to run his hands lightly and lasciviously over Ellen — everywhere.

ELLEN:
>   If my body could grow younger,
>   Mind be cleared, and soul made stronger,
>   I'd wish, I'd hope —

M.C.:
>   — Sssh! Hope no longer.
>   You cannot live unless you love.
>   Unless you're loved, you cannot live.
>   Your life should change. It will! It must!
>   Shall I bless you? Give me your trust.

ELLEN:
>   Yes, yes, I do! My pain's so deep,
>   So long, so hard, I cannot weep:
>   To breathe is pain! Bless me with sleep.
>   I'm empty. I'm cold as can be.
>   Come near. Touch me. Warm me. Heal me!

Tenderly, he bends over her, and kisses her, hieratically: on her knees, her navel, her breast, her mouth — one phrase to each kiss.

M.C.:
>   Be calm..

ELLEN:
Dear heart!

CHORUS:
Splendid!

M.C.:
Be whole.

ELLEN:
Dear heart!

CHORUS:
Wondrous!

M.C.:
Be true.

ELLEN:
Dear heart!

CHORUS:
Awesome!

M.C.:
Be free!

ELLEN:
Dear heart!

CHORUS:
Sublime!

M.C.:
With this kiss, I thee part!

CHORUS:
    Ah!

The M.C. closes the lid, picks up a monstrous saw and begins to cut the box in half with long, measured strokes. On each downstroke, he chants. Unseen, the Mist. of C. alternates her chant on each upstroke. Dim at his table, and still frozen, Frank echoes them mournfully.

TRIO

M.C.:
    One! for your money!

MIST. OF C.:
    One! for your loving!
FRANK:
    One! for your body!

M.C.:
    Two! for your show!

MIST. OF C.:
    Two! for his lies!

FRANK:
    Two! for your soul!

M.C.:
    Three! are you ready?

MIST. OF C.:
    Three! is she living?

FRANK:
Three! Where's your beauty?

M.C.:
Four! let us go!

MIST. OF C.:
Four! now she dies!

FRANK:
Four! gone below!

CHORUS:
Ah!

ELLEN: [her voice distant, echoing, chambered: offstage and in
the theater]
Calm, how calm it seems, this darkness!
Long, how long I've sought such wholeness!
Truth! Truth with you — I know you're true!
At last I've reached the end: I'm free!

*The M.C. vents his last burst of scornful, hilarious laughter. It is the
end of his act. Lights out.*

*Lights up, the dance floor is darkly illumined. No coffin to be seen.
Fuur couples are dancing a funerary yet erotic ballet; it is a parody
of the tango: they are souls glued face to face — with no hope of
animal climax. Towards the end of this dance, the Mist. of C. becomes visible beside the piano, Frank at his table. Dazed, he sips at
his glass. She hums the tune of the dance. Frank looks up and
speaks out to her across the room.*

FRANK:
Where is my wife?

MIST. OF C.:
    Who was your wife?

FRANK:
    Ellen. We came together.

MIST. OF C.:
    Ellen? You never knew her.

FRANK:
    That's not true. What do you know?

MIST. OF C.:
    She loved you, Frank. Isn't that so?

FRANK:
    Why not? Is that all?

MIST. OF CER.: [wearily]
        es, That's all. Isn't that enough?

FRANK: [exasperated by it all]
    What is love!

MIST. OF C.:[laughs]
    Oh Frank! What *is* love? What is *love*?
    That is a foolish question, Frank!
    You've led a most successful life:
    The brilliant young executive,
    But you've grown bored the way you live,
    Bored bored by parties you give,
        Bored bored bored — with bed and board and wife!
    Oh Frank, what is love?
    Now you're thinking of a change, sir:

You want to learn if love should burn,
If love can kill, or merely chills
Like wasted hours, and wilts like flowers.
        So you really want a change, sir?
You understand, it's danger?
Oh Frank, what is love?
Are you ready for its danger?
Those dreadful powers you must find?
I wonder just what's on your mind.

FRANK:
    I want to know if I've been blind.

MIST. OF C.:
    I wonder just how brave you are.
    — Come to me, Frank. Not very far.

*During the last lines of her song, she has been approaching Frank.
As he takes up her invitation, her dare, she is beside the table,
looking powerfully down at him*

FRANK:
    I'll come. And then?

MIST. OF C.:
    And then....

FRANK:[to himself, desperately]
    What can I lose?

MIST. OF C.: [agreeing with him, sardonically]
    What can you lose?

FRANK:
        Only my wife.[to himself]

MIST. OF C.:
    Only your life. [to herself]

She leans over him They exchange their kiss of greeting: they taste; they savor; they commit. An occult, long-drawn moment, augmented by dread, passion, danger, terror — and mockery.

Silence.

FRANK:
    Who *are* you?

MIST. OF C.: [mysteriously]
    You know who.

[Optional pantomime during DUET. Suddenly Snake Arms coruscates down from the cloakroom, across the stage front, to disappear at left rear. She has vanished into a mirror. The Homonculus appears, following uncertainly. He stands baffled before the mirror, trying to find a way into it.]

The Homonculus steps into the mirror and vanishes.

Frank takes the Mist. of C. by the hands. The lights dim, then brighten in another key as a clock begins ticking the last minutes of the old year. Spotlight up on the Mist. of C. and Frank. At arms' length, they survey one another with intense interest. They are at the center of the dance floor.

DUET:

FRANK:
    There is a way, I hope, to find

MIST. OF C.:
A way, you hope,

FRANK:
The time and place where we can be

MIST. OF C.:
For us to find

FRANK:
Ourselves again — to see the face

MIST. OF C.:
The secret place

FRANK:
And form of life we truly love.

MIST. OF C.:
Of life and love.
I am the way you hope to find

FRANK:
I know you are

MIST.OF C.:
The face and form of truth you love.

FRANK:
The only one

MIST. OF C.:
Frank, you and I can only be

FRANK:
Who knows that life

MIST. OF C.:
Ourselves again when we are done.

FRANK:
and love are one.

MIST. OF C.:
There is no more, dearest, to say.

FRANK:
What more is there, dearest, to say?

They kiss again. It is terrifying. Then, silence. The clock begins to strike twelve.

CHORUS:
Down rings bell!
Out rings old!
In rings new!
Up rings hell!

The Mist. of C. welcomes both Frank and the New Year. The Chorus dances about them with naive gaiety, in voice and gesture antiphonal.

MIST. OF C.:
Now all your lies are washed away!

CHORUS:
Now all our lies are washed away

FRANK:
Our lies...!

MIST. OF C.:
As though your life begins today!

CHORUS:
As though our lives begins today!

FRANK:
Life! Today!

MIST. OF C.:
Your flesh is clean, your limbs are light!

CHORUS:
Our flesh is clean, our limbs are light!

FRANK:
Our flesh is light

MIST. OF C.:
Your hearts are pure, your lusts are right!

CHORUS:
Our hearts are pure, our lusts are right!

FRANK:
Hearts pure! Lusts right!

MIST. OF C.:
And so your joy flames hot and bright!

CHORUS:
And so our joy flames hot and bright!

FRANK:
Joy flames!

MIST. OF C.:
Your past is dead: live long this night!

CHORUS:
The past is dead: live long this night!

FRANK:
The past! Tonight!

MIST. OF C.:
Your past is dead: it died last night! [she points awfully at Frank]

FRANK:
My past is dead — she died last night!

Bacchanal by dancers. Mist. of C. and Frank, at the center, draw hypnotically close to each other for their third, and deepest, kiss. They merge and fade into darkness. At the same time, there is a projection much larger than life above them: we see a kind of "negative" that shows Ellen and the M.C. in similar embrace. There is a terrific flare of light. Then, as the curtain closes, there is darkness, except for the glow of the shadow lovers.

Act II

The Cool Waters, One year later, again on New Year's Eve.

Scene 1. A TV studio. Early on New Year's Eve.
Scene 2. A void. A few hours later.
Scene 3. The Cool Waters. Immediately following.

SCENE 1

A television studio. Anæsthetically white: a heavenly, blank, clear white in contrast to the obscurity of ACT I. Sparsely furnished, like a laboratory equipped for an "abstract experiment," an investigation of the soul's dynamics. At left, a small stage at rear center, a glassed-in "Control Room": the glass will become a movie screen. From the right, the long-barrelled zoom lenses of the cameras jut out (the TV-cameramen are invisible). Through the glass of the Control Room are seen glowing, Pulsing banks of dials, switches, meters. The light is not harsh now, but grows from ordinary white to blinding intensity as the scene progresses to its "Revelation." By then everything glows with inner radiance: walls, seats, even the people! The studio audience is composed of couples wearing informal street attire. They sit profile, leaving front of stage for the aisle, which runs right front to left rear. As the curtain goes up, the Headwaiter is on-stage, now as The Announcer; he wears a chest-microphone that looks like a great ruby, and a neat pair of earphones. "Snake Arms" is at rear corner of the studio stage, now as Usherette, a caryatid who holds nothing over her head. She is naked, and shimmers in her trance. Frank is in the audience, inconspicuous until called forward as "The Contestant."

HEADWAITER:[rapidly, insanely]
    Ladies and gentlemen and all our friends out there!
    Twelve months exactly have elapsed.
    Once again it is New Year's Eve,
    And we await the Master and Mistress of Our Ceremonies.
    And now, Children of the West, you and you and you,
        welcome all!

["you" and "you" indicate both audiences]

    We present the PERSONAL-UNIVERSAL QUIZ!
    Prizes for everyone everywhere!
    But first, here's today's UNIVERSAL-PERSONAL RIDDLE:
    Can you solve it? Ready? Watch! Listen!

The Homonculus appears in a hitherto invisible niche of the studio-stage, between microphones and Control Room. Later, Ellen will be revealed standing there in it as though in an up-ended coffin.

HOMONCULUS: [clarion-voiced]
    I spring from wells
    I fall from stars
    Sometimes suspected
    Often rejected
    Never perfected.

    What am I ? [Announcer and Chorus echo: *What am I?*]

    Eagerly sought [more intensely]
    And cheaply bought

Everywhere taught
Anywhere lost
Regained at great cost.

Where am I?   [echo: *Where am I?*]

And I am heard   [most intensely wrung out]
And I am seen
And cannot be willed
And cannot be filled
And cannot be killed.

Who am I? [Announcer and Chorus echo, bemused: *Wh o am I?*]

ANNOUNCER:
    Remember remember remember
    Guess it by midnight
    Or lose the prize, the prize

The Homonculus fades away. The Announcer turns to welcome the Quiz Masters as their theme music accompanies them in.

ANNOUNCER:
    Now clap your hands, friends, if you will,
    For Jack, our Host! Our Hostess, Jill!

Seated firmly, the audience performs a brief ballet of applause: they clap hands once, hold out right arms in mechanical salute, clap again hold out left arms. A hungry yet mechanical adoration. The Quiz Masters are, of course, the M.C. and the Mist. of C. He, in black Madison Avenue pinstripes, looks sinister and slick (perhaps a moustache); she, hatted and veiled, in modish Lady of TeeVee costume, commercially sophisticated. They are epitomes of the glittering glib entertainer and his harridan accomplice: of the Conversers, Panelleers, Quizzers, Soothers, Advisors, and Pundits.

Action for The Quiz begins slow and broad, quickening, or seeming to, imperceptibly to the climax: the theophany of Ellen.

When the Quiz Masters announce that they will give a prize, the niche is faintly illumined: a body visible in it becomes clearer as the scene develops. It is Ellen, apparently dead. As Frank's agon contin-ues, she glows more intensely, until she is fluorescent. Frank will have been staring at her, or through her, into the blinding light that fascinates him, though he has not understood or seen what it is. Finally the shrouding will drop, and she will be given to him She is the inconceivable goal toward which he has been driven, and with which he is rewarded for having endured their pitiless baiting.

M.C. & MIST. OF C.: [together, with brisk, false generosity]
    To our lucky, clever winners
    We give the finest of worldly goods.

MIST. OF C.:
    To you lucky, clever sinners:
    Tours, homes, clothes, cash, cars, frozen food...

BOTH:
    Et cetera!
    Tonight, our Anniversary Jackpot
    To the contestant we've chosen by lot:

MIST. OF C.:
    One who wants what he cannot have

M.C. :
    One who wins what he cannot hold

MIST. OF C.:
    One who lost what was the better

M.C. :
    One who found what will be worse.

BOTH:
    One who's waited for an end to pain
    While twelve long months have passed him by:
    A helpless, empty, broken man,
    Who's satisfied to live or — die.

M.C.:
    There he is! Step up, sir! Don't linger!

He points at Frank, and the studio audience, excited, looks for his subject in their midst.

MIST. OF C.:
    Your name! What is your name, sir?

She trolls him up to them by a hypnotic waggling of her long-nailed finger. Emerging from stage-audience, so that only now are we aware of him, Frank is nearly unrecognizable: dark, drab, savage, full of the powers of knowledge, But lacking understanding and satisfaction: a man consumed by passion. His mien, one of stoic desperation. His concentration of self is impressive yet his voice is calm with resignation. He steps before them. They look down upon him, retaining the advantage of those on a dais.

FRANK:
    Frank Singer.

M.C.:
    Your occupation?

FRANK:
>No occupation.

MIST. OF C.:
>Come come come, my dear sir! Nothing?[mischievously]

FRANK:
>Of any account.

CHORUS:
>Ah! [sighing wistfully]

To amuse the studio audience the Quiz Masters begin a rapid, teasing attack on Frank.

M.C.:
>You're not exactly sure
>If you're rich or you're poor?

FRANK:
>I —

CHORUS:
>Oh!

MIST. OF C.:
>You're not sure which is which:
>when you're poor, when you're rich?

FRANK:
>I —

CHORUS:
>Ah!

MIST. OF C.:
    You balance your budget
    Yet live beyond your means?

FRANK:
    I —

CHORUS:
    Oh!

M.C.:
    Your means are ends, it seems?
    You mean your ends are dreams?

FRANK: [rattled]
    I, I —

CHORUS:
    Ah!

M.C.:
    Why are you here?

FRANK:
    I do not know.

M.C.: [sneering at him to studio audience]
    He doesn't know.

CHORUS:
    Oh!

MIST. OF C.:[in an other-worldly voice, Cassandra-eloquent]
    What you do not know will kill you!

M.C.:
  What do you want here?

FRANK:
  I do not know.

M.C. & MIST. OF C.:[jeering at him, worse than before]
  He doesn't know.

CHORUS:
  Oh!

MIST. OF C.: [again, sibylline]
  You do not know the truth, yet you lie!

FRANK:
  Which of us is not a liar?
  Isn't that the way we all are?

MIST. OF C.:
  We do not want *your* suggestions!

M.C.:
  You're here to answer *our* questions.

FRANK:[contrite, but sullen]
  I know.

M.C. & MIST. OF C.:[scornful, contemptuous]
  He knows.

CHORUS:
  Oh!

M.C.:
    You know nothing; [peremptory]

MIST. OF C.:[following few lines repeated ad lib]
    You have no one.

FRANK:
    I —

M.C.:
    You want something

ALL:
    You know nothing.

MIST. OF C.:
    You seek someone.

FRANK:
    I do.

M.C.: [mockingly]
        We shall see, Mr. Frank Singer.

M.C. & MIST. OF C.:
    Each request in our examination .
    Must be answered without hesitation.

M.C. snaps his fingers. The stage goes dark. Then a projection of deep space appears. In the following sequence Frank comes abundantly alive and names the various phenomena shown. Images of what he names flash on the screen. They are those views of deep space produced by the space telescope. They change in slow-motion: millions of light-years are traversed through oceanic depths of space. The vision is magnificent.

CHORUS:[with stupefaction]
   Ah!

M.C.:
   What are these? Little stars?
FRANK:
   No. Not stars. Galaxies.

*There are inflections of pain and grief in his delivery of the abstruse
information: we hear Frank's deepest spirit expressing the woe and
wonder, the misery of consciousness: it is God's prophet's voice: rapt,
superhuman, almost divinely remote.*

FRANK:
   I see: the world outside the world.
   The Universe of Universes:
   Each star I see is not a star, but a universe.
   Universes in forms diverse: spheroidal, discoidal,
   Spiral, irregular and mixed:
   Each vaster than our dusty Milky Way,
   On the edge somewhere
   We ourselves are whirling, turning.
   Turning, turning, turning
   And, each universe contains also:
   Gas, particles, debris, planets,
   Stars, star clusters, large clusters, small clusters,
   Universes dense or sparse,
   Some near, some far, far, and all more distant than we
      can know:
   Universes bright or faint, universes heavy, light,
   Dark or luminous....

Frank falters, staring about puzzled as the M.C. prompts him.

M.C.:
    And...?

FRANK:
    And only a dozen universes are as close as a mere million
    light-years,
    But see: through the Bowl of the Great Dipper:
    Look: a million galaxies!
    In each, a billion stars:
    And remember, there are billions of galaxies,
    Shining, shining, shining

CHORUS:
    Ah![in genuine admiration]

The lights glare brighter, and then sink to ease our eyes. It hurts.

M.C.:
    Yes. Of course. *Space.*[he is rather blasé]
    — And these?

*Total darkness. Now we see a projection showing the complex beaded
track, being made in slow motion, or subatomic particles traversing
a Wilson Cloud Chamber, this image enlarged immensely.*

CHORUS:
    Ah!

FRANK:
    I see — I see: the world inside the world.
    Invisible matters made visible:
    Pieces of pieces of pieces:
    The molecules, atoms, radiation quanta,
    Protons, Electrons, Neutrons,
    Mesons that live but l-millionth of one second,

Neutrinos, Anti-neutrinos, Anti-protons, Anti...anti...
An infinite plurality dwindling away, away —
Into nothing, nowhere —
Burning, burning, burning!

CHORUS:
Ah! Ah! Ah!

Lights flare suddenly; a silent explosion. The Quiz Masters relent.

M.C.:
Yes. Of course. Time. [again, blasé]
Time is — ?[insidiously]
FRANK:
— what happens.
And what happens is — time. [he goes dead again]

M.C. & MIST. OF C.:
What is eternal?

FRANK:
Death is eternal.

M.C.:
And what you cherish?

FRANK:
Is what must perish. [somewhat curious now]

M.C.:
Yet this dead earth?

FRANK:
Brings life to birth.[waking a little more]

M.C.:
> And life persists?

FRANK:
> And life persists? [his eye is caught by a shrouded form now
> noticeable in the niche, a draped statue]

M.C.:
> Because?

FRANK:
> Because?

M.C. & MIST. OF C.:
> Think! Our prize is not for the blind.

Frank attempts to push on to the answer.

FRANK:
> For life persists
> Though death insists,
> For life consists of — ?

M.C.: [prompting hard]
> Of?

MIST. OF C.: [urging him]
> Of?
> Can you win it?
> You've one minute!

An intense passage of time. Frank cries out in impotence.

FRANK:[paralyzed]
> Of?

The time is up. A knell. The lights blind.

MIST. OF C.:
>You must answer!
>You *must* answer![most urgently]

Frank stands silent, inarticulate. The Chorus speaks for him.

CHORUS:
>He cannot know.
>No means death.
>But life grows:
>Life says Yes.
>Could he feel Yes,
>Could he hear Yes,
>Could he know Yes,
>He would breathe it:
>He would sing it!

FRANK:
>Like men who love — ?

M.C.: [half-prompting, half agreeing]
>Yes? Your word is *Love*?

MIST. OF C.:
>Yes! He knew: it's *Love*! [quickly congratulating him]

FRANK: [stunned]
>What? *Yes* comes to this — *Love*?

CHORUS:
>Who needs words
>You read in books?

We want money,
We want looks!

M.C. & MIST. OF C.:
>   Yes! That is bliss: Love! [mawkish]
>   Yes! Love sings its own song! [maudlin]
>   I knew it all along:
>   You knew it, she knew it,
>   We and you and they —
>   Even he knew it!
>   Yes! Whatever is, Love is there!
>   Yes! all is bliss, everywhere!

CHORUS:
>   Everything is bliss, everywhere!
>   How long we've waited.
>   How hard we've prayed.

M.C. & MIST. OF C.:
>   Shut your doubting eyes
>   And you will now receive
>   The unexpected prize:
>   The gift you can't believe.

CHORUS:
>   Shut your doubting eyes,
>   And you will have your prize.

M.C. & MIST. OF C.:
>   That word so hated
>   Must be obeyed!

Frank shuts his eyes as if in prayer. The veil drops. Ellen stands there, a "bridal" statue in a white gown through which her form shines. Her eyes are closed in deep sleep. Slowly, her hands unfold and rise, expressing wonder and joy; then sadly they fold into tranced repose. As Frank cries out, her eyes open and she gazes tenderly at him

FRANK:
   Ellen, it's you! Is it you?

Ellen sings a pathetically sweet hymn to the reawakening of love and joy. Frank is enraptured, and remains stock-still, until the Quiz Masters have had their last word and departed.

ELLEN:
   Am I the woman you once knew?
   Am I your Ellen? Who are you?
   When we were young and love was joy
   We thought our life a simple toy:

   Though time was long
   And space was wide
   Love never died
   But we were wrong.

   Nothing is sure if love can die,
   What else is there but you and I?

   We were alone:
   No days, no nights,
   Dark heats, cold lights:
   The world was gone.

   We did not know when we were torn
   That love can die, yet is reborn:
   By grace restored
   To its sweet place,
   Returned the face,

The heart adored.

Imagine yourself, alone again
Wondering why you are filled with fears
And your head on the breast of that siren
While her voice like cold fire burns your ears

And imagine me with him once more
In his arms — that ultimate power!
Oh! He flames like ice, and kills at the core!
Beyond all hope, in love with horror.

Imagine...her voice...
Cold flame...her breast...
Like ice...his power...
Hope...and horror...

We must take the gift we're offered:
The reward for what we've suffered.
Oh...!

The face you see, the face I see,
The only worlds for you, for me:
Not far — but near,
Not dim — but clear.
Do you know where
Our life is, dear?
Do you know, dear,
Our love is — here?

M.C.:
What a pleasant surprise for you, audience!

CHORUS:
Oh!

M.C.:
To be present at this sweet reunion.

CHORUS:
Ah!

MIST. OF C.:
May you learn from their strange experience

CHORUS:
Oh!

MIST. OF C.:
That love is your only communion.

CHORUS:
Ah!

Aside, to each other, and for the benefit of the audience in the theater, the Quiz Masters remark with consummately wicked smiles:

DUET

M.C.:
That the test of love
Is the quest of life.

MIST. OF C.:
But the best of love
Is the jest of life.

M.C.:
And never know the worst:

MIST. OF C.:
　　Both life and love are — cursed!

*They depart briskly. Frank's concentration on Ellen is interrupted
by the Announcer, who holds out pen and contract. Without glancing down, Frank signs.*

ANNOUNCER:
　　Just to say she's unharmed,
　　Will you sign here, please.

He turns and inanely addresses both audiences:

　　Join us again to show what you know
　　And win *your* Jackpot from *our* Rainbow!

He exits.

*Ellen descends slowly from her niche, and comes downstage to Frank,
pausing during their words. After Frank's ìYes,î they turn and pace
out together d.wn the aisle, from left rear to front right, stopping
majestically a few times, as though they were leaving the wedding
altar. Lights will steadily diminish.*

FRANK:[impulsively]
　　No matter why you went away,
　　I love what I have won:
　　A new life begins!

ELLEN:[serenely]
　　Frank, can, you forgive
　　And love me, as I love you?

FRANK:
Can we confess we lost our heads —

ELLEN:
Nothing to confess.
We were careless.
We're still young
Love shall make us strong.
Don't look back!
I could not bear it.
Will you promise?[anxiously]

FRANK:[desperately]
Yes! I swear it!

They leave. Shadows have developed and the stage is almost dark as they pace ceremoniously out through the dimming fire of the EXIT.

Segué into Scene 2. Exalted transitional music also voices its own echo, becoming a suspended terror, providing the "walk" that follows with a suggestion of self-doom, the sound of a failing heart — which is voiced by the unseen Announcer.

SCENE 2

A few hours later.

Frank and Ellen emerge before the curtain. They are in the formless void, hardly moving. They might seem blind and asleep, inching forward. Their duet is poignantly stoic. They are ascending the holy mountain whose top cannot be reached. Ellen has more strength than Frank — that is, more faith, from which the strength of her illusion derives. At least she has the foreknowledge of what will be seen and known at the summit. During the segué, the Announcer's voice will be heard through a microphone.

ANNOUNCER:
    Blind
    We have come into the formless void
    Blind
    We are walking, blind,
    Into a gale of nothingness

    Where will we arrive?
    Forward, we must go forward
    Step by step by step

    Is it a mountain we are climbing
    Is it the holy mountain we are climbing
    Whose top can never be reached?

    It is the sound of the heart
    Failing
    In the dark, in desolation
    The heart conscious of nothing but itself
    Failing
    Hearing nothing but itself
    Failing
    For there is nothing but itself
    Failing

The voice fades as Frank and Ellen advance over the stage.

DUET

ELLEN:
    I see our life ahead:

FRANK:
> I see no life ahead:

ELLEN:
> Always our tomorrows

FRANK:
> Because our tomorrows

ELLEN:
> Filled with happy hours

FRANK:
> Come with bitter hours:

ELLEN:
> Because we live together:

FRANK:
> Always, dying together:

ELLEN:
> Nothing but living

FRANK:
> Nothing but living

ELLEN:
> Simply as we are, loving,

FRANK:
> Simply as we are, loving,

ELLEN:
> Hoping to love, in peace —

FRANK:
Hoping to love, in peace —

ELLEN:
Forever.

FRANK:
Forever?

They face each other, at a standstill, their souls struggling.

ELLEN:
Is there some word, some way to reach you?

FRANK:
Is there no word, no way to teach you?

ELLEN:
To come near to you, and be dear to you?

FRANK:
To make clear to you that my love for you

ELLEN:
Before it is too late, too late, too late?

FRANK:
Is like our life: we wait, and wait, and wait

ELLEN
Before we die, Frank, before we die, we die?

FRANK:
Until we die, Ellen, till we die, we die.

They move forward again, even more slowly and painfully, if possible — as if steeply uphill.

ELLEN:
  I want to live and love — to love and live.

FRANK:
  I cannot live for love — I won't love to live.

ELLEN:
  We must try, dear, we must try, must try.

FRANK:
  I Don'tknow why, dear, Don'tknow why.

ELLEN:
  Until There's nothing more to do

FRANK:
  And so There's nothing more to do

ELLEN:
  But go on - — as if we went together

FRANK:
  But go on — as though we went together

ELLEN:
  Giving everything

FRANK:
  Although There's nothing

ELLEN:
Until the end, the end, the end....

FRANK:
It is the end, the end, the end....

They stop again, looking at each other fixedly in need and despair. They have almost reached the right side of the stage.

ELLEN:
Or else.

FRANK:
What else?

ELLEN:
What else?

FRANK:
Or else?

ELLEN:
I understand

FRANK:
I understand.

ELLEN:
He understands. [to herself]

FRANK:
She understands. [to himself]

BOTH:
We understand:

FRANK:
Ellen?

ELLEN:
Frank?

Now they kiss, the ultimate formality. It is their last recognition and acknowledgement of each other. Nobility, nobility! Their greeting is their parting. What follows is remembrance, mere echo, as ghosts would sound, drifting away on separate currents of emptiness.

ELLEN:
Shall we love again?

FRANK:
Love? Again?

ELLEN:
What else is there?

FRANK:
Love? Again?

ELLEN: [a last statement]
There's nothing more!

FRANK: [blank cynicism]
Nothing more?

ELLEN: [despairing]
Is there nothing more?

FRANK: [bleak skepticism]

Nothing? More?

Suddenly the Homonculus appears in the No-World, drifting opposite to their direction, But faster.

HOMONCULUS:
Oh! Where is the sound of the human voice?
Am I alone? Am I alone in the silence of my mind?
I cannot hear another human voice!

He fades off left, his hands to his ears in pain. Bitter lighting on Frank and Ellen.

ELLEN & FRANK:
We died, yet live again
Not knowing how or why.
How long the way to life!
How short our time.

ELLEN: [alone])
Frank, Don't deny me!
You're silent?
Speak to me! Speak, love!
Who else is there? [she has realized]

FRANK:
Who else?

ELLEN:
Someone?
Something?
No one?
Nothing?
Answer me!

FRANK: [cold, hollow]
　　Somehow, somewhere, our lives went wrong.[
　　Love once broken's never strong.
　　I cannot go on. A dark voice
　　Calls, calls me back. I have no choice.

During this last frozen exchange, the Mist. of C. has become visible through the scrim at upper left stage. She is elevated a foot or so. She holds the floor microphone's snake-head in one hand at her breast. No more of her is seen than head and shoulders.

ELLEN:
　　You don't want me as I was before?
　　Have we reached the end?

FRANK: [singing, musing, through her and at the Mist. of C.]
　　I look at you, and think of our past.
　　How simple life was. That' sall passed.

ELLEN:
　　It's she. You're obsessed.
　　What has she done to you? You're possessed.

MIST. OF C.: [as from another world]
　　He's gone beyond you. What have you to give?

Ellen turns and answers her, though she cannot see her.

ELLEN:
　　My constancy. What have you to give?

MIST. OF C.:
　　Perfect freedom. When he lies on my breast,
　　In darkness, silence, he'll be free: he'll rest.

ELLEN:
Whoever you are, whatever you say,
If Frank loses me, he loses the way.

MIST. OF C.:
Where I go, he goes — wherever that be.
Whatever he seeks — he'll find with me.

ELLEN:
You care nothing for him: your words are lies.
You'll use him till you're finished — then he dies.

MIST. OF C.:
And you? You need him only for yourself!
He doesn't want his life: he hates himself.

ELLEN:
Forget his promise? Cut our last ties?

MIST. OF C.: [contemptuously]
Call! Call to him. He won't hear your cries.

ELLEN:
My love! [repeat these lines a*d lib*]

MIST. OF C.: [repeat these lines *ad lib*]
He doesn't hear you!

The music calls, and Ellen gestures imploringly. Frank drifts off to rear right. Ellen, at right wing, disappears. At next moment, Frank is seen behind the scrim, which is disappearing. We are back in the Cool Waters. The Mist. of C. is singing her Torch Song. Frank falls into the front-table seat where we see him standing. He is alone; he drinks. The Mist. of C.'s costume, although much the same as that of the preceding year, is phosphorescently prinked out with black. Also, fatal jewelry.

The couples, who have grown distinct at the other tables, are in despon-
dent attitudes. The women are each Ellen: same dress, same hair, same
face. Their escorts are Frank. These men drink heavily while their com-
panions sit immobile before full glasses as if but shades of themselves
and unable to drink mortal liquor. As this scene moves to its climax, the
men slump imperceptibly into morose drunkenness; finally they sit col-
lapsed, some forward, some backward. Towards the end of her threnody,
the Chanteuse sings to Frank, and he looks up yearningly at her. She
stands over him by then, looking down compassionately. The place is a
vacant hell, immemorial. It is indeed the Cool Waters.

SCENE 3

MIST.OF C.:
   It is born, but it dies.
   Though it dies, it is born.

   Not for you, not for me.

   There was no way to know
   There is no way to go.

   Not for you, not for me.

       Our hope is all consumed.
   Love cannot be resumed.

   Not for you, not for me.

FRANK: [breaking from her gaze, he snaps his fingers]
   Here! Another champagne!

A new bottle appears in the bucket. He is being truly served now.

The Mist. of C. looks at him; she is sad. During her pleading she seems very much a human person.

MIST. OF C.:
> Darling, won't you, for us, be glad?
> Let's drink. Our New Year. Don't be sad.

FRANK: [tonelessly]
> Darling, sorry. Do I seem sad?
> It was your song. Let's drink, be glad.

They clink glasses. They drink.

MIST. OF C.:
> Haven't you heard that song before?

FRANK:
> No. Was it me you sang it for?

MIST. OF C.:
> Yes. Don't think of her.
> She's gone. You've shut that door.
> You can't go back.

FRANK: [gestures about him]
> Must we go on?
> I can't forget, won't forgive
> This place — the way we live.
>
> From silence we came to light,
> To singing and light, passion and light.
>
> We think and hope, try to pretend
> We are not frightened of that end —
> Emptiness! where dead lives are tossed:

That cold silence — darkness — in which we're lost.

Void worlds! all void! Voids for which we lust,
Timelessness! Where we drift like dust....
Nothing remains the same,
Not even the old games.

As if we should believe ourselves,
As if we could invent new selves
And go on. Could we go on? How?

   — What time of the world is it now?

MIST. OF C.:
   Late.

FRANK:
   Late?

MIST. OF C.:
   Too late.

FRANK: [to himself]
   For love, or hate?

MIST. OF C.:
   What did you say?

No answer.

   I'm bored.

No answer.

   Let's dance. [entreating]

FRANK: [to himself]
  No other way?

Resigned, he rises to dance. But as he does so, he realizes his situation, and cries out:

  I've lost my chance!

She cajoles him to her while she backs to the center of the stage. There is no doubt that she is ordering him to dance with her. Because he would not say Yes freely, he is now compelled to obey her. He is damned. Nevertheless she is attractive, very much so, and attentive and tender. She holds herself out for the, to Frank, fatal embrace. He enters it, and they dreamily begin to dance in a frozen way.

TRIO [Headwaiter also sings, unseen]

FRANK:
  Though you know I hate you,
  I know you will love me.

MIST. OF C.:
  Though you know I love you,
  I know you will hate me.

HEADWAITER:
  Though she knows he hates her,
  He knows she will love him.

FRANK:
  How can I ever stand such love?

MIST. OF C.:

You cannot understand such love.

HEADWAITER:
He cannot understand such love.

FRANK:
That is not the way it should be.

MIST.OF C.:
But that is the way it must be!

HEADWAITER:
That is not the way it should be.

FRANK:
Your love, my hate?

MIST.OF C.:
Your hate, my love?

HEADWAITER:
His hate, her love.

Frank wakes with a start and recognizes her. He is shocked.

FRANK:
No! Not you! No! Where is my wife?

MIST. OF C.:
Yes! For you! Yes! You've lost your life!

She laughs diabolically: it is the laughter of her consort, the M.C., as we recall it from ACT I.

Frank drops his arms. Music strikes for midnight, and action draws to a close. Frank goes from table to table. The spotlight follows through vapor and glare. At each table his simulacra repose drunk as death, his Ellens expectantly fresh, cold, and unreal. Frank calls out, only to be answered inanely by these women.

FRANK:
Ellen!

First GIRL:
Yes, dear?

FRANK:
Ellen!

Second GIRL:
Yes, dear?

FRANK:
Ellen!

Third GIRL:
Yes, dear?

FRANK:
Ellen!

Fourth GIRL:
Yes, dear?

It is midnight. The music withers into its last sigh. Frank returns to the triumphant Mist. of C. She stands in an attitude of serene magnificence. Smiling the wise smile of wisdom and despair, she waits. Frank reaches out for her, as to a last resort and solace, But she holds up a denying hand. She scorns him He has turned from her to his false Ellens. The shades of Ellen come dancing from their tables to surround him. After each chorus, one girl pushes him into the arms of the next. He is sobering up fast. Finally he stands stunned: the doomed one.

The Mist. of C.'s invocation to the New Year is valedictory, prophetic, macabre. When the dancing begins, the M.C. appears, elevated, at the back wall, faintly illumined by running fire on his person. Beside him, as Prize and as Consort, is the darkened shadow of Ellen herself. They sing with the Mist. of . Frank and Chorus accompany antiphonally.

MIST. OF C., M.C., & ELLEN:
Your mind was soft! Your heart was tight!

FRANK:
My mind was soft! My heart was tight!

CHORUS:
Mind soft! Heart tight!

MIST. OF C., M.C., & ELLEN:
You wished you could! You wished you might!

FRANK:
I wished I could! I wished I might!

CHORUS:
You could! You might!

MIST. OF C., M.C., & ELLEN:
Be freed from love, life's awful blight!

FRANK:
Be free of love, life's fearful blight!

CHORUS:
Of love, that blight!

MIST. OF C., M.C., & ELLEN:
Your love seemed black! Your hate seemed white!

FRANK:
My love seems black! My hate seems white!

CHORUS:
What's black is white!

MIST. OF C., M.C., & ELLEN:
Love brought you joy! Love gave you fright!

FRANK:
Love brought me joy, But gave me fright!

CHORUS:
Love's joy is fright!

MIST. OF C., M.C., & ELLEN:
Since right was wrong, since wrong was right!

FRANK:
My right was wrong My wrong is right!

CHORUS:
Your wrong is right!

MIST. OF C., M.C., & ELLEN:
You feared its length, you feared its height!

FRANK:
I lost my strength! I lost my sight!

CHORUS:
Lost strength! Lost sight!

MIST. OF C., M.C., & ELLEN:
May all your lies return to stay!

FRANK:
Have all my lies returned to stay?

CHORUS:
Lies! Lies! Lies! Lies!

MIST. OF C., M.C., & ELLEN:
So all your lies return to stay!
You know your life must end today!

CHORUS:
And now your life will end — this way!

They close in on Frank, their nails out-thrust.

FRANK:
My loves, my pains: my life! all end today!

CHORUS:
The end! The end! The end!

*Short, murderous bacchanal. They strip him. They tear him to pieces.
The light is going. The last one to be seen during this frenzied dance
is the Mist. of C., who stands with arms stretched out in command:
her dress shimmers with running blood. What is left of Frank lies at
her feet: a heap of disjecta membra. Cigarette butts burn in ashtrays, and blood stains the floor. The Homonculus moves slowly and*

hesitantly through the debris, and pronounces an Epilogue in a
pale, abstracted voice.

HOMONCULUS:
   If you can guess the reason why
   Winter comes when spring's gone by
   Or know what makes our hopes all lies
   And think that love, true love, must die:
   You've seen Just what meets the eye!

   Ah! But have you? Look at me:
   A thing like you, made to see
   To walk and talk, as though free —
   And so I am! So is she!
   Such is our necessity. [he sees Snake Arms coming towards
   him]

Snake Arms has glided in out of the darkness. She is a glittering,
gilded, faceless sylph. She dances in shrinking circles around him At
the close of the next stanza, she moves into his arms.

   If life is death, then lead is gold.
   Ice will burn the heart yhat's cold.
   But — There's more than can be told:
   What's not born is very old,
   And we shall keep what we can't hold!

They fade into invisibility, so that the gold girl is the last thing that
can be seen. He goes on singing, and his voice is covered by the
gradually louder voice of the Announcer, the unseen, who sings this
last stanza with him

   Such terrible beauty! It comes!
   From everywhere, to us it comes!
   Eternally, to us it comes!

Blinding! Deafening! Drowning! Comes!
This terrible beauty! It comes!
It comes! It comes to us! It comes!

Darkness.

A gray, antelucan light comes up on the deserted stage. Ellen, seated again at her old table, stares up into emptiness, profiled, frozen. Cigarette stubs send up thin lines of smoke from ashtrays at the tables. There is silence. The M.C. is visible at left rear. He moves towards center stage as he sings, until at the close he occupies it fully.

It always ends this way.
For woman and for man.
For man and for woman
There is no other way.

Ellen, hear what I say!   [Ellen does not move]

You live, you die, in the cave.
There are the worlds outside,
There are the worlds inside.
You have only the cave.
Here you must make your life
Or else you lose your life.

Ellen, hear what I say!
There is no other way!

You are silent, Ellen.
At last you've reached the goal
You've feared that you would find:
How lonely your lost soul,
Your emptied heart and mind!

You are silent. Ellen.
Ellen, hear what I say
It always ends this way!

You are free now, Ellen.
Your husband is no more.
Ellen, do you hear me?
I tell you, you are free
Frank I cannot restore.
Do you hear me, Ellen?

I, who am more than human,
Can make him less than human... [he picks up what was
Frank's arm]
Like all of those who want
But know not what they want:
Something ridiculous
Like my Homunculus...   [he laughs]
A thing like you: made to see
To walk and talk, as though free....

And so he is! So is she!
Such is their necessity. [he laughs again, harder]

*At the mention of his name, the Homunculus has appeared, and
moved hesitantly through the debris of overturned chairs, et cetera,
looking for something. Snake Arms appears too, vaguely, opposite
him in the darkness: a glittering, gilded, faceless sylph.*

[speaking to Ellen, his tone a damnation]
And you shall be the goal
He seeks but cannot find.
You shall be his lost soul,
His emptied heart and mind!
And so you make your life.

There is no other way.

He drops Frank's arm back on the heap. Now he turns to face and address the theater audience. He is baleful, fatal.

> Soon you too shall join us
> Here in the Cool Waters.
> Here in the Cool Waters
> You'll become one of us:
> Something ridiculous —
> Like my Homunculus.
>
> And so you'll lose your life.
> There is no other way.
>
> For man and for woman
> It always ends this way.

Snake Arms glides into the open arms of the Homunculus, and they fade.

Total darkness.

CURTAIN

THE ANNIVERSARY

OPERA IN TWO ACTS

BY

Ned Rorem

1962

LIBRETTO by **JASCHA KESSLER**

ACT I

"THE COOL WATERS", a nightclub. New Year's Eve. The present.

ACT II

One year later:
1. A T.V. studio - early on New Year's Eve.
2. A VOID. A few hours later.
3. "The Cool Waters" - immediately following.

Frank Singer . . . . . Baritone
Ellen Singer . . . . . Soprano
M.C. . . . . Bass
Mistress of Ceremonies . Mezzo
Headwaiter . . . . . Tenor
(also Announcer in Act II, and offstage voice)
Homonculous . . . . . Counter-Tenor

CHORUS . . . . . . S.A.T.B.

NON-SINGING RÔLES:

Piano player . . . . performs on stage during first and last scenes
Cloakroom Girl . . The Snake-Arms of Act I. The gold serpent-sylph of the Epilogue. (A dancer)
DANCERS . . . . Couples who, in Act II, make up the television audience
A man and woman . At front table during opening song.

ORCHESTRA:
2 flutes (1 inter. picc.)
2 oboes (1 inter. Eng. Horn)
2 clarinets (1 inter. Bass cl.)
1 bassoon
1 Saxophone (alto inter. with tenor)

3 Horns
2 Trumpets
2 trombones

PERCUSSION: incl. timp, B.D., Sn.dr., tom-tom, bongos, ratchet, w.b., slapstick etc.
Vibraphone, Xylophone, Guitar, Tubular bells - etc.
HARP
GRAND PIANO - (on stage)

FOR ALL DETAILS SEE LIBRETTO PRINTED SEPARATELY

"THE ANNIVERSARY" was commissioned by the N.Y. City Center Opera through the Ford Foundation.

NED ROREM
NEW YORK, CALIFORNIA - 1962

ACT I

NED ROREM

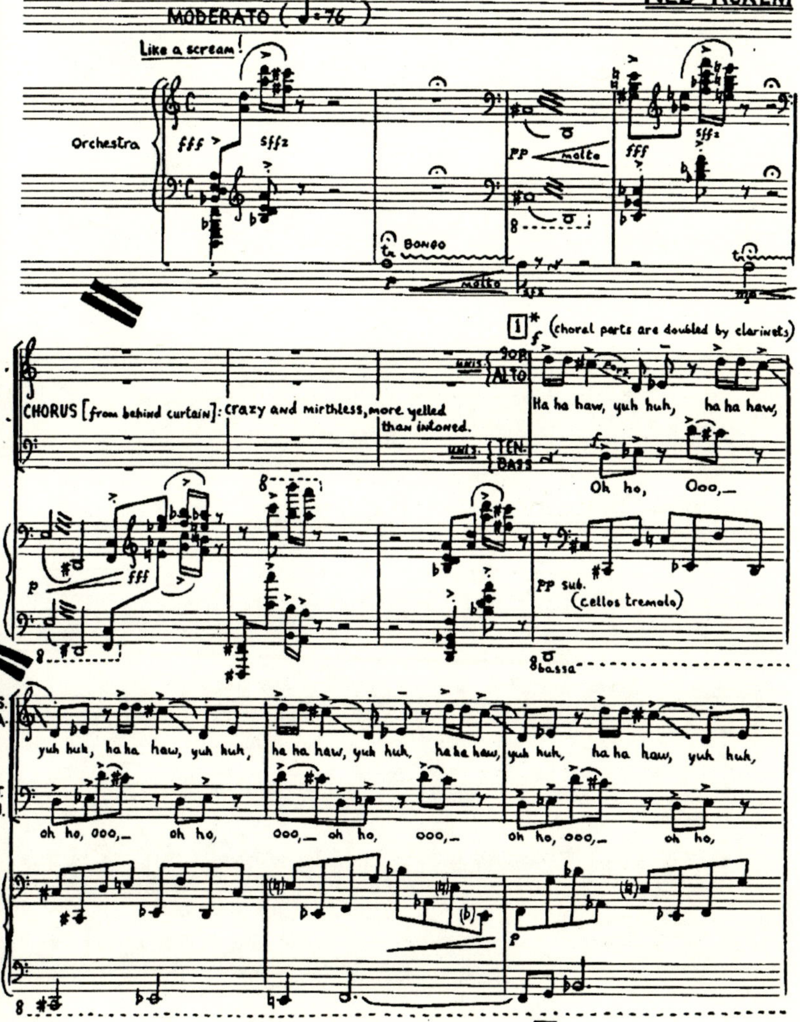

*Piano is heard from on-stage until 3

(shouted!)
S.
A.
ha ha haw, yuh huh, ha ha haw, yuh huh, ha ha haw.
Happy New Year!
Ha ha haw, yuh huh, ha ha haw,
T.
B.
(shouted!)
000, — oh ho, 000, — oh ho, 000. — Oh ho, Ooo, —
(xylo.)
mp sub.
8
2
yuh huh, ha ha haw, yuh huh. ha ha haw, yuh huh, ha ha haw, yuh huh, ha ha haw, yuh huh
oh ho, 000, — oh ho 000, — oh ho, 000, — oh ho, 000, — oh ho
sfz
(shouted!)
ha ha haw, yuh huh, ha ha haw, yuh huh, ha ha haw.
Happy New Year! Ah!
000, — oh ho, 000 — oh ho, 000. —
(shouted)
fff marcatissimo
Ped.

3 **ALLEGRO MOLTO** (♩ = 144)
Doppio Movimento

Behind curtain is sound of chatter, screaming, buzzing, cheering, which continues loudly until **5**

CURTAIN rises slowly on dark stage....

4 strings tutti (+ brass interpol

Mistress of Ceremonies is dramatically spotlighted against the piano.
A few couples are seen dancing in the shadows — slowly, despite the fast music.

The guests' wordless noise subsides as they await the Mist. of Cer.'s song.

TEMPO I°

RIT. MOLTO

fff
8
Quiet dancing continues as, with closed eyes, she now begins.......
Mist. of Cer.:
5
RIT.
mf
A Tempo (like a Torch Song)
mp
When mind and bo-dy had no pain___ The sun_ shone_ on lovers'
MODERATO (languid and bluesy) 𝅗𝅥 = 63
sffz
hold until faded
p
hours: Now falls the black___ and bitter rain_ On this isle___ of shining
mp
flowers. In the dark___ the world is turn-ing And the years_ dim___ like old de-
mf

Lyrics under the staves:

sires: Yet all night long____ stars are burn-ing Far through cold space, e-ter-nal

PANTOMIME (see libretto):

A man at front table is so fascinated by the song that he ignores his partner back his shoulder. She turns elsewhere for h

fires. The city will rise____ proud and bright, Stone and

Her eyes fall on a silhouette at rear "office exit": the M.C.
She rises somnambustically to go toward him (as her partner
remains staring at Mist. of Cer. who continues singing)

steel can-not feel____ sor-row; But love is____ born and

Hypnotically the girl moves through the dancers — upstage.

dies____ each night. What of you____ and me____ to

The girl (back to audience) halts before M.C. He rips down her dress, as tho shucking an ear of corn, and for a moment we see her naked spine.
A Tempo
mor - - - row? The black rain falls. The
M.C. beckons with authority and she steps into the red-glowing chamber. He slips in after her.
world is turn-ing. In the dark-ness Stars are burn-ing. Fall - - ing,
At front table the girl's escort is oblivious of her disappearance.
turn-ing, shin - - - ing, burn - - - - - - - - ing!
BONGO
Dancers have stopped a moment to listen as the singing grows frantic. But the sense eludes them and they resume moving calmly.
Stone and steel Cannot know pain But love is

Mist. of Car.
appass.
ff
born — And dies — in pain. — What —
f
sf mp sub.
As song closes, the man (now alone at table) rises uncertainly and goes to Mist. of Car. who vanishes with him into the
Mist. of Car.
f
mf
Rit.
of — you? — What — of — me? — What
fp sub.
mf espr.
RIT.
p
Mist. of Car.
you? What of me?
Spotlight fades —
CHORUS applauds. Stage grows lighter.
A Tempo
p
mp
mf
RIT.
At song's close Frank and Ellen have entered and now remove their wraps, assisted
the Snake Arms.
8
ALLEGRO MOLTO (♩=152)
mp
p
strings

Headwaiter shows them to a little front table, all the while singing about them, pointing, etc. — although they hear nothing of what he says.
f
ff
fff
mp
9
HEAD-WAITER: mf
(poco staccato)
I see them everywhere, I'd know them anywhere: The
Poco Meno Mosso (♩=126)
(brass)
mp (pizz.)
man you'd like to be, Our he-ro from the start: Hand-some, clev-er and free, No
f
stronger than his heart! And the woman, what is she? She'll al-ways play her part: Her life's the mys-ter-

Disappearing. . . .

Anyone too. Anyone

If he seems anyone, She is anyone too.

He seems anyone; She is anyone, too.

Headwaiter vanishes, and is replaced by M.C. who appears at the table of Ellen and Frank. Evidently he knows all about them (for he is a mind-reader), but they are not startled by his sudden apparition nor his particular knowlege. With bored sophistication they greet him from their seats. He remains standing thruout the following.

too.

M.C. Good

Anyone too.

11 Lo Stesso Tempo, ma meno deciso
ELLEN:
Good even-ing.
FRANK:
Good even- ing.
M.C.
even-ing.
Mister and Mrs. . . . .
[He mindreads]
Singer, I be-lieve?
Vln.
Vla.
C.B.
EL.
How did you know?
Fr.
yes, that's so!
M.C.
My tal-ent, I could say, for names. A use-ful gift, sinc
[Shrugs]

[shrugs]
Freely
[mindreads]
I play games. For ex-ample... Now let me think... Frank... and...
(segue)
pp
Ellen laughs and claps.
From the outset their is a bold flirtation between her and M. C.
12
[coy]
mf
Is there something else you've learned?_ I like secrets
El-len? I'll bet your drink._
A Tempo
Fls. (flutter)
sn. dr.
mf
mp
pizz.
where I'm concerned._
Noth-ing I say will sur-prise you._ What-ev-er I know, you know too.
w.w.

E.I. I'm not sure I know what you do. If you'll tell me, then I'll tell you.

Fr. What point learning what we

Hrns.

Fr. know? Why not tell us what we don't?

S.A. pp [whispered] If he seems any-one, She is anyone, too.

T.B. pp [whispered] He seems anyone. She is anyone too.

γ Bongo

What you do know, you ought to know. You won't know what you don't know.

Take pi-ty, everyone!

Take pi-ty.

[14]

[Ignoring Frank and cajoling M.C.]

But I think I want to hear.

[Spoken: in strict time]

I don't think I want to hear.   I don't think I want to hear.

[spoken]

Why not?   No, he

strings

That's true.
you've been mar-ried sev-en years._
Sev-en long and hap-py years.
mf
Why_ not?_
15
mf [to herself]
There is no reason we
Why not?_
M.C.
And have you an-y cause for tears?
should.
[to himself]
What is the reason we should?
M.C.
You're sure you have no cause_ for_ tears?

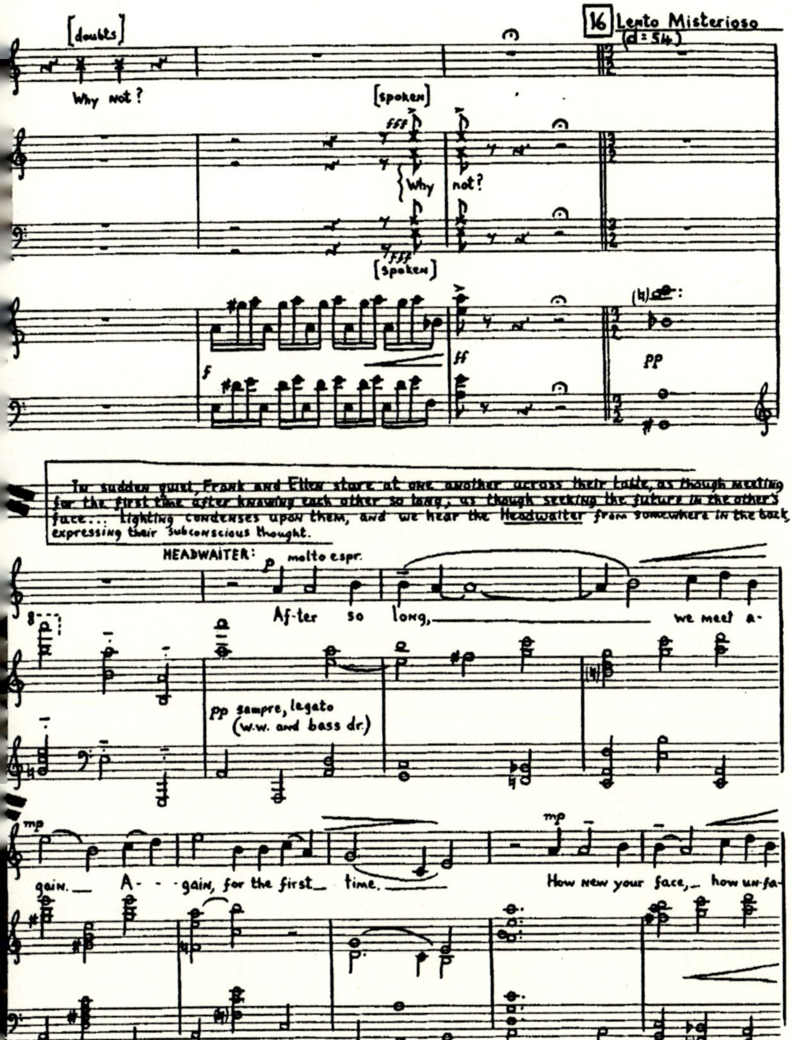
[doubles]
Why not?
16 Lento Misterioso
(𝅗𝅥 = 54)
[spoken]
fff
Why not?
fff
[spoken]
f
ff
pp
In sudden quiet, Frank and Ellen stare at one another across their table, as though meeting for the first time after knowing each other so long, as though seeking the future in the other's face... Lighting condenses upon them, and we hear the Headwaiter from somewhere in the back, expressing their subconscious thought.
HEADWAITER:
p molto espr.
After so long, we meet a-
pp sempre, legato
(w.w. and bass dr.)
mp
gain. A- - -gain, for the first time.
mp
How new your face, how unfa-